Letters from the Spanish Civil War

LETTERS

from the

SPANISH

CIVIL WAR

A U.S. Volunteer Writes Home

EDITED BY

Peter N. Carroll AND Fraser Ottanelli

THE KENT STATE UNIVERSITY PRESS
Kent, Ohio

Library of Congress Catalog Card Number 2013012314
ISBN 978-1-60635-174-1
Manufactured in the United States of America

Carl Geiser's letters are reproduced courtesy of Linda Geiser
and the Tamiment Library, New York University.

LIBRARY OF CONGRESS CATALOGING-IN-PUBLICATION DATA
Geiser, Carl.
[Correspondence. Selections]
Letters from the Spanish Civil War : a U.S. volunteer writes home /
edited by Peter N. Carroll and Fraser Ottanelli.
pages cm
Includes bibliographical references and index.
ISBN 978-1-60635-174-1 (hardcover) ∞
1. Geiser, Carl—Correspondence. 2. Spain—History—Civil War, 1936–1939—
Participation, American. 3. Spain—History—Civil War, 1936–1939—Prisoners
and prisons. 4. Spain—History—Civil War, 1936–1939—Campaigns. 5. Spain.
Ejército Popular de la República. Abraham Lincoln Battalion—Biography.
6. Prisoners of war—Spain—Correspondence. 7. Prisoners of war—United
States—Correspondence. 8. Soldiers—Spain—Correspondence.
9. Soldiers—United States—Correspondence.
I. Carroll, Peter N. II. Ottanelli, Fraser M. III. Title.
DP269.47.A46G462 2013
946.081—dc23
2013012314

17 16 15 14 13   5 4 3 2 1

*The editors dedicate this book to their colleagues of the
Abraham Lincoln Brigade Archives (www.alba-valb.org),
a nonprofit national organization devoted to the
preservation and dissemination of the history of
the North American role in the Spanish Civil War.*

CONTENTS

PREFACE AND ACKNOWLEDGMENTS

Carl Geiser had a strong sense of his own history. The only book he wrote, *Prisoners of the Good Fight,* carefully documented the experience and context of his own POW status during the Spanish Civil War. After that project, Geiser worked with family members and friends to transcribe and annotate the letters he sent home from the war. In preparing the letters for this volume, we preserved Geiser's earlier notes and carefully checked his transcriptions against the original manuscripts now held in the Abraham Lincoln Brigades Archives (ALBA) collection at New York University's Tamiment Library. We have indicated corrections to accidental word omissions by bracketing any additions. We silently corrected obvious spelling and punctuation errors. We have also retained Arabic numerical footnotes (1, 2, 3, etc.) that he added when the letters were transcribed in the early 2000s along with his additions that are identified by [CG:]. Our own editorial footnotes are given as endnotes with roman numerals.

In preparing this edition, we would like to acknowledge Geiser's first wife, Sylvia Segal, who not only saved all the letters but then returned them to him years after their divorce. This project would have not been possible without the support and assistance of Carl Geiser's children, Peter, James, Linda, David, and Gary, along with Geiser's close friend, Christopher Brady. A trained historian, Brady played a crucial role in helping Geiser organize and provide his own annotations to the letters. Several members of Geiser's extended family offered essential information; they include Bennett and Grace Geiser, Ruth Yarman, and John Schmidt Cristia Sullens. We appreciate the assistance provided by the late Michael Nash and Gail Malmgreen of the Tamiment Library. Several colleagues helped us identify the people and organizations that Geiser mentions in his letters. Special thanks to James Fernández, Robert Cohen, and Juan Salas of New York University; Sebastiaan Faber of Oberlin College; Helen Graham of Royal Holloway, University of London; Jyrki Juusela of Helsinki; and especially Christopher Brooks who developed the biographical directory for the U.S. volunteers, which is available at the ALBA website at www.alba-valb.org/volunteers/browse. We also extend thanks to Ann Fraser Ottanelli who checked the original letters against the transcript as well as Marianne Bell and Judy Drawdy of the Department of History at the University of South Florida for clerical assistance.

Introduction

"Probably you are a bit surprised to hear I am in Spain fighting with the army of the Spanish Republic," Carl Geiser wrote to his brother, Bennet, nine days after he crossed the border into Spain on May 1, 1937. "And so I suppose you want to know why I am here." Geiser's politics were no secret to his family, but the new recruit had been prudent, so far, to conceal his mission to Spain from his close relatives. Now that he was there, Geiser felt no reluctance about speaking out. His decision to risk his life in a foreign land was not a sign of restless adventure or youthful ardor, but rather a mature choice that reflected both his deep-seated personal values and developing political beliefs and experience. He was 26 years old.

Carl Frederick Geiser had come from a small rural town, Orrville, Ohio, where he was born on December 10, 1910. His family had migrated to the United States from Switzerland at the end of the nineteenth century. Carl was the oldest of six children with a brother, Bennet, and four sisters: Marie, June, Ellen, and Irene. Orrville in rural Wayne County, fifty miles south of Cleveland, was part of Ohio's Amish country, where people with strong religious views predominated. One of the town's major businesses was (and still is) the Smith Dairy company founded by Carl's maternal uncles in 1909. Carl's father farmed eighty acres, and the boy grew up working on the farm, performing a range of tasks from tilling and hoeing, taking care of animals, and hunting as well as participating in community activities like corn husking, threshing, and barn raising.

Geiser had fond memories of these early experiences. In a letter from Spain to his sister Irene he wrote, "Your description of life and work on the farm makes me almost homesick for it again. Perhaps what appeals most to me about it now is its peacefulness. It would be quite a contrast to my present life, and many times much peacefuler, and quieter."

While his father's side of the family was Mennonite, Carl regularly attended the Christ Reformed Church along with his maternal grandmother. He took an active role in church activities, driving neighbors to services on his uncle's Model T and even becoming a popular Sunday school teacher. The family was hardworking, frugal, churchgoing, and politically conservative with a strong sense of community, and, while they had little formal schooling, they held education in high regard.

For Geiser, growing up in Orville, Ohio, provided more than just an idyllic childhood. While in later years he embraced political views at odds with those of most of his family, in many ways, Geiser's ideals were the product of the small-town communal values of his youth. At the end of October 1937, while recovering in a hospital from wounds he received from a mortar shell, Geiser reminisced in a letter to his wife about Halloween:

> It brings back a thousand delightful memories of life in Ohio . . . especially of masquerade barn parties and dances, with corn stalks and brilliantly colored fall leaves, and cider and pumpkins and pumpkin pie and square dances. How beautiful these things become with time, especially when one is bedfast far away from them. Such traditions and customs need not die out, but in fact, can and should become more joyous than ever in the country side.

As Carl's children remembered years later, while in many ways he "was decidedly different" from those who had raised him, in others their father was "cut from the same cloth."

Carl's father died in the influenza epidemic at the end of World War I, and his mother passed away shortly afterward of tuberculosis. The children were divided up among their large extended family. Carl and his sister Marie were taken in by his widowed maternal grandmother for whom he took care of her sixteen-acre farm. Raised in a German-speaking environment, Carl learned English in school. Through the eighth grade, he attended a one-room schoolhouse and excelled in his studies. In 1928, after he graduated with the highest grade any boy had received from Orrville High School, Carl enrolled in the YMCA School of Technology (later Fenn College and now Cleveland State University) in Cleveland, where he majored in electrical engineering. This program, which alternated classroom work with actual employment, enabled students—for whom a college education might otherwise be unattainable—to finance their education while gaining practical work experience. Carl was an electrical engineering major. In his words, he went to college convinced that "he could become a millionaire through hard work."[1]

The onset of the Great Depression swiftly undermined his illusions. With the collapse of the job market and the erosion of student funds, Carl, along with thousands of college students across the country, began to question the logic and value of capitalism. Years later, he recalled how he first encountered socialist ideas from a fellow student in an economics course. In addition, the worldwide economic calamity stimulated a dramatic change in international relations, including the consolidation of Fascism in Italy, the rise of Nazism in Germany, and the Japanese invasion of Manchuria, all of which increased fears of an impending world war. These concerns over a faltering capitalist system, fascist expansion, and the threat of war led tens of thousands of young Americans to participate and join in a range of activities sponsored by young Communists and Socialists.

In college, Carl's embrace of radical politics progressed quickly. In 1931, as head of the local branch of the Baptist Young People's Union, he openly questioned the morality of the church's reliance on John D. Rockefeller's benevolence; soon after, Carl's support of racial equality got him expelled from the Christ Reform Church in Orrville. In the spring of 1932, Carl was removed as editor of the school newspaper, *The Cauldron,* because of his sympathetic coverage of the World War I veterans, the so-called "bonus marchers," as they passed through Cleveland on their way to Washington, D.C., to demand immediate government assistance. But the experience that had a decisive influence on shaping his political thinking was his trip to the Soviet Union as part of a student delegation. Carl saw the Soviet experience as a flourishing alternative to economic depression and an effective bulwark against the threat of war. He also took advantage of the trip to visit relatives in Switzerland and to go hiking in the Alps. Upon his return to Ohio, Geiser joined the youth organization of the U.S. Communist Party, the Young Communist League.

Not long before traveling to Soviet Russia, Carl had become a member of the Communist-led National Student League (NSL). Founded in 1931, the NSL was a militant organization that agitated for student rights and benefits, such as financial aid, defense of academic freedom, and free speech, as well as support for striking workers and organized labor and opposition to racial segregation and campus military training under the Reserve Officer Training Corps.

As one of the local leaders of the NSL, Geiser helped raise money to organize the Ohio Student Congress against War and Fascism held in Cleveland over Thanksgiving weekend in 1932. A few weeks later he was part of the Ohio delegation to the NSL-sponsored National Student Congress Against War and Fascism held in Chicago over the Christmas holiday. The national congress marked the beginning of a relationship between young Communists and other socialist, liberal, pacifist, and religious groups around a common antiwar program. By the mid-1930s, however, increasingly concerned about fascist aggression in Asia, Africa, and Europe, the NSL began to link opposition to war with anti-fascism. In April 1935 the NSL was among the sponsors of nationwide demonstrations that involved tens of thousands of students in over one hundred schools across the country. Marching behind banners proclaiming "Down With Imperialist War" and "War is Un-Christian," communist and socialist students united with a wide range of groups and individuals from religious organizations, sororities and fraternities, high school students, college administrators, and local government officials.

To give a voice to this multitude of groups and provide a common front for all democratic student organizations against fascism, communist and socialist students merged their organizations and founded the American Student Union (ASU) in Columbus, Ohio, in December 1935. The ASU successfully brought together diverse groups and was well received on campuses across the country. While its peak membership never exceeded twenty thousand members (with the strongest pockets at the City College of New York, Brooklyn College, and the University of Chicago), the influence of the ASU over the student body was considerable. Its members and leaders were among the brightest and most politically active students, and its various activities for students' and workers' rights, along with its broader anti-fascist sentiment, assured the ASU broad support among liberals.

The 1932 Chicago NSL convention was a turning point in Geiser's personal and political life. At this event he met his future wife, Sylvia Segal. Affectionately referred to as "Impy," possibly for her diminutive appearance, Sylvia had a graduate degree in biology and was a teacher in the New York City public school system. The convention also selected Geiser as its representative at the Latin American Congress against War and Fascism held in Montevideo, Uruguay, in February 1933. Financed partially with money he received from Mexican muralist Diego Rivera, Geiser traveled to Montevideo where he gave a speech condemning the United States for "not contributing to peace." His fiery words enraged local U.S. consular authorities and got him briefly detained by Argentine immigration officials.

Back in the United States, Carl moved to New York and married Sylvia. For the next three years until Carl left for Spain, most of their activities were centered on politics, although they spent their free time hiking in the Adirondacks. Sylvia combined union organizing with teaching to support the couple, and Geiser became a full-time activist, going on speaking tours to colleges from New England to North Carolina, campaigning against the threat of war, in favor of the Scottsboro Boys (nine black youths unjustly accused of rape and sentenced to death in Alabama), and serving as the youth secretary of the American League against War and Fascism. Founded in the fall of 1933 in New York, the league was an important vehicle through which Communists promoted their foreign policy. In order to provide a forum for young people concerned with the threat of war, the league established a youth section, which campaigned against the militarized structure of the New Deal's Civilian Conservation Corps, opposed compulsory military training in schools, and participated in student antiwar strikes. At first, the appeal of the league was limited by its insistence on linking anti-fascism with the struggle against capitalism. At the end of 1934, however, the league endorsed a broad-based anti-fascist unity. This new priority increased the league's appeal as it now offered a platform for many personalities—including prominent religious figures, labor leaders, liberals, and non-Communist left-wingers, even members of President Franklin D. Roosevelt's cabinet—to express their opposition to Hitler and Mussolini and support for "collective security." In addition, the organization promoted a range of activities, such as the boycott of trade with Japan, protests against the Italian invasion of Ethiopia, and, eventually, support of the Spanish Republic. In 1937, to express its more positive outlook and belief that antifascist wars were justified, the organization changed its name to American League for Peace and Democracy.

While involved in broad-based activities, Carl also took an increasingly prominent role within the communist movement. A member of the "Nathan Hale" club of the Young Communist League (YCL), he was also the organization's education director for Bronx County. In 1936, not long before going to Spain, Geiser was elected to the National Committee of the Young Communist League.

For Geiser, the decision to take up arms against Fascism was the climax of an individual itinerary that had begun long before the outbreak of the Spanish Civil War in July 1936. For him, as for many other men and women from around the world, this faraway conflict became the symbol of the global fight against exploitation, oppression, and racism. As Franco's army, with critical military support from Hitler and Mussolini, rolled through the Spanish countryside, the slogan "Madrid will be the tomb of fascism" embodied the certainty that events in Spain would foreshadow the global defeat of Fascism and Nazism. Eventually, together with over 150 Ohioans, Geiser joined 2,800 volunteers from the rest of the United States in the fight to defend the democratically elected Spanish Republican government against its fascist foes.

The Spanish war began as a domestic dispute. In 1931, Spain's historic monarchy had abdicated and been replaced by a republican government. But the new regime inherited political and social divisions that had weakened Spain's national unity for decades. Stated simply, the very idea of political democracy threatened the interests of powerful segments of Spanish society. Opponents of the new republic included the pro-monarchy aristocracy, the landlords of vast agricultural estates, the Catholic Church, which dominated villages and small towns (and typically aligned with the landowners), and the professional army. Complicating matters further, the world depression accentuated the economic disparities that separated wealthy elites from the impoverished peasants and urban workers.

Leaders of the new Republic hoped to accelerate political democracy by harnessing universal suffrage; broadening land ownership by dividing huge estates controlled by the aristocracy; diminishing the influence of the Catholic Church in political affairs; introducing public education, civil marriages, and allowing women a role in public activities; and weakening the power of the professional army, top-heavy with officers. Consequently, each of these groups believed that the Spanish Republic threatened the traditional and spiritually "pure" Spanish nation. Meanwhile, both rural and urban workers organized around trade unions, agricultural collectives, and radical political parties (both Socialist and anarchist), and pressed the government for immediate changes, such as redistribution of land, the right to strike, and social welfare assistance.

For the next five years, Spanish politics seesawed between liberal reformers seeking to build a secular democracy and a reactionary coalition that fought to stop social change. Often, the resulting contention swung outside the political arena, leading to violent protests, labor strikes, police attacks, assassinations, even armed rebellion. In October 1934, the government summoned the army's Foreign Legion under Gen. Francisco Franco to suppress an insurrection of coal miners in Asturias. The troops crushed the civilian uprising; thirty thousand people were imprisoned. As Spain approached national elections in February 1936, a coalition of left parties struggled to gain power against an equally motivated group of conservative ideologues.

Although conservative parties captured nearly half the votes, the parliamentary victory overwhelmingly went to the self-described Popular Front—a loose alliance of Republicans, Socialists, and trade unionists as well as regional parties representing Catalans and Basques (both of which stood for regional self-government). Significantly, few Communists were elected to the Cortes (Parliament) and none became part of the government. Yet the phrase "Popular Front" was no accident. Once Hitler rose to power, he intensified rhetorical attacks on the "Bolshevik" danger of the Soviet Union to European peace and order. Recognizing the threat of Nazi Germany, the international Communist movement responded by altering its position on world revolution. Instead of standing for the overthrow of all "bourgeois" governments in the name of socialism, Communist leaders argued that the threat of fascism demanded cooperation with other antifascist classes and parties. Spain's Communist Party numbered less than ten thousand in 1936; but to the reactionary groups in Spain, any signs of communist political activity indicated a perilous threat to the social order.

Frustrated by their failure to control parliamentary politics, the top officers of the Spanish army—led by Francisco Franco, Emilio Mola, and José Sanjuro—now began to plan an overthrow of the government. During the next four months, political rhetoric from both the left and right extremes of the political spectrum grew louder, often spilling over into spontaneous violence—riots, shootings, assassinations. Such extralegal activity underscored the weakness of the republican government, reinforcing those who claimed Spain needed stronger authority. The conspirators saw themselves not merely bringing down an elected government but also the principles of mass democracy; in their estimation, they would save Spain from itself.

The rebellion erupted on July 17, 1936, in Morocco, a Spanish colony in North Africa, and spread to Spain the next day. The coup instantly undermined the government's military authority. But to the surprise of the rebel generals, significant portions of the armed forces remained loyal to the Republic and joined with civilian militias organized by labor unions to subdue the rebellion in Spain's major cities. In the capital, Madrid, and in Barcelona, a stronghold of industrial workers, unions, and left-wing organizations, the loyal forces defeated the rebels. Government leaders believed that the insurrection would shortly collapse.

Within a week, however, Spain's civil war escalated into an international conflict as other European powers attempted to benefit from the crisis. General Franco's appeals for military assistance from Hitler and Mussolini won a sympathetic response in the form of airplanes to ferry Spanish soldiers and Moroccan conscripts from bases in North Africa to southern Spain. Such indispensible aid enabled the rebellion to continue, and the rebel army began marching toward Madrid, leaving behind a trail of slaughter and destruction. Over the next months and years, Italy and Germany would provide immense military support to the rebellion, including soldiers, aircraft, tanks, ammunition, and supplies. Carl Geiser's letters frequently comment on the omnipresence of Nazi and Fascist military hardware.

Republican appeals for foreign assistance, by contrast, ran into a stone wall. Britain and France, suspicious of Spain's Popular Front and fearful of confronting Germany and Italy in military competition, announced policies of non-intervention and refused to provide aid to either side. By August 1936, they had persuaded most European countries, including Germany and Italy, to formally endorse a Non-Intervention Treaty. However, neither Hitler nor Mussolini abided by that agreement, and London and Paris chose not to challenge their noncompliance. France did open its borders briefly for material aid to reach the Spanish republic, but the strength of conservative groups within France halted such assistance.

The Soviet Union, under the dictator Joseph Stalin, supported the principles of the Popular Front as a way of gaining allies in an antifascist bloc and, in that spirit, initially joined the Non-Intervention Committee. But as the fascist powers openly flouted the agreement, Stalin decided in September 1936 to send military assistance to the Republic. The hazards of shipping military goods from the Soviet Union—Italian submarines patrolled the Mediterranean Sea and sank ships heading to the Republic—limited the amount of material aid that reached Spain. Stalin also dispatched military advisers, pilots, and tank drivers to assist the republican army. Such assistance, however, remained a small fraction of the offerings Franco received from Germany and Italy.

Stalin's great symbolic contribution was the idea of encouraging volunteers from all over the world to go to Spain to form an International Brigade to fight within the republican army against the fascist rebels. "It is the cause of all progressive mankind," he announced, and communists and non-communists, men and women, from over fifty countries made their way to Spain. Recent estimates suggest that as many as thirty-five thousand volunteers participated in the International Brigades. Others enlisted in the crusade as medical workers—doctors, nurses, ambulance drivers, and laboratory technicians—creating an international assistance program that built hospitals and clinics to aid both soldiers and civilians who suffered trauma or illness during the war. Carl Geiser's description of his medical treatment in Spain indicates both the high quality of medical services and an unfortunate lack of adequate equipment and supplies in the embattled country.

As the nations and political groups of Europe responded to the Spanish Civil War, the United States remained cautiously uninvolved in this era of non-intervention. In response to anarchist takeovers of factories in Barcelona, Roosevelt's State Department warned against aiding the left-leaning Republic. U.S. public opinion generally sympathized with Spain's elected government, especially among liberals, anti-Hitler Jews, anti-Mussolini Italian Americans, African Americans, and trade unionists concerned about fascist expansion. Such groups supported numerous humanitarian aid programs, sending contributions to help the Spanish people. On the other side, the Catholic Church followed the lead of the Vatican and supported the military rebellion as a check against the spread of communist ideas and influence. As a fundamental part of Roosevelt's New Deal, U.S. Catholics had inordinate political influence on presidential policies; Roosevelt needed the Catholic vote for reelection. Regarding the Spanish Civil War, the White House remained quiet, content to enforce U.S. neutrality laws.

News about the formation of the International Brigades reached the U.S. Communist Party in October 1936, and party leaders began recruiting volunteers to go to Spain. They were still in the planning stages when the first Internationals from Germany and France reached Spain in November and provided critical support for the defense of Madrid. Six weeks later, the day after Christmas, the first contingent of U.S. volunteers—slightly fewer than 100 men—sailed to Spain. Since their mission was illegal under U.S. neutrality laws, they kept their purposes secret, landed in France, took a train to Spain (the French border was still open), and prepared for battle.

In January 1937, Congress extended the Neutrality Act to include Spain's civil war, and the State Department began stamping U.S. passports "NOT VALID FOR TRAVEL IN SPAIN." But recruitment for the International Brigades continued during 1937 and 1938, eventually numbering approximately 2,800 volunteers, including 150 medical personnel. Since the Communist Party organized the transportation of U.S. volunteers, most of the first recruits were party members or from the Young Communist League. Subsequently, significant numbers of Socialists, liberals, trade unionists, and anti-fascists of every stripe entered the ranks. In the end, approximately two-thirds to three-quarters of the volunteers defined themselves as Communists (though some did so simply because it was the easiest way to get to Spain).

The background of the volunteers also reflected the social and economic context of the 1930s. The recruits came from every state except Wyoming and Delaware, but most inhabited the large urban centers. A large number were immigrants from Europe or the children of immigrants who came to America in the decades before World War I and settled in the cities. They were not mercenaries; they were not paid for their services. Those who could not pay for their transportation to Spain obtained tickets from the Communist Party. Relatively few had any prior military experience; some had never fired a weapon before going to Spain. At the beginning of the war, they had time to fire three shots into a hillside before entering the front lines.

Ethnically, the U.S. volunteers represented nearly every European nationality group (over seventy types). Their numbers included nearly one hundred African Americans and Native Americans, as well as Asian Americans and Latin Americans living in the United States. This racial and ethnic mixture reflected communist attitudes about equality and the primary importance of economic class over national or racial background. In Spain, African Americans would command white troops for the first time (by contrast, in the U.S. Civil War white officers commanded the black regiments).

Economically, the volunteers came from every class. Carl Geiser's letters mention David McKelvey White, for example, who was the son of a former Ohio governor. Others Geiser knew in Spain were college graduates (as he was), such as George Watt and Robert Merriman. Most volunteers described themselves as "workers" or, typically during the Depression, "unemployed." Over 80 percent were unmarried, a large percentage considering the median age of the volunteers was 28.5, but that also reflected Depression conditions, which saw the average age of marriage rise. One-third of the volunteers were over thirty-five, which underscores that they were not impulsive youth looking for adventure. Rather, they were politically mature and had a clear awareness of the war's stakes. Geiser's letters to his brother, Bennet, provide a lucid explanation of why a young man from rural Ohio would take up arms in a foreign country.

Once in Spain, the U.S. volunteers formed into a separate battalion that became part of the Fifteenth International Brigade. The first recruits named themselves the Abraham Lincoln Battalion—not only because of the six-teenth president's fame for emancipating slaves but because Lincoln was the leader of the legally elected government in a civil war, facing the same type of rebellion that confronted the Spanish republic. By the time Geiser arrived in Spain, enough North Americans had arrived to form a second contingent named the George Washington Battalion.

After the Battle of Brunete in July 1937 (Geiser's first taste of combat), casualties were so high that the two battalions were merged as the Lincoln-Washington Battalion. An additional battalion was also formed. In one of his letters, Geiser speculates it would be named after Tom Mooney, a labor activist then imprisoned in California. Instead, it was named after two nineteenth-century Canadian nationalists (William MacKenzie and Louis-Joseph Papineau) and known as the Mac-Paps. Other North Amer-icans found themselves in the John Brown anti-aircraft company or the Regiment de Tren (transportation) or were attached to another battalion because of their language skills. On the U.S. home front, the volunteers were known collectively as the Abraham Lincoln Brigade.

In his first letter to his brother, Geiser summarized his reasons for being in Spain: First, "because I want to do my part to prevent a second world war. . . . And secondly, because all of our democratic and liberty-loving training makes me anxious to fight fascism." The language was double-edged: Geiser spoke as a Communist, seeing the menace of fascism to civilization and social progress; he also spoke as an American, "liberty-loving," eager to spare his native country the agonies of another war. "We ought not to think that if the fascists take Spain we are safe," he continued, "no more than we ought to think our house is safe if their neighbor's is on fire." Three years later, President Franklin D. Roosevelt would use the same homey metaphor of the neighbor's house on fire to plead for U.S. intervention on behalf of Great Britain. But, by then, the world war Carl Geiser predicted had begun.

Carl Geiser's letters from Spain are part of a much larger body of cor-respondence sent by volunteers from the battlefields of Spain to their families and friends back home. Recipients of such letters often treated them as treasures, firsthand eyewitness accounts of the most impor-tant international events of the day. They shared these scribbled (rarely typed) documents with their own families and friends, sometimes transcribed them to protect the fragile manuscripts, read them aloud at political gatherings, or sent them to newspapers and magazines for public consumption. In Los Angeles and San Francisco, in Philadelphia and New York City, local supporters who formed the Friends of the Abraham Lincoln Brigade anthologized these letters and sold booklets for a few cents to raise funds to support the Spanish Republic.[2] Other edited collections have appeared in print more recently, but Geiser's compilation in this volume is perhaps the largest written by a single volunteer from any country in the International Brigades.[3] Taken together, these letters provide vivid personal descriptions of the first military conflicts of World War II.

Although, like Geiser, the writers of these letters seldom had literary ambitions, their style is usually fluid and clear, despite great varieties of orthography and punctuation. Moreover, they knew that their compositions had to be cleared by military censors who blacked out descriptive passages that might have value to the enemy. For these reasons and reflective of their own ideological commitments, the letters tend to express an optimistic view of the war, passing over complaints about life in the army. To reassure their loved ones at home, the soldiers sometimes disguised their actual experiences (injuries, exhaustion, inadequate food, real danger) rather than depict adversity.

Geiser's correspondence, however, reflects one volunteer's deeply held beliefs in anticipating an ultimate victory against his fascist enemies. His optimism is authentic, even, sometimes, to the point of self-deception. Only during one period, when recovering from wounds in a hospital, did he complain about the quality of medical services and resented the prolonged period of convalescence. Like many other injured volunteers, Geiser wanted to return to active duty and rejoin his comrades as quickly as possible. His letters are also distinctive in their primary focus on his political and ideological motivations for going to Spain. Unlike many of his comrades, who linked their participation in the war to some personal issues (ethnic background, economic situation, or romantic desires, for example), Geiser's most intimate letters remain statements of reason, logic, and political persuasion. He never addresses a specific moment or turning point that obliged him to go to Spain.

Self-restraint and optimism fit nicely with Geiser's appointment to the rank of commissar of the Lincoln Battalion. In that role, he expected to articulate the views and opinions of the political and military leadership. His statements aimed to encourage similar self-restraint and optimism among the rank and file, thereby tightening morale in the fight. But the target of these letters is specifically his readers on the home front, exhortations to support the soldiers in battle by winning wider support for them among the general population and political leaders in Washington. Realizing the imbalance of military power in Spain, Geiser tried to awaken his friends at home to the menace of a fascist victory in hopes that they, in turn, might influence U.S. policy.

CARL GEISER'S LETTERS

Sunday [April 18, 1937]

Dear Impy:

Just finished watching "Charlie Chan at the Opera," for we have movies every other day or so. And now I will take time out to write you a while.

Everything is going marvelously. The only thing missing is you (and especially since there is not even one pretty girl on board—they are practically all English girls and very plain.)

This is by far the best boat I have ever traveled on, 3rd here exceeding Tourist on the Hamburg American Line.[4] The Georgic boasts 27,000 tons, but is a bit slow. We'll probably hit Ireland (Queenstown or Cobh) on Tuesday & Havre Wednesday—and then on to Paris.

The food is good. A special menu card for each meal—and quite a wide choice, and quite well prepared.

We have had excellent weather so far—the 2nd day out was a bit stormy—and a few became seasick, but not I. The majority of us haven't missed a meal.

There is a slight problem to entertain ourselves—of course, I read "Babbit[t]"—and then "the Good Earth" by Pearl Buck which was well worth reading. Now I am in the middle of "Adventures of an Alpine Guide" written by Christian Klucher. It makes me very homesick for the Swiss Alps, especially since he speaks of the Matterhorn, Wetterhorn and Jungfrau, both of which can be seen from my Grand uncle's window—I don't know exactly how long it will be before I get to them, but I hope quite soon.[5]

Besides this we play Ping-Pong, Shuffle Board, and a few similar games. Tournaments are being run off in these. I was eliminated in the first round of Ping-pong but am in the Shuffle Board finals (15 entered). My opponent is a Polish lawyer—a slight man with glasses. The final play-off is tomorrow.

I have also learned how to play Stud & draw poker—but of course no gambling.

The passengers are an excellent group. My table is made up of a group of young fellows—on my left is the Polish Lawyer, on my right a Swede from Michigan on his way to Sweden, an illustrator on his way around the world, and a Brooklynite on his way to Roumania [sic] I believe.[6]

There are many other interesting people on board—and quite a number of Irishmen & Scotchmen. The English crew look[s] like a fine bunch although several scarcely seem more than 14 years old.

My only mishap so far has been a sprained wrist obtained while man-hugging [Geiser changed "manhugging" to "armwrestling" when later transcribing the letters] with the illustrator. But it is much better now.

I often think of you, and wonder what you are doing. I certainly left you with a handful of work. But I know my Impy will come through with colors flying.

(60 hour Intermission)

Took the shuffleboard championship—supposed to play for 2 out of 3 games, but took the first one in spite of fact score was 16 to 2 for me (game was 21). Now everyone is trying to beat me, but so far none have been able to.

Today, 200 miles of the Irish Coast, we are rolling delightfully. So Willie, the Illustrator, and I have been amusing ourselves at Shuffleboard, making all kinds of trick curves when ever the ship lies on one side or other.

It seems our first stop is Cobh, Ireland, instead of Queenstown, which we should reach tomorrow afternoon. & Then Havre by 7 Wednesday evening, making our sea voyage eight days long. There are over a thousand people on board including the crew. Joe, the waiter at our table, who bummed the freights in the States tells us he is going to the 20th Anniversary Celebration in Moscow on November Seventh. And he seems like such a nice chap!

We have a few splendid Scotch types onboard, a head 15 inches long & 6 inches wide. And then there are many others as well.

It's 9:30 now about 5:30 New York time. So I suppose you are either preparing your supper, or going out somewhere for it.

Ray, the Swede, who sits next to me, writes 3 full pages a day to his girl friend—can you imagine that? It sets a very bad example for the rest.

The ocean has been rather quiet all day long, and very grey, reflecting the gloomy sky. We were following about 100 yards behind a strong shower of rain for quite a long time this morning, but it seemed we travel about 2 or 3 miles an hour more slowly than the clouds. And still we haven't seen a ship, or a whale, or an iceberg.

By the way, I wasn't able to take Herman's present along with me. Tell him he should bring it over.

CUNARD
WHITE STAR

ON BOARD
"GEORGIC"

Sunday

Dear Impy:

Just finished watching "Charlie Chan at the opera", for we have movies every other day or so. And now I will take time out to write you a while.

Everything is going marvelously. The only thing missing are you (and especially since there is not even one pretty girl on board - they are practically all English girls and very plain)

This is by far the best boat I have ever traveled on, 3rd here

[HANDWRITTEN ON CUNARD STATIONERY; CONTINUED ON PREVIOUS
LETTER ABOARD THE *GEORGIC*]

Wednesday Afternoon [April 21, 1937]

Dear Impy—

It turned out Cobh & Queenstown are the same place—Queenstown being the Irish name.[7] We anchored in its harbor last night at 7 and the passengers were taken off by tender to the city.

In about 3 hours we will be in Havre, from where I intend to mail this letter.

Played several very tough games of shuffleboard this morning, but won them all, & this afternoon the Polish lawyer entertained us with stories. Babbitt I have donated to the Ship's Library. Klucher's book was certainly inspiring. The praise given him by his Herrs whom he led over the Alps reveal him as perhaps the greatest Alpine climber up until the present.

We are now entering the Channel, and it is quite smooth. It is supposed to be quite rough ordinarily, but this is the second time I am crossing it in good weather. This morning the Berengaria overtook us.[8] I understand it is now making its final trip. Today we constantly pass all kinds of boats, mostly freighters and a number of sailing sloops.

For the last few evenings we have been playing a very interesting game, played with cards, called Fantail. The aim is to get rid of your cards first. The winner has the privilege of whacking the others over the wrist with his 2 fingers the same number of whacks as the latter holds cards. The top of my wrist is consequently a bit tender, but not really sore. My other one still bothers me a bit.

Last night I received an ashtray as a prize. So I gave it to an old gentleman who took a fancy to it.

Thursday morning, April 22

So now I am in Paris. Arrived here at 11 last night after a 3-hour train ride from Le Havre, during which the Polish lawyer insisted on entertaining us with dirty stories. But we had a sandwich on the train that was a knockout, a thick slice of ham between a loaf of bread sliced in two.

Since I haven't been out in broad daylight yet, I can't know what the city looks like, but I hope to see part of it today.

I'll be writing you by every Post, but in the meantime, don't worry, for I am getting along splendidly. And I am wondering how you are getting along with all those things I left you to do. Eliza undoubtedly will help you a great deal. In the meantime, keep your chin up.

With love, Carl

[HANDWRITTEN]

May 9, 1937
Albacete, Spain

Dear Brother Bennet & Grace:[9]

Probably you are a bit surprised to hear I am in Spain fighting with the army of the Spanish Republic. And so I suppose you want to know why I am here.

But before I do this, I'll let you know I am well, busy and happy, and quite safe for the time being.

The reasons I am here is because I want to do my part to prevent a second world war, which would without doubt, draw in the United States and seriously set back our civilization. And secondly, because all of our democratic and liberty-loving training makes me anxious to fight fascism, and to help the Spanish people drive out the fascist invaders sent in by Hitler & Mussolini.

You probably have 2 questions, or rather objections to my being here. One, that the fight here is between the "Reds" and the church & democracy, and 2 that my being here tends to draw the USA into war.

If these things are true then I actually should not be here. And if you think they are true, you have been badly and maybe purposefully deceived. And in the time I have been here, I have been able to ascertain without doubt, that the fight here is between democracy and fascism, and not between communism & fascism or democracy.

Last July 16, an uprising was begun against the democratic legally elected Republican government of Spain. It was organized and financed by Hitler & Mussolini. Fortunately the leader of the uprising was killed by a plane crash as he was returning from Berlin to Spain.[10] The uprising was supported by few Spaniards, notably the big landowners who have starved the Spanish people for generations, the largest capitalists, the nobility, and the majority of the Army, especially the officers, and certain sections of the hierarchy of the Catholic Church who were rich & powerful & often held large lands.

The uprising would have been squelched within a short time, if Hitler & Mussolini had not sent in tanks, airplanes, weapons, and men, until today they are literally invading Spain.

What would happen if Franco, Hitler, & Mussolini were victorious? It would mean that fascism would be stronger everywhere, & fascism means war. Democratic France would be encircled by fascist states preparing for war. The conquest of Spain is part of the fascist preparation for a new world war.

On which side is the church? The great majority of the Catholics are on the side of the government. How much the fascists love Catholics may be seen from Franco's wiping out of a village of 10,000 in Basque territory which is completely Catholic.[11] Also you know what Hitler is doing to the Church in Germany.

So you can see, it is a matter of checking fascism and war, of preserving democracy & peace. We ought not think that if the fascists take Spain we are safe, no more than we ought to think our house is safe if the neighbor's is on fire. Protect yours by helping your neighbor put out his fire. That is why the idea of "neutrality," of keep out of Spain, is very wrong and harmful. Everyone who wants democracy and peace must help the Spanish government, and right away. Frankly, if the Spanish government is victorious, Germany & Italy will be surrounded by more or less democratic countries, and we shall have an excellent chance of avoiding another world war.

I am a member of a machine gun crew in the American Battalion of the International Brigades. And the members of the International Brigades that had come from 52 countries, (I don't know if there are any more countries) and are representing the working people of his country, and here to fight fascism & war. And it looks now, with the continued support of the peace & democracy loving people of the world, that the Spanish government will win in time, and that fascism will be greatly weakened. But our powerful democratic Republic of the United States is not doing enough, is not carrying its share of the fight for peace & democracy. The rich & reactionary men of the USA, who too want fascism, have many Americans deceived and inactive. That is something we have to change.

A few words about my life here. At present I am perfecting my knowledge of the operation of the machine gun. Food is plain, not enough of course, it consists mostly of soups, beans, rice, bread, bully beef & wine. Since there is a shortage of water one has to drink wine. Milk, eggs, chocolate, most vegetables, pastries, are not served and can be bought only occasionally. Soap is also lacking, and we feel this more than anything else. But on the whole, the food is good, the weather quite warm & sunny & the exercise very beneficial.

Quite a few of my friends are here both from New York & Cleveland. And our relations with the Spanish people are very, very cordial.

I wish I could write to all my friends in Orrville, but it is not possible, and I shall have to trust to you to tell them I am here, and why. I hope you will especially tell Marie, Amos, Rose, & Gus.[12] Tell them all I send them my warmest regards.

You can write me here—

    Carl Geiser

    Socorro Rojo Internacional[13]

    Place Altozano

    20 G.P.

    Albacete, Spain

And I hope you will write very soon.

& give my regards to Leonard also.

    Very sincerely,

    Your Brother, Carl

P.S. 12 oranges for 4 cents, so we eat them all day long.

They grow them here and they are plentiful.

By the way, I don't need any money or anything else. The best way you can help me is by helping the people of Orrville know the truth about what is happening in Spain.

    Carl

[TYPEWRITTEN]

    Socorro Rojo International

    Plaza Altozano

    20 G.P.

    Albacete, Spain

    [May 19, 1937]

Dear Impy,

Gee, this is only my third letter, and I know you are looking for one each day. But I am finally settled for a few days, and will be able to write to you oftener. And, of course, I hope that in a few days or a week I will hear from you, and what you are doing.

First of all, I am well, and getting on fine. The food is good, but of course there is no great variety. But there are oranges galore. You get about a dozen for three cents, though they are small, but very good. The main liquid is wine, always grape, since water is not very plentiful and some not very good.

Soap is very scarce and can not be bought, nor can any luxuries, such as chocolate, butter, gum, American cigarettes. But nevertheless, life is pleasant and stren[u]ous.

Believe it or not, but I am in a Machine Gun Company (and political leader of a section, 29 men) and with a very fine bunch of fellows—especially one, a U.A.W. member from Detroit.[14]

Yesterday I met Andy for a moment, though I have not had a chance to talk with him. I haven't heard of Paul yet, though I have met a number of other friends.[15]

As you know, things are going well for democratic Spain, and especially important is the step taken by Catalonia, dissolving its autonomy and becoming an integral part of Republican Spain.[16]

It certainly is stimulating to meet people from every country in the world, all here to help the legal government of Spain drive out the fascist invaders, thus weaken world fascism and prevent a new world war. All recognize that the battle they are fighting now helps keep the rest of the world, including their own country-men, out of war. And take it from me, the International Brigade are powerful disciplined anti-fascist fighters. You have read of their bravery. But that isn't the half of it. 40 men, several machine gun crews, spent over 2 weeks at the front, and only 1 man hurt. Lincoln casualties, I am told, for the past week were only 7. That means real fighters, disciplined and trained.

Well, Imp, time is scarce here, and afternoon drill is due, so I will close. Don't worry and say "Hello" to all my friends for me.

With love,
Carl

May 20, 1937.

Dear Impy,

I must confess that time has never flown so rapidly for me as at present. I haven't written for four days, but it seems I wrote only yesterday.

Am very well, and my hand has a lot of blisters from pick and shovel work. For it seems most of the work of a machine gun crew consists of digging pits, holes, trenches, etc. Have been chosen editor of our company wallpaper.[17] Our first edition is due day after tomorrow. We have a surprising number of fellows who have had experiences on wallpapers. I think we will get out quite a good one. But there are all kinds of difficulties. As yet I haven't been able to obtain white unruled paper, thumbtacks, glue, etc. because stores don't have these materials. But we always manage to dig up something, somewheres.

One doesn't appreciate the suffering war entails for a population until you are right there. Even if you pass up such things as the bombing and murder of civilians from the air, and the casualties at the front, you still have many things as the following: our company wanted to handle a real get together next Sunday evening and we (. . .) [the last part of the previous sentence was erased but remained legible].

[Rest of letter is missing.]

[HANDWRITTEN]

June 3, 1937

Dear Impy:

My first real rainy day in Spain, and it is quite a relief. The crops were badly in need of water, and this means much for the harvest in this region. Just now the comrades in my gun crew are kidding about what they would do on a rainy day at the front, about how much they would be willing to pay for a taxi to take them home from the gun pit, etc.

Here it means we have a little extra time for lectures and indoor classes. This morning was devoted to a lecture on gas warfare. Although the fascists have not used gas yet, perhaps because they are not supplied with masks for their own men, we are preparing ourselves if they do use it. All of us have masks, and are fairly well prepared to meet a gas attack. We know how to recognize the different types and how to deal with them.

Yesterday we had a lecture on defense against tanks. And we are quite prepared to stop them. Our whole defense is built against tanks. Besides this we have pits or traps, hand grenades, and special ammunition.

There has been a marked change among us here. At first we were hoping we would get some training before going to the front, though we would have gone without any if need be. Then after a few days training and we appreciated how much we did not know, we were still more anxious for training. But now we feel we are prepared to go to the front, and are anxious to get our baptism of fire. In addition, these few weeks has given us complete confidence in our officers, and they certainly are quite capable. My section leader spent four years in the German Army in 1914–18, wounded 4 years.[18] Our Company Commander has had plenty of experience on the front. Others have had quite a bit of experience in the army of the USA. And with the modern tactics that are being developed here we are all set.

Just now our discussion is raging about the subject of digging dug-outs, trenches, making tea, etc. how to dig in sand and timber etc. and now it's on tobacco and making charcoal for smokeless fires. Which reminds me that yesterday we each received a piece of chocolate from the Friends of the Lincoln Battalion.[19] It was good.

By the way, I haven't received a letter from you yet, although fellows have gotten letters dated on the 19th of May. But I am still waiting patiently.

Incidentally, I am No. 5 man in my crew which is the next most responsible post to that of Corporal, and am also being trained in signaling.

You, of course have read of the bombardment of Almeria by the Nazis.[20] It seems to me this ought to be about the last straw. Do the Catholic teachers still refuse to see why they must support the Spanish Government. People must realize that if the Nazis are permitted to do this with impunity, they will go still farther, that nothing will be too low for them. The role of fascism certainly is made clear by this action.

You must be near the end of the school year when you get this. And getting ready for the summer vacation. I hope you are not entertaining any idea of coming here, for it is impossible to enter Spain. And even more impossible for me to leave. And don't let anyone tell you different, for I know. Anyway, I'll probably be quite busy this summer.

Just now, the subject is unmentionable, but quite hilarious.

Did I write you, I thought I had scabies (a trotskyite itch) but it turned out to be flea bites. They are under control now. But don't worry about me, for I am feeling fine.

Give my regards to all
  With my love
  Carl

P.S. My address is always the same regardless of the particular place I am at.

[HANDWRITTEN]

June 5, 1937

Dear Impy: a few minutes after I mailed my last letter, I received yours, and certainly was happy to hear from you. And 2 hours later, I met Irving W. and Pretty. You could have knocked me over when I saw Pretty. Both of them arrived here without difficulty and are well. But they just came in time for I think our Company is leaving this place today, although one never knows until one is on the way.[21]

I am glad you didn't write until you were certain and you addressed it quite properly. Now to answer some of your questions.

Yesterday they took out about a third of the men from my Company because a higher standard is demanded of us than of the Infantry. For if one man in a crew doesn't do his duty, it may have very serious results. Each machine gun crew is made up of 5 or 6 men. There is the Corporal, the first & second gunner who are responsible for the gun, and then 2 or 3 more Ammunition Carriers who are responsible for supplying the gun with water & ammunition. I am the last man, responsible to see that no one ever leaves any ammunition behind, for keeping in touch with the ammunition dump, to see that everyone in my crew keeps in line and Communication between my crew and the section leaders—there are 3 or 4 crews to a section, and 10 to 12 to a Company.

Probably you are worried because the machine gun crews were called "suicide squads." But actually, you are relatively safe, if you properly camo[u]flage your position and know your gun & work hard, which means use that pick & shovel every night.

Am glad to hear you plan to go to Cornell for the Summer. I hope you'll go through with it. Let me know your new address. And am glad to hear you are all set as for the furniture, etc., are concerned, though I am almost tempted to remind you of some remarks I made when you bought it.

I am writing to my branch to tell them I heard they are doing good work.[22] It is certainly nice to hear they are going ahead. It means much to me here.

By the way, the name of our Battalion is the George Washington. I think the next battalion will adopt the name of Mooney.[23] But the name Washington is much better for us, for it signifies our own struggle for national freedom and brings to mind the support we received at that time. And it certainly should help the American people understand why we are here.

How did the elections come out in your union? How large is it by this time? And how many in your club from your place?

You can write to Marie, for I have written her as well as Bennet. By the way, open all my mail & answer it for me.

Must close if I want to get this into the mail before we leave.

> With all my love
> Carl

[HANDWRITTEN]

Friday, June 11

Dear Impy:

Just received 3 letters from you dated the 21, 23, & 25th. The regularity of the mail can be judged from the fact that I received yours of the 20th six days ago.

Am glad to hear you moved to Aunt Adele's, and that everything is taken care of as far as the apt. is concerned. And give Herman my thanks for helping you. I mean to write him again, but writing letters takes time.

Hope you will send me the picture, but the smaller it is the better, otherwise I won't be able to take it with me, and there is no place to leave things.

I don't remember answering Ellen's letter.[24] Please write to her, and also send me her address, I am writing to Arnold, but I am afraid it may be a bit late for his Commencement.

By the way, you said you enclosed writing paper. It must have dropped out in the Censor's office for it never reaches me. But never mind, for I have no trouble getting paper.

I appreciate the news about the CIO.[25] It seems things will soon come to a showdown. Well, there is no more question about who will be victorious than there is about who will win the war. Can you imagine, over a thousand deserters to our ranks in the month of May alone. And wait until we start a real offensive.

We are still standing by, and continuing our training, but ready to move at any moment. I received a letter from Paul, (it seems he is in a Machine Gun crew also) and he seems to be doing very well.[26] It's possible that I may see him there in a few days. I certainly hope so. His Battalion has been at the front for over 3 months straight, so they must be pretty tough now. I understand whole days go by there without a single casualty, for both sides are dug in very deep.

Yesterday forenoon we had a large Maneuver and tonight we are going out from 8 to 6 in the morning practicing a night attack. My gun crew is one of the best if not the best in the Company. And if we get a new corporal as I hope we will today, it will be the best. Unfortunately, our present corporal is an IWW member, and has Constitutional objections to giving orders, besides drinking a bit heavy.[27] But the other 3 besides myself are all you could ask for. And our Section leader, Herman, who had 4 years Machine Gun experience in the world war, is tops.[28]

More men are here, and the 3rd American Battalion is already well under way.[29] But they are giving us quite a thorough training in the use of gas masks, for it is quite likely the fascists may try to use it as a last desperate move. So far we haven't been touched, but the other night fascist planes flew nearby but our chasers drove them off.

Harvest time for grains is already here. The Barley is being cut, by hand, of course, and the Spanish beans are ready too. And the weather reminds me very much of the Adirondacks especially since our work is almost all done in pine woods. Incidentally, the pine nuts are very good to eat.

Have some sewing to do before this evening, so will write more in a day or so.

Of course, I wish you could come here this summer. But it is impossible so go to Cornell. And I may see you before the year is up.

With all my love,
Carl

[HANDWRITTEN]

June 13, 1937

Dear Impy:

Didn't have time to mail this where we were, so I'll add another installment. We are now close enough to the front to hear the artillery fire and I expect to see Paul any day now. It looks quite certain that we will join his Brigades in a few days. Am looking forward very much to the next few days when we get our first taste of fire, and our first chance with the fascists.

This part of Spain, that is the Central Plateau, is quite interesting. While generally quite level, it is cut by steep broad valleys. There is a great deal of wheat grown here, and even sugar beets. And all night long, a number of birds call to each other. I was on guard last night from 12 to 2, and it was very pleasant listening to the birds, looking at the stars, and standing guard at the entrance to our camp.

We are at present quartered with a Company of Britishers, some of whom I had not met before. They are a swell bunch of fellows, most of them being Welshmen and great singers. Majority of them are coal miners.

Did you receive Andy's letter?[30] He says he wrote to you and is waiting for an answer. One of the men in my gun crew is a larger edition of Andy, except that he doesn't drink. Incidentally, Andy has straightened out pretty well on that point.

Our food seems to improve as we approach the front. That is good, for I suspect I am getting something like hives, but it is nothing serious, from our standing diet. This morning, we had a fine swim. The water was 8 to 10 feet deep and very swift, so it was great fun. I could swim 100 yards in a very short time.

If I am not mistaken, you have a Birthday pretty soon, or is it in Sept.? And soon it'll be four years, just about the time you get this.

I hope you can read these letters for they are all written on my knee, since no table is available.

> With all my love,
> Carl

[HANDWRITTEN]

June 16, 1937

Dear Impy:

While waiting to move up into the second line this morning, I have a little time to write a few letters.

Probably by this time, you know we are in the 15th Brigade along with the Lincoln Battalion. Yesterday the military leaders of our Brigade spoke to us, and certainly made a fine impression.

The 15th has a mighty good record, for they helped stop the drive on the Jarama front last February 12–15th when the fascists tried to encircle Madrid.[31] So we have plenty to live up to.

Imp, I have undertaken the most serious job of my time, that of political leader of my Company.[32] And it will mean the hardest work of my life. Our Company now is rated as the best Company in the Battalion, partly due to the fact that we are more or less a selected group. In addition, our Company Commander, Comrade Garland, is one of the finest men I have ever met, and is both respected & loved by his men, and he has an excellent attitude towards political work, and makes a fine political report as well as military.[33] So this makes my task a bit easier. But I'll have many things to tell you when I see you again.

We certainly are glad to read about the cigarettes & Chocolate the F of LB are sending us.[34] And we are going to make certain they reach us, for such things usually go astray. You can not imagine how much cigarettes help us, even though I don't smoke.

So far, I am quite well, although I acquired a touch of Barbers Itch, but it is under control. It hasn't hurt me, only the salve doesn't improve my appearance.

Paul and his Company finally are on leave, and I hope to visit him tomorrow.

But I have work to do, so will close. Of course, you realize I await a letter each day & am very disappointed when I don't get one.

     With all my love,

     Carl

[HANDWRITTEN]

June 20, 1937

Dear Impy:

Thanks for the clippings in your letters. They are very useful for our wall paper and thanks for sending me soap, only I am afraid it won't get here. If you want to send me anything, sent it to the "Friends of the Lincoln Battalion" in N.Y. and they'll forward it to me through their channels. Last night we were very much surprised for we received 4 packages of Lucky Strikes per man. And we hear Chocolates are coming. These things certainly help.

Well, we are only some 7 or 8 kilometers from the front now, and at 12 noon and 7 P.M. a dozen shells land in a small town a kilometer away. You can hear them whistle as they come. The town is practically evacuated, but there are several hospitals there, for it is right behind the lines. But only a few of the shells actually land in the town. We are hoping to go to the front line soon, for now we are in a reserve position where we can hear rifle & machine gun fire, but can't see it.

I am quite well except for slight attacks of diarrhea once in a while, though I haven't had it seriously yet, so many have. It's a very interesting ailment, and is due to the great difference in temperature between noon and four in the morning. So they are going to issue flannel belts to wrap around the abdomen to prevent chilling of the intestines at night.

By the way, you can send me something directly, and that is a copy of the C.I.[35] There is one here for several hundred men, so one never gets to see it.

My work as political leader keeps me quite busy. I also teach 4 classes a day, 2 in Spanish & 2 in map-making and reading. In fact, I am writing this letter in installments. Just at the moment, I am waiting for several other Comrades to meet, in order to go to the Social Local People's Front Committee to offer our help to harvest the wheat, which is now ready for cutting.[36] Only ¼ of the usual number of men are available for this work, the rest being in the Army. The fascists are sending over incendiary shells now trying to set the fields on fire, but so far they have not been successful here.

Very antiquated methods of harvesting and threshing are used, dating back to the methods used 3,500 years ago. Wheat is cut with a small hand sickle. I haven't seen even a cradle used around here. Threshing is done by plac[ing] the wheat bundles on a hard packed piece of ground, and then driving over it with a mule pulling a plank with obstructions underneath. Then the chaff is thrown into the air to separate it from the grain.

Ralph Bates spoke to us last night and told us how the peasants go into No-Man's Land, or even behind Fascist lines, to harvest certain crops at night. Bates is the best speaker I have heard here, and holds the attention of the men completely.[37]

Tuesday, June 22

Will try to finish the letter for you now. I was very happy to receive your letter of the 4th. By the way, I haven't received a single letter from anyone else yet.

No, I am not smoking, and don't think I shall, but I have very many friends who do. But I am learning to drink wine, for that is served twice a day at meals. But give our grocer my thanks for the soap, only I hope they come through.

I should think the aid for the Basque children can do much to enlighten some of the more misguided Americans.[38] The situation about Bilbao looks tough just now, but far from hopeless.[39]

Am enclosing a drawing you may find interesting. [not found]

When are you leaving for Michigan? Keep me informed of your address. And give my regards to all our friends.

With all my love,
Carl

[HANDWRITTEN]

June 27, 1937

Dear Impy,

Am enclosing a letter for Johnny Little. Please forward it to him. But read it first, so I won't need to repeat some of it for you.[40]

Received a letter from Bennet. It's a waco. I think he may join the Liberty League.[41] Anyway, he says the idea of my being here to prevent a world war is ridiculous, that U.S. must have nothing to do with either side, and that when I get through, I can come home and think "What a fool I've been." He also tells of great prosperity in Orrville, all factories having men, every one busy, and goes on to say he thinks a revolution is around the corner. Such a feeling during prosperity is certainly indication of the period in which we live. However, his letter is quite friendly in spite of all this. So I shall send him a long reply. It is also quite evident from his letter he is seeking some escape thru religion.

We are still standing by in our reserve position. The other night during that terrific storm, the fascists launched an attack in this sector, but didn't get anywhere and the day before yesterday we were bombarded, not with bombs but with leaflets from the fascists, can you imagine. It was to the effect that Bilbao has returned to Spain, etc., but their leaflets have little effect, for truth is against them.

You ought to see us whenever a plane is sighted. We have to remain absolutely still until it passes, and planes are usually seen 3 to 4 times a day. Usually ours, but often one can not tell.

Yesterday, we were cutting wheat again with hand sickles but the thistles give one a nice prickly hand. It'll all be harvested in very few days now.

This morning, I was informed that the General Staff has officially approved my appointment as political leader of my Company. So far, am getting along quite well. Especially since the food has improved, more cigarettes are available, and yesterday we received quite a bunch of pamphlets. Andy, by the way was temporarily political leader of an infantry Company in our Battalion while the regular P.L. was in a hospital. His tent is only about 15 yds from mine, and we see each other often. He says he has written to you, and will write again.

Impy, these clear nights out in the open remind me of our trip thru the Adirondacks last summer. I certainly hope we can repeat that again soon. But in the meantime, there is much to do.

With all my love,
Carl

[HANDWRITTEN]

June 27, 1937

Dear Brother Bennet:

Certainly was glad to hear from you. Your letter came in less than 3 weeks. And I am heartily in favor of a reunion some time. But we will have to set the date far ahead for it seems we almost cover half of the world now.

Am very glad to hear that Orrville is prospering, and that the Dairy is doing well. Though I am quite surprised to hear you speak of a revolution coming that can't be stopped, at the same time you talk of this great prosperity. Perhaps it is because 10 million are still unemployed in spite of the fact that prosperity seems to be back. For many millions are not helped by this prosperity, especially in the large cities.

Is Marie living in St. Louis, or just visiting there? Isn't she teaching school anymore? And is June working in Cleveland or studying?[42] I certainly should like to see them again.

I sent you another letter a few days ago, but will write again to take up some of the points in your letter.

You are right, there are 2 sides to every matter. What are these two sides? Things look different to one man than to another. Why do they look different. For instance, if a banker goes to Soviet Union, and sees what has happened to bankers, he thinks it is a horrible country. But a worker goes there, sees there is no unemployment, medical service is free, his children are paid for going to school, wages are steadily rising while prices fall, there is full democracy for him but none for capitalists, he says, "Hmm, not so bad, not so bad."

According to Henry Ford, labor unions are very, very bad. But his workers think they are fine, and like them. In other words, what is one man's meat is another man's poison. These are the two sides of every question. And you have to learn which is your side. I know both sides, and I know which is mine. And millions of Americans are gradually learning this as well. Think this over.

You say our going to Spain to prevent another World War is ridiculous. When the communists, and they were the only ones, said in 1927 and 28 that another depression was coming, every one else called them ridiculous.[43] But who was ridiculous? When the Soviet Union announced its first 5-year plan, everyone scoffed. But they finished it in 4 years, 3 months. Now we say that Italy and Germany are preparing for war to get whatever they want and that if the rest of the world doesn't stop them, we will have a second world war. Bennet, in a few years, perhaps even before, you'll see the truth of this. I only hope enough Americans can understand this before it is too late.

I am a bit surprised at your unwillingness to defend Democracy. Don't you think it is necessary anymore? You almost scoff at the idea. You say the average man will believe almost anything he is told. No, Bennet, the average man has good common sense, and can not be fooled for long. And a democratic government is absolutely necessary for our welfare and we must help Spain maintain its Democracy. The volunteers on the Loyalist side make it clear that they are only here to help drive out fascism, and when that is done, want that the Spanish people themselves democratically decide what kind of government they want. Bennet, if fascism is victorious here, democracy is weakened in the United States, and the danger of another World War becomes extremely serious.

There is one other thing you forget. The war here is not between two governments, but between the Spanish Government, supported by the majority of the people as proven in a democratic election, against a handful of landlords & capitalists who engineered an uprising against the government with the help of war materials and men from Hitler and Mussolini. Why does the United S[t]ates refuse to sell arms to the Spanish Government? It sells arms to Italy to conquer a weak country like Ethiopia, but when the legal government of Spain tries to put down a reactionary capitalist landlord uprising, they refuse to sell it arms. Isn't this strange? And hadn't we better do something about it?

Just a few words on the Church. You write, "It seems to be an organization to muddle in affairs which are none of its business." I am afraid you swallowed some propaganda. Do you mean that your religion does not apply to all fields of activity. Is it something only for Sundays, and to scare little children with the fear of hell if they don't do so and so. Do you think that Christ would say, "War is none of my business?" You know that Christ would be against war, against every injustice no matter where, that he would be ashamed to see his followers say, "That has nothing to do with the church."

That is a capitalist idea, for the christian religion interferes with his business activities. But for the masses of people, there is not the conflict between their religion and their every day activities. In fact, the mennonite religion especially should be a help to the working people if they worked for its application everywhere.[44]

And didn't Christ send his disciples out to all corners of the world? And is it not the suffering of the Spanish people something for every Christian to share? How can you as a Christian say, "I don't think we should help the Spanish People"? Perhaps, Bennet, it is you who look at things from one side and from the Capitalist side at that, when you are a worker. You see all this is not a matter of being high minded, but of being practical, and thoroughly honest in every phase of life.

Anyway, if we were face to face, we could discuss these matters very much better. In the meantime, a few more words about our life here. I think I wrote you that we are helping the farmers harvest their wheat. It'll be finished in a few days. If you could only see what kind of a government there is here, and the kind of laws. All land has been given forever to the people who work on it. No one can be evicted from the land as long as he works it. Of course he must pay a certain tax to the government, but it is a very reasonable one. The peasants are really happy. Just at this moment, there is one harrowing the field in front of me, and you ought to hear him sing.

But Bennet, I have a thousand and one things to do. Today, I was informed that my appointment as Political Leader of my Company has been approved by the General Staff. And so I don't have even a single free minute now.

Write often, and give me plenty of news about Orrville. Give my sincerest regards to Grandmother, and all my friends in Orrville.

Most Sincerely,
Carl

My address
Socorro Rojo Internacional
George Washington Battalion
Albacete, Spain

[HANDWRITTEN]
Address: S.R.I., Plaza del Altozano, 27
Albacete, Spain
June 30, 1937

Dear Impy:

Just a few words to let you know I am well, and that all is going fine. There really is no exciting news except all kinds of rumors which are wrong 9 times out of ten.

Les Grumet, whom I knew from the NSL in Pittsburgh, was here 2 days ago.[45] He is with the Medical service now, and he knew Paul, and some of my other friends. Bernie saved his life one night by taking him to a fire when he was practically frozen. He has the greatest praise for Bernie.

We are still in our reserve position about 15 minutes by truck from the front line. Nothing exciting, except that a good part of the 10,000 Italians landed at Malaga 2 weeks ago are now on this front.[46] This morning there is a lot of artillery fire quite a ways to our right. But at present we spend most of our time perfecting our knowledge of the machine gun, grenade, digging gun pits and going through small maneuvers.

The other evening the political and military leaders of the Lincoln Battalion had been invited as our guests, for supper, and for a joint meeting, for we have many questions to ask them. But unfortunately, they were unable to come. But I am hoping to go there soon and to see Paul.

You may wonder how we took the news of the fall of Bilbao. Actually, it only made us more determined and serious, without any thought that this presages a fascist victory. On the contrary, there is no doubt that fascism will be smashed. But we do realize that how long it will take us, and how much it will cost us depends very much on the action of the people outside of Spain. If U.S. would treat Germany and Italy as aggressors, which they are, it certainly would help Great Britain make up her mind. And what is also very good news is that the British Labor Party has decided to oppose the non-intervention policy, and I think it can change the policy of the British Government on this issue. But in the meantime we are improving our military power.

There have been some scant news which seems to indicate there are big doings in the States in connection with the steel strike. There are rumors of a national General Strike and what-not. Anyway, it must be cementing the forces of the People's Front.

By the way, I haven't received word from my Branch yet, tho I expect a letter each day. The wrist-watch they gave me certainly is handy for watches are in very great demand here.

Imp, don't forget to enclose a picture of yourself once in a while. The two I have of you are good, but were almost washed away in the flood the other night. And don't forget to write every other day.

With all my love,
Carl

[HANDWRITTEN]

Fourth Company
Geo. Washington Battalion
International Brigades, Spain
July 3, 1937

C. Lundquist
Box 69, Sudbury
Ontario, Canada

Dear Comrade:

On July 2, 1937 it was decided by our Company Disciplinary Court to inform you that Comrade [Tauno] Lindle has not proven himself to be a disciplined anti-fascist soldier. Comrade Lindle is being punished for his third offense of drunkenness by having this letter sent to you, and by a fine of 20 days pay.

Drunkenness is a very serious offense in our International Brigades, especially in a machine-gun Company where it may cost the lives of many men. However, we are giving Comrade Lindle another opportunity to prove himself by permitting him to remain in our Company. If Comrade Lindle through his future actions proves himself to be a good anti-fascist soldier, we will inform you of that with great pleasure.

Comradely,
Signed by Commander Garland
Pol. Com. Geiser

[HANDWRITTEN]

July 3, 1937

Dear Impy:

Just received your letter of June 12 and will answer right away, although it is so dark I can't see the pad.

Imp, by the time you get this, you'll be reading of a big, audacious and powerful drive.[47] And we'll be right in the center of it. You should feel the air. Expectant, confident, waiting for the word, "Adelante." I shan't be surprised if we break the back of fascism.

These evenings we spend either marching or sleeping under the stars on the ground. We have passed the stage of Barracks.

You should see the effect on our Spanish Comrades when I tell them of a party where 6,000 pesetas is raised for them. But, Imp, it is getting so dark I can't even see the lines let alone the words, and it seems possible we may sleep here tonight, so I'll be able to finish this in the morning—Salud.

July 4, 1937

Dear Impy—

Met Paul this morning, all browned and hardened. The Lincoln Battalion has certainly done some tough fighting, especially when it first went into action. For a number of reasons, I think our Battalion will be even stronger than the Washington. Paul is very well, but insists he is only going to be a rank and filer, and doesn't want responsibility. I'll talk with him awhile.

Just came from a meeting of Company & Battalion political Commissars. It was truly inspiring. I don't think I am giving any secrets away when I tell you that this is the first offensive by the Government and should relieve the pressure on the Basque Country, stop the shelling of Madrid, and with a lot of luck, smash Spanish fascism.

You ought to be here, hear and see the tremendous preparations. Equipment & men galore. We certainly should do plenty. Just now Paul's Company is only several hundred yards from us.

Of course, don't think everything is rosy. We need more machine guns and all kinds of equipment. Even the Dimitrov Battalion has several men without shoes, and this country is bare and rocky.[48] It's going to demand plenty of the men.

By the way, some deserters from the fascists on the Jarama front didn't believe Bilbao had fallen for they had been fooled too often. And they reported that many were only waiting for a strong gov't offensive to desert the fascists.

But, Imp. Believe it or not, I had a swell swim and shave this morning. Am feeling fit, without even a serious cut on my hand or the diarrhea and no lice yet. It's grand, only our food truck is already 1 hour and 15 minutes late and I am very hungry. Coffee and bread at 6 in the morning, and then nothing until 1:15 in the afternoon makes you appreciate food.

Are you sending me your picture. Am awaiting it, and if this offensive goes as we hope it will, I'll be seeing you in a couple of months.

With all my love,
Carl

[HANDWRITTEN]

July 14th, 1937

Dear Impy:

Your letter of the 24th of June came at a most opportune time, when I was dead-weary after 7 days of steady fighting, usually in the front line. Imp, you must write me every two or three days this summer, for your letters lighten me very much.

I haven't written you since the 4th because we have been at battle in the big offensive since then, and I have been much too weary, tired & dirty, not to say lacking paper and equipment to write you.

As you know, our offensive has been victorious, and is still continuing. But believe me, Imp, war means suffering, horrible and nerve wracking. I have never been so exhausted in all my life. Our machine gun company lost 3 commanders and 4 section political leaders, all wounded. As you know, this kind of fighting means much greater casualties than ordinary trench warfare.

Just now we are in a reserve position, which means we are ready to move into the trenches, or to the front lines, in a few minutes notice. But it gives us a chance to sleep, to rest and my first shave and bath since the 4th. And just now it looks like we are going up again after 8 hours here.

You read about 700 soldiers deserting en masse to us 2 or 3 days ago. This is the kind of action that helps us very much and we hope it will increase during the next few weeks. Opening of the French border will help us greatly for while we have great sources of arms, there are many things we could use, such as field glasses. The fascists use them to spot our positions, while we try to locate them with our naked eye.

You ought to see how brave our boys are when they lie shot on the stretchers, as long as they are conscious, they speak firmly and think only of the battle. By the way, Paul is well, but Andy is dead. A sniper must have got him when he sat down to rest for a moment. Anyway he was found sitting down with his head nodding forward a bit. He did very well here. Pretty & Irving are in the 3rd American Battalion which did not take part in the offensive yet.

As you probably read, our Battalion was in the thick of it from the beginning, and we took part in the taking of Villanueva de [la] Cañada, and now are about Mosquito Hill, the highest point between here and Madrid. As soon as it is taken the going should be much easier.

But, Imp, I hope to get back to tell you many more things of our fighting here. As for myself, it is doing much to steel me physically & mentally.

Only one thing, write me every two or three days, for when one is out in that terrifically hot sun, oftentimes without food & water, with bullets flying all about, and you are exhausted to the bone, a letter from you means very much to me.

The best of luck for your trip to Cal. this summer!

With all my love,

Carl

[HANDWRITTEN]

July 14, 1937

Dear Herbert:[49]

Am writing to you instead of to Arnie in the hope that I will hear from you and the Branch a bit oftener.[50] I finally received a letter from Arnie, but it was a long time coming. However the news it contained about the work of the Branch is very interesting and cheering.

I have just been through 8 days of fighting, most of it being in the front lines, and the rest in the second or third. Our Battalion was in the offensive from the very beginning. In a way, I wish you could have been here, but then again, you missed a lot of suffering & pain. War, especially when you are on the offensive, is the hardest kind of work imaginable, in which you work without rest, food, & often water, in sun so hot water standing in a pot burns you. It is to say the least, hell. But we have to fight here if we want to defeat fascism, and so our comrades fight on bravely until they drop, either from a bullet or exhaustion.

As you know by this time, our battles here, north & west of Madrid, the capture of Villanueva de [la] Cañada in which we took part, and the others have been of extreme importance. The demoralization which it is causing among the fascist forces is tremendous. Two whole battalions have already come over to us en masse. And during the last 2 days, the fascists lost 25 planes & we 5. The biggest air battle, with 70 planes taking part, occurred right over our head, although so high it was hard to follow. The fascists lost 10 planes and we lost 1.

Just now I am trying to write this under a bush. 300 yards to the north fascist shells are falling. And every couple of minutes, fascist planes fly overhead. The fascists are desperate, so they are throwing shells and bombs about madly, without a well-thought out plan, but which doesn't make it any less exciting for us.

I don't believe Pretty had a chance to take part in this offensive, for I believe his Battalion is still in training. But he'll soon be here, I imagine.

I certainly am glad to hear the Branch is collecting funds for Spain. We get American cigarettes and chocolate every now and then. But it seems to me that also very important is to educate the young people that the U.S. neutrality policy is wrong, that the Spanish government must have the right to buy whatever it needs in the U.S. And Herb, there are plenty of military equipment that we need here. The Spanish government must have the right to buy from the U.S.

But I must dig a hole for protection against artillery and aerial fire, and camouflage our company equipment, so must close.

Please write at once, with news about the Branch, yourself, Vince, Florence, Charlotte, Mollie and everyone else.[51]

Most sincerely,

Carl

My address:

Carl Geiser

Geo. Washington Battalion

Albacete, Spain

[HANDWRITTEN]

July 15, 1937

Dear Impy,

While I have the chance, I had better write you another letter. We are still in a reserve position.

Today the Lincoln & Washington Battalions were amalgamated. Our Battalion Commander is Comrade Marcovich, our Political Commissar is Steve Nelson, and what a swell guy. Our Company Commander is Syd Levine, from New York.[52] I stay on as company political leader.

But this gives us a really powerful machine-gun company, and a real bunch of fighters. You ought to see the shield of one of the Lincoln MGs. It has been hit at least 15 times by bullets. The guys who were behind were undoubtedly very glad for its protection.

We are in a very interesting spot at the moment. Planes are overhead almost half of the time, and we have to stay ducked in the bushes. In addition there is shelling on both sides, but it seems they haven't discovered us here yet, so none have landed very close.

We are all feeling much better and a bit rested now. Everyone is sleeping and writing letters and bathing and reading reports of our fighting and getting an idea of what we did.

Paul is sleeping about 15 feet from me. He has lost 40 pounds and is a powerful athletic person now. But he refuses to be more than a rank and filer, so called, or more properly, a militia man.

Your trip to Cal. interests me very much. Look over the country, so when I get back and we can make a trip across, we'll know where to go & what to see. It certainly should be a great trip, especially since you are traveling with Tima. But don't forget to write me, and let me know where to address you.

It's 10 to 7 now and we are waiting for supper. We have gotten good food today, rice & coffee this morning, & Rice and Roast Beef this noon. Rice is appreciated because it is so filling and nourishing.

Imp, if it is convenient, enclose an Inprecor in your letters, for we seldom see one here.[53]

May write you more tomorrow. In the meantime, here's all my love. & Don't forget a photo.

> Comradely,
> Carl

[HANDWRITTEN]

July 16, 1937

Dearest Imp:

Well, Imp, you see when I have time I write you every day. By this time I am quite well recuperated and beginning to enjoy life, especially since we haven't been shelled or bombed all day long.

You ought to meet our Battalion Political Leader, Steve Nelson, former Political Leader of the Lincoln Boys. He is one swell guy. When the Commander of the Lincoln Battalion was wounded in some very stiff fighting a few days ago, he took over command. Two hours later, under pressure of a fascist counter attack, the adjacent Spanish Battalion broke and began to run back. The Adjutant of the Lincoln Battalion said he was going back to get reinforcements two hours away. A Company

Commander came up and said he couldn't control his men any longer. If the Lincoln boys would have retreated then it would have meant a very serious break in our lines and prepared the way for a serious flank attack on us. Nelson appointed a new Company Commander on the spot, took over the battalion, and with the help of our present Company adjutant who put up a machine gun on the advancing fascists, the line was held and the fascists forced to retreat. So with a ma[n] of this caliber here, it means the Washington-Lincoln Battalion will be a powerful one.

In a few weeks the grapes are going to be ripe. And that means our problem of water & sugar will be taken care of at least in part. Besides other fruits are ripening, so we are looking forward to plenty of fruit.

I finally received a letter from my Branch, and what a fine one. It certainly is heartening to know that they are doing so well. And today we each received a bar of Baker's Chocolate with Almonds. You can't imagine how fine it tasted. And any one who receives a package is immediately surrounded by a group of admiring friends.

Come to think of it, probably by the time you receive this you'll be in California, for you can't possibly get it before August First. Time certainly flies.

But it's getting on in the day, and I have to run around to see all my group political leaders on a few matters.

Don't forget to write often.

With all my love,
Carl

P.S. Last night from 10–12 I spent on top of a hill on watch with a machine-gun, as the moon slowly sank down, and it certainly made me lonesome for you and the Adirondacks, or even the Palisades. It really never gets very dark here, and as I told you before, the stars stand out beautifully.

Carl

[TYPEWRITTEN]

July 23, 1937. Sunday

Dear Sylvia,[54]

You can't imagine how glad I was to get your letter.[55] Despite the swell people here and the love for your comrades that grows stronger each day, still you want to know that those back home keep you in mind. No, my parents still don't know.[56] The last letter Sarah sent says that the deception is still a success. What a load off my mind it would be if my parents were revolutionists.

Carl looked swell when I saw him, which wasn't often. He was always busy—either out mapping or having to go to a meeting. Only once did we have time for a real long intimate conversation and I felt lousy then because I wanted to overwhelm him with details about you and it was plain that he, despite his typical restraint, was yearning for more and more news about you, and all I could tell him was that we had eaten together at your Aunt's and that you had looked well. His outfit moved out very soon after I hit town. You ask about our strenuous life and it reminds me that for the first time I saw Carl tired, really tired. He came in one rainy night from mapping and he sat down on his bunk and said, "Tonight I'm really tired. Tonight I feel tired for the first time!"

As for me, yes, it was hard going at first, just as it was for most of the fellows, because of the change in climate and diet. Everyone gets diarrhea, and besides that I got a spell of weakness which kept me listless for three days. The first two weeks here I lost twenty pounds. But now I'm okay, and I've stood up under big strains. Not only ordinary maneuvers, but a four day maneuver which closely resembled first line conditions— digging trenches, living in trenches, continually under fire, attacks and withdrawals, night patrols, etc.—in four days none of us, I think, slept more than ten hours. The morale was very high. The last evening of the maneuver I remember very distinctly. The whole battalion sang the International. Singing it in our helmets and bandoliers, we felt our power. It's the final conflict all right. By the way, I stood up so well under this test that I'm proud to write you that I was complimented on being a good soldier. This praise (from my commander) was especially heartening because I made some very serious errors here, which resulted in severe criticism.[57] But it was a lesson I needed, and if I come back in one piece, I'll be a Bolshevik with a real understanding (for the first time) of party organization and discipline. Right now I'm a group leader—the equivalent of a sergeant. That doesn't mean I'll last as one—there are continual shifts, which is very good, I think, because the men—and don't forget the caliber of these soldiers—acquaint themselves with different duties.

The fall of Bilbao has not disheartened us here at all and all I hope is that this mood you speak of does not hurt the collection of funds, and the aid in general. It's funny, it's not that anyone minimizes the fall of Bilbao, but there's such a sense of confidence, such an absolute lack of demoralization, and so clear an understanding of the conflict. I suppose the clearest expression of this emotion is Del Vayo's statement, "I believe in our victory because I believe in our people!"[58] Yes, I'm certain it's this faith in the masses, and especially in that section of them which has been victorious, that section of them which is the ace in the hole for the world proletariat, dear Sylvia—which is the basis for our casual confidence, and for our scorn of the fascist bastards' arms.

From a military point of view, I suppose you read the article by Golubov in the D[aily] W[orker].[59] The article states that the fascists think in terms of some big victory—Bilbao or Malaga—while we think in terms of a general offensive on all fronts.[60]

Of course, the fighting is very bitter. The bulletins we get every day report that and our army is not as coordinated as we would like it to be. But they will learn on the other fronts just as they did on the Madrid front. And we in the International Brigade are serving as an example of discipline and of coordination, above all. And we will succeed in our task, everywhere and anywhere, our tactic of surrounding the enemy, getting him in the rear, cutting him to pieces, giving him only this alternative of be killed or surrender.

Well, Sylvia, write again and soon. I hope to spend my birthday at the front and to greet Carl there. My address is [no address included]
So long there comrade, and I want to know why you went to Michigan. Gee, it's so hard for me to say how grateful and happy your letter made me. You're swell, Sylvia.

Irv

[HANDWRITTEN]

July 26, 1937

My dear little Impy,
I received your post-card of "El Greco," Thanks very much even if it did remind me very much of my 5 years in Cleveland. Soon I expect to get a letter from you giving more details about your trip.

Since I wrote you last, we spent several more days on the front in some of the worst fighting I have seen [seven handwritten lines redacted].[61]

Impy, the American people can be proud of the role and the way their representatives in the International Brigades are fighting. In spite of the fact that they are completely exhausted (I haven't been able to eat for 5 days because of Stomach trouble of some kind), have inferior weapons to that of the fascists, are fighting in a boiling sun, they are still being used as shock troops, and they only leave the trenches when carried out wounded or completely cracked-up.

Yesterday, we finally started out for a rest, but were halted and are still in a reserve position. If we have to go back, it will be very hard, but we will do it. At this moment we are in a position where the fascists send over as many as 30 huge bombers at a time, and you ought to see the earth, rock and steel fly. But yesterday, I saw something I'll always re-member with relish. Twelve huge fascist bombers were coming towards. I and 3 other comrades were lying in a ditch. They were flying very low, and I was watching them very closely, for you can see them drop their bombs and know whether they are going to land very close. They were flying in this formation.

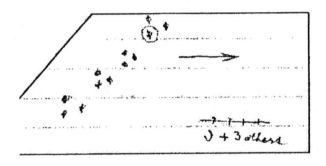

I notice the 3 in the lead beginning to drop their bombs and could see they would drop some 250 yards to our left. But those in the rear were going to come uncomfortably close and I told my comrades, "Here is where we get it" and I watched the bombs fall. All of a sudden I saw a huge red explosion above us exceeding any 4th of July fireworks I have ever seen. At first I thought they had dropped some shrapnel bombs that burst in the air overhead. But then I noticed a fascist bomber was miss-ing, the one I have encircled. And I noticed all kinds of debris slowly spiraling around and falling to the ground. AND then we realized our anti-aircraft guns had scored a direct hit on one of the bombers and it had exploded. The rest of the planes were unloading their bombs now too, but were frightened and veered off to the left so that bombs didn't come closer to us than a hundred yards. Boy, did we thank our stars for that hit! It was all that saved us.

Am trying to get up enough energy this morning to shave and bathe. I certainly need to do both. If we really do go out for our rest, it'll really give me a chance to recuperate & clean-up. You ought to see me now. You probably wouldn't recognize me.

But don't forget to write me often, for your letters are a great help to me.

With all my love,

Carl

[HANDWRITTEN]

July 30, 1937

Dear Bennet:

Believe it or not, I am in a hospital, but I am not wounded. Just completely exhausted and suffering from non-functioning of my stomach. But a few days here with proper food will put me on my feet and feed again.

I haven't heard from you for quite some time. Hope you'll write soon. By the way, you can expect a visit from Sylvia some time near the end of August. At the moment she is in Detroit, both studying and teaching. She'll be able to explain a lot of things to you. Kiss her once for me, by the way.

How is Leonard and his mother? You know, I would like a picture of him. I can imagine he is of a pretty good size now, and can appreciate your pride in him.[62]

According to the papers you've had some hot weather. Must have been good for Uncle John's business. By the way, what does John think of my being here? And Kate? I'll bet he doesn't even like to think of it.

As you know by this time, the Spanish Army put on quite a powerful offensive west of Madrid. The American boys were right in the front ranks of the whole thing, and were used where ever there was an important job to do. We certainly have earned a fine reputation for the fighting Yanks among the Spaniards. But it cost us plenty, not so many killed but about half wounded.

But [if] you want a kick you should be in some situations as we were. One time, our machine gun was placed in a line of Spanish troops. There was a rumor that the fascists had broken through on our right flank and were cutting in behind us, so all the Spaniards ran. Of course we urged them not to, and said we were going to stay there until we got orders to move. So we were left all alone, holding several hundred yards of trench with one machine gun. That was a real thrill. And when the Spaniards came back 2 hours later, when they found out the rumor was false, were they ashamed.

Bennet, if you could be here for only a few hours you'd learn a lot, especially if you were to enjoy a little aerial and artillery bombardment with us. Now, there is nothing like an aerial bombardment by about 20 big bombers over you. The ground shakes like an earthquake, and smoke and dust so thick you can't see. And every single one of these planes, cannon, shells and bombs are either German or Italian. For Mussolini and Hitler are definitely out to conquer Spain for themselves and to set up a fascist government here.

What right have we got to be here, democracy-loving Americans? By what right did Lafayette help us in 1776, or Van Steuben, or Kosciusko? Every honest and sincere person must be on the side of the Spanish people.[63]

Who are in the trench opposite us? Italians, Moors and Germans, and a few Spaniards. But what do these few Spaniards do. In one town, 600 of them killed their officers and came over to our side in a body, and were they glad to be with us! Day before yesterday Franco fired 200 shells into Madrid. He knows he can't take it, so he'll ruin it instead. No Franco means all kind of race hatred, low wages, no democratic rights, and what is most important to you and me, will sell out Spain to Hitler and Mussolini who must have it to carry out their plans for a new world war to divide up the world as in 1914–18.

And Bennet, you don't save yourself by letting your neighbor's house burn down, let alone the fact that it is very far from being Christian in Spirit. It seems to me if you would read the Bible more from the Standpoint of what it says you should do today, instead of what it prophesies for the future, you would come nearer to the truth. I feel if one does what one feels is his duty today, he need not worry about the future. Christ would certainly never say, Let's have nothing to do with Spain, let them take care of themselves. Did you ever read of the brotherhood of man? By any decent standard we have many obligations to the Spanish people.

But write me a long letter again about what is happening in Orrville, and what you are doing. I'll try to write at least every other week to let you know I am well.

Most Sincerely,

Carl

July 31, 1937

Dear Impy:

Now that I am taking a rest, I feel inclined to write you every day. You ought to see what a great educational work I have carried on during the last 36 hours on my friends in the States about Spain. I must spend about 8 hours a day writing letters now.

Just finished quite a detailed letter to Ellen, and think I'll send one to Irene also.[64]

Am feeling much better, suffering only a bit from gas. A little Milk of Magnesia ought to fix that. But there are one or 2 kids around here among the Americans. But we'll fix them before long. They are satisfied with nothing and disgrace us by their ungrateful & rude actions, to say the least.

Bernard Ades, the noted Constitutional Lawyer from Washington, D.C., is also here recuperating.[65] Then there are quite a number of British, Germans & other nationalities, for it seems this is sort of a rest home for our Brigade, where they also provide a certain minimum of medical and dental treatment.

This morning I took a walk of about 2 miles before breakfast, which comes at 9. The scenery is extremely lovely at that hour, and I hope I shall have the opportunity the day before I go back to climb a mountain about 3 miles away that stands out alone, above the tree line. I want to do it some morning bright & early. I think from it the view should be more than magnificent.

The people here are very generous to us except the storekeepers. And because we are up so high, although no fruit is available, we are able to purchase real honest to God cows milk, diluted about half and half. But even that is something to rave about.

While I am here, it is very unlikely that I will receive any mail for it comes direct to my Battalion and I told them to hold it there for me. So I spend part of my time wondering what you are doing, what success you are having, and when I'll see you again. But appearances indicate the war may go on for some time yet, tho one can never tell. If we could resume the offensive quickly, and the democratic nations come out a bit more firmly in our favor, things might happen. Especially since there are numerous reports about open revolt at several places in rebel territory. The fascist disintegration might take place quite quickly with the proper stimulation.

Am enclosing a German clipping of some interest. One side deals with land statistics that are very pertinent and the other with the fight against illiteracy in the Army.

[Clipping not among letters]

> Till tomorrow—
> With all my love—
> Carl

[TYPEWRITTEN COPY]

July 31, 1937
15th Brigade Rest home

Dear Aunt Sylvia,

I hope this letter won't shock you too much, but I am finally getting around to writing some of my friends in the States whom I have so long neglected, especially you.[66]

The reason for my writing at the moment is the fact that I am in the rest home of our Brigade, where I was brought 36 hours ago, suffering from complete exhaustion and digestive difficulties. Today I already feel much refreshed, and hope that in a few more days to return to [m]y battalion.

There are many things to tell you. As you know during the last 3 days the International Brigades took part in the big offensive. We were either in the 1st or 2nd line for three weeks straight, and Aunt Sylvia, there is nothing harder than such fighting. It must go to the credit of our boys that for all that time, where there was a hard job to do, a strategic position to hold, that is where we were placed.

Because of the large numbers wounded, for relatively few were killed, the Lincoln and Washington Battalions were merged. My part during all of this until I came here, was to be political leader of the Washington Battalion, and then of the joint one.

But you ought to see our rest home. It was only opened 3 days ago, and used to be the home of some rich Spaniard. It is way up on the side of a mountain range, and the air and scenery is magnificent. Of course, although we are some distance from the front, we are constantly reminded of the war by the scarcity of objects. Almost all food is rationed. Sweets and tobacco can not be bought; in fact, our purchases are limited to writing paper, wine and cloth, and by some freak, a glass of milk at certain hours of the day. But it is a great relief to be here and rest and sleep.

Aunt Sylvia, if you could see what a terrific sacrifice the Spanish people are making in lives, in comfort, in materials, to check international fascism (we often heard the Italian soldiers shouting at night, "Viva il Duce" and singing Italian songs. German shells and bombs rained all around us.) The American people must do much more to help this heroic people. First of all make it possible for them to buy arms and war materials as they are legitimately entitled to do.

But Aunt Sylvia write and tell me how you are getting along and what is happening in New York. My address is

[Rest of letter missing]

[HANDWRITTEN]

Aug. 3, 1937

My Dear Impy,

Am writing you this in a bar, can you imagine that. But it's quite alright for I am waiting there for the morning papers to arrive. For if you are not on hand when they come, you don't get any. But in the meantime I spent 9 pesetas for a bottle of Malaga to bring back to camp with me. And I'll be very popular as long as that lasts. Malaga is a sweet wine, very good compared with what we ordinarily receive.

I borrowed this pen to write with, and it must have seen at least six years service already & consequently is a bit weak.

When I proposed that I return to my Battalion he wanted to know what my hurry was and suggested I climb a mountain near here. That is just up my alley so I plan to do so tomorrow leaving here at 4 A.M. with my breakfast, and will be back by dinner time.

Several others are being obliged to return today against their will, because of their shameful actions and wrong idea that if you don't kick, you don't get what is due you.

We have 3 books to read here; one is None Brown by Richard Morly (punk) another Matormi's Vineyard by Oppenheim Collins, which is very interesting because it deals indirectly with Mussolini's ambitions nearly bringing about a war with France in 1940, stopped in part by the "Red Shirts."

And the 3rd, is the complete works of Shakespeare, which I am reading at my leisure and enjoying greatly.

There is nothing much new as far as the war is concerned, especially since here we seem to be comparatively out of touch with it. There are of course numerous rumors about the I.B. but none of them are worth repeating. We have a very appropriate name for them here and since there are so many contradictory ones, when something does happen, one of the rumors was right.

I have written to Bennet that he should expect a visit from you. Suppose you will see him shortly. Hope you plan to spend at least a day in Orrville.

> Here comes the mail, so
> With all my love,
> Carl

[TYPEWRITTEN COPY]

August 5, 1937

Dear Impy—

Am writing this while waiting transfer from our base hospital to the Battalion. Things are badly organized for the moment since everything has been moved, but I hope to be back in a few hours.

(Four hours later)—am now waiting at the Brigade headquarters for transfer to Battalion, so I'll continue.

Yesterday I climbed the mountain of which I wrote in my last letter. I left at 5 A.M. and by 8:30 was having breakfast on top, with a magnificent view in spite of some murkiness. The way valleys drop steeply down reminded me very much of the Swiss Alps. And I had an excellent breakfast—a can of milk, a loaf of bread, a tin of sardines and half a bottle of Malaga.

But on my way down I was taken into custody by some Spanish solders quartered near the mountain who thought I might be a spy. But a telephone call to the hospital settled everything. All in all I walked about 27 kilometers from 5 to 1, or 8 hours, and it was well worth it. By the way these mountain sides are abundantly supplied with springs. And on the adjacent side there were a number of glaciers, not very large ones though, the largest being, perhaps, 75 yds long.

Last evening we had a long ride of over 100 km from the Rest Home to our base hospital. It ended at 2 A.M. after we almost drove into the front. We could hear the trench mortars and small 75s popping constantly. It sounded as if someone was trying to make an attack, but it was probably only a lot of firing.

Now I am waiting very impatiently here to return to my Battalion where I can get your letters and I'll continue this one after I read yours.

Well, it seems as if my friend forgot and marked my mail hospital and sent it back, so I guess I can kiss it goodbye. So I'll await further mail.

It's very nice to be here with the Battalion. We are getting a rest in a small town and there is even a chance we may get to see Madrid for a few hours. Today we have had some very welcome surprises, for a shipment arrived from the Friends of the Lincoln Battalion. It began last night with an issue of Raleigh cigarettes, continued this morning with Rice Krispies and milk (the first I've had in Spain, even though we were short of milk) and this noon with canned peas, carrots, asparagus, and sardines, which were very, very good. Then this afternoon we received an issue of Toilet Paper (wow), hazel nuts, soap and towel. And I understand a further surprise is in store for us at supper. Just so it comes regularly! We enjoy it greatly. This noon Paul and I ate out and, in addition to vegetables we had a tortilla made of eggs, potatoes and onions baked in a frying pan, and it tasted very good. Here the people told us how they lived. Bread is plentiful, so are beans. But there has been no meat or butter for a long time, and sugar is very scarce. Soon the grapes and melons will be ripe. Now they are harvesting the wheat. All the young men are away at the front.

Paul is feeling much better now and is political delegate of this group of 9 men. He also looks well.

But it's supper time and time for today's mail to come in.

> With all my love,
> Carl

[HANDWRITTEN]

Aug. 9, 1937

My Dear Impy:

For the 3rd consecutive day I have received a letter from you, and it has made me very happy. Especially your letter describing your midnight picnic was particularly inspiring. It must have been a grand night and altogether, you must be having the time of your life. I'll bet the days go very fast.

But I am afraid that you did some worrying, for judging from your letters you know I was in the offensive and for 2 weeks I wasn't able to write you. But let me assure you you need not worry when you don't hear from me for a week or two; for there are often times when it is impossible to write for lack of writing materials, or because there is no outgoing mail, etc.

But now I am feeling very well and even plan to go fishing for perch in a river about 4 miles away. And we are getting excellent meals now while the shipment from the Friends of the Lincoln Battalion lasts, yesterday we had 2 cups of milk!

A number of Americans joined us recently, including Pretty. You should see him, actually looks like a soldier.

Irving is remaining with the McKenzie Papineau Battalion. I must write him, for according to Pretty, rumor had it I was dead, in fact Pretty was very much surprised to see me. Incidentally, never believe any rumors you hear, 99 out of a 100 are false.

Am enclosing a copy of "Volunteer for Liberty" [not among letters] which has a number of excellent and informative articles.[67]

By the way, vegetable crops are ripening here, so now there are potatoes, tomatoes, grapes & melons available. So about once a day we eat at the home of some citizen, for which we pay them well. We usually get a Tortilla, consisting of a Potato and egg omelet. Eggs are the only proteins available here, meat being exceedingly scarce.

Incidentally in a small town here, not half the size of Orrville, there were over 200 Volunteers. Yesterday I was talking with a group of about 9 women, exchanging some of that soap you sent me for eggs. And all except one had either sons, husbands or brothers at the front.

By the way, thanks a lot for that soap. You can do wonders with it here. I am sending the Robinsons a letter of thanks for it.

> Will write you tomorrow,
> With my love, Carl

[HANDWRITTEN]

Aug. 10, 1937

My Dear Little Impy:

Am writing you from Spain's Capital, Madrid, where I am on a 48 hour leave. It has a million inhabitants, and is a beautiful city, even though all the windows are broken in the principal buildings and many gaping holes to be seen where shells have landed. The streets are very broad, in marked contrast with most Spanish towns, and there are a number of beautiful buildings.

But Imp, the sight of sandbags everywhere, of boarded windows, and broken windows, makes one feel sad. And inside the stores, no food is to be bought, and often the shelves are quite bare. But certain things can still be bought, especially clothing, tools & equipment. This afternoon alone I spent about 200 pesetas, including some 60 for a pipe, tobacco pouch, etc. Yes, I am going to try smoking a pipe, that is, if I can get some smoking tobacco. It seems that it can not be bought, but on occasions, there is a small ration of it. So there is no danger of my becoming an inveterate smoker.

In addition to that, I bought a pocket book, for my old one has been resewn many times, and this pen, which I find is not so good.

We priced some chocolates, 70 pesetas. A pound—over $6.00 according to the present exchange. Needless to say, I didn't buy any. But good wines & liquors are quite reasonable. A good bottle of Muscatel is 5 pesetas, & of Malaga 9. But believe it or not, we were unable to buy any bread.

Paul Wendorf is also here, getting a special pair of shoes made up. All Spanish sizes are too small.

But let me tell you what our room for the night is like. It's a double room, my partner being Ben Findley of Turtle Creek, Pa.[68] We have single beds with beautiful golden covers & what fine springs and mattress. We have 2 stuffed armchairs and 1 sofa, 2 marble topped writing tables, 4 chairs, a huge clothes closet, a dressing table with full length mirror, a private bathroom, with toilet paper and all, for all of which we are paying 3 pesetas or 25 cents a piece. Of course there is a catch in it. It's located where most of the shells fall, in fact every one of our windows are broken, and since most people prefer safer places evidently, we get lovely rooms very cheaply.

Of one thing there is sufficient, and that is books. There are many book stores and innumerable small outdoor push wagon book stalls. But so far, I haven't found any English ones.

But Imp, I am awaiting your letters to learn of your progress among the autoworkers, and your lively descriptions of your experiences. And also you must write me of your visit to Orrville, if you made it.

I may write you again tomorrow, and give you a better picture of Madrid, for I have only been here a few hours yet. But during this time we saw a talkie of Charlie Chan at the Circus. It is interesting to note the clever use of Spanish words, so that although the actors are actually speaking English, you hear them speaking Spanish and it almost jibes perfectly with the movements of their mouth.

Everything is closed here in Madrid by 9 P.M., and all lights out at 10. But recently there have been no further night raids, and there was no shelling at all today. I hope this continues.

So until tomorrow, with all my love,
Carl

[HANDWRITTEN]

Aug. 13, 1937

My Dear Impy—

Received a letter from you last night when I returned from Madrid, and again on this morning, and that certainly is nice. Your decision to write every day is tops with me. And I'll try to do at least half as good on an average.

By the way while I was in Madrid, I saw something I thought you'd like, and then besides I remembered your birthday is on the 14th, or is it the 17th, of next month. I hope it will reach you by then [gift unknown].

Yesterday, Ben (my best pal here) and I visited a number of interesting things in Madrid. Our hotel was on the main street only 3 blocks from Puerta Del Sol, the main square, and only about 400 yds from our hotel there is an excellent barricade, 5 feet thick of concrete and cement blocks right across the street. We went on a little further, and convinced ourselves there is really an iron ring of fortifications around Madrid that will never be broken.

A little further along, in territory where no one is permitted except the soldiers on duty, although we didn't know this, we saw the Imperial Palace, and from a parade grand balcony, we were able to see the Casa del Campo battlefield. We could hear rifle & machine gun fire, though no bullets were whizzing by us. We were able to see some trenches, though they were no longer occupied.

Just as we were to leave, an officer approaches us & takes us to the Captain of the guard to whom we show our papers and who nicely explains to us we are in a front line position, and could not remain there. So we were escorted out. Generally speaking, the buildings close to the front are not destroyed but are damaged, especially with windows broken and holes in the walls. But I can imagine that shortly after the fascists are driven out of artillery range, the city will soon appear quite normal again. Life now goes on as if nothing were happening, with streetcars and subways and stores crowded, and people wandering about everywhere.

Do you remember Robbie, waterfront organizer? Well, he is our Battalion Political Leader now. I think he will do quite well.[69] Steve Nelson is now our Brigade Political Leader, and is receiving praise from all sides. The new men who joined us are being assimilated into our Battalion. There are a couple of tough guys in it. Chances are that the front will reveal their softness they now are protecting by their pseudo-hardness. But on the whole, they are a good bunch.

Yesterday I started to break in my pipe. The biggest trouble is getting pipe tobacco. At present we use Spanish cigarette tobacco, which works after a fashion.

But more tomorrow.

> With all my love
> Carl

[HANDWRITTEN]

Aug. 15, 1937

My dear Impy:

I received four letters from you in 24 hours, so probably I won't get any for a day or so more. But I find there are a number of things I haven't answered.

You asked whether I was in the offensive Matthews described.[70] We were right in the middle of it for 21 days. As I wrote you, it was the most excruciating and exhausting experience of my life, from the first night when we marched, or more accurately, ran up for the attacks in the morning, until that solid 4-hour march out without 1 minute's rest. We have been given to understand that in future offensives, and you can be certain there are going to be more of them and much more powerful ones, we will be relieved much sooner. And it was only our revolutionary consciousness that kept us going the last time during the last 10 days. And it has become obvious to all, that this is not enough to keep antifascist soldiers in such condition that they can continue attacking, but that rest and food are required as well.

But Imp, I can tell you that our next offensive will make the past one look small, both because of the experience of the men and of the command. Our Battalion is much larger and stronger, and much better prepared.

I am writing with a pencil now, for I have just heaved the pen as far as I could. I just bought it, of Spanish make, for 18 pesetas, ($1.50) and it isn't worth a damn.

Your comments on your class are very interesting, and I can well understand them. Believe me, you can also notice it here. The best disciplined men and most reliable fighters come from the strata of workers you are working with. Frankly, the seamen here have been a bit of a disappointment. Among them were some of the finest, as for example Harry Hynes, with whom I worked until he was killed.[71] But there were a number of "tough," "rank & file," swaggerers, who when it really got be tough, were not to be found up front. Andy, tho, I must say, did very well, as section political leader, and he was always where the going was tough.

About your question, on the farmer & his milk. The ½ cent increase by the farmer may and probably is due to an increase in the amount of [words missing] socially necessary labor. But of the 2 cent increase by the middleman, only this ½ cent and perhaps a slight fraction more, is due to socially necessary labor. The rest is only gravy for the middleman which he can extract because of his monopoly hold on the market. This 2 cent increase is extortion and unnecessary. But I am afraid my answer is too late for by this time you are back in N. Y.

I received a letter from Frank, on the I.R.T.[72] He's sending me cigarettes and candy. But he is the only person I have heard from except 1 letter from my Branch, and 1 from Bennett. So write often.

With all my love

Carl

[HANDWRITTEN ON LETTERHEAD]

Aug. 16, 1937

SOCORRO ROJO INTERNACIONAL

CORRESPONDENCIA DEL COMBATIENTE

MADRID

Dear Impy—

Many thanks for your picture, though I must admit it does not do justice either to yourself or the falls. But nevertheless, it is a pleasant reminder.

I haven't received any picture of myself yet, although several have been taken. But when I get one, I'll send it. I think you may still recognize me.

What is this about Leo's "La Voz"? Is it a daily? I hope it can give "La Prensa" some real competition.[73]

Am sending you a package of 3 magazines, one on Guadalajara, and 2 copies of a magazine on Canute, the bad soldier.[74] It is an excellent piece of educational work and perhaps can be used to raise some funds for Spain.

Evidently the Lovestonites and the various other scum are still up to their scurvy tricks.[75] It is no secret here, especially after the mysterious escape of the Trotskyite Nin from prison, that these scoundrels still have some agents left, and have some very injurious influence on some Anarchist leaders. I have never hated them as I do now. They are truly the contemptible agents of fascism in our own ranks, covering themselves with their pseudo-revolutionary words.

I can full well understand the meeting of the Soviet workers condemning the Trotskyite traitors and supporting the measures against them. I know it does my heart good every time I read of the execution of some of these spies, either here or in the USSR.[76]

And I suspect that in Spain, things would go more smoothly were it not for them. And the worst of it is that certain Anarchist leaders support them, & attack the CP & the USSR. Everything is not well yet in the

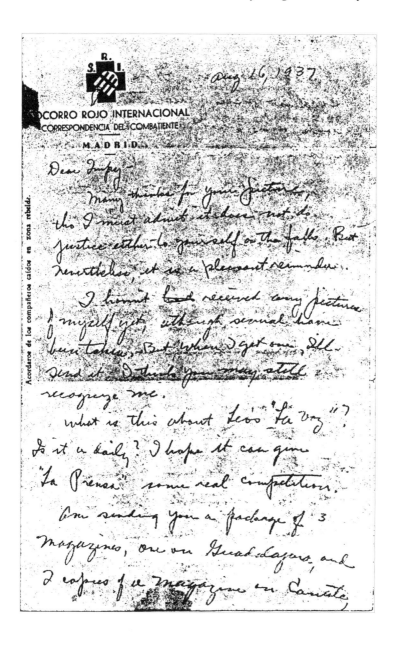

Anarchist ranks. When the matter will come to a head I don't know, but it is obvious from all the newspapers except the Anarchist ones, that the government is prepared to deal with any eventuality. And it certainly will have the support of the army to the people.

Today's Mundo Obrero has a photograph of a letter sent by a lead[er] of the Poum [POUM] last October to Gil Robles offering a special intelligence service giving him information about the activities of the C[ommunist] P[arty].[77] It also carries the news of the expulsion of 52 Trotskyites from the American C.P.[78] That is fine.

By the way, let me know if the packages arrive without difficulty.

The military head of our Brigade spoke to me several days ago, and informed us that our Brigade was one of the best in the Spanish Army, and our Battalion one of the best Battalions. We certainly earned this reputation.

Awaiting word from you & with all my love,
Carl

[HANDWRITTEN]

Aug. 22, 1937

My Dear Impy:

Have not written you for several days, since we have been doing a little traveling, getting prepared for our next offensive.[79]

Though I may not sound as enthusiastic as the last time, I think it will be even more successful, and certainly we shall capture more ground there at the Center, where we took 120 square kilometers of very important ground.

Also I am made more confident in beginning this offensive than the last. At present I am Company Observer, for the Machine-Gun Company. My work is to watch the enemy lines, their movement, fortifications and firing points, and the relation of our position to these, whether we are properly placed. It is a really interesting work & one which calls for plenty of initiative and careful work.

I am always forgetting though that by the time you receive this, the first phase of the offensive will be over, and we will be at rest again.

I haven't seen Irving, and I don't know exactly where his Battalion is. I sent him a letter officially denying the rumor that I was dead which was circulating in his camp.

Pretty is a Battalion runner, where he enjoys himself immensely running around all over delivering orders from the Battalion staff.

The question of political work here is very interesting and this work is much needed. Wherever it is neglected a bad situation immediately arises, where the men complain against every inconvenience. In a capitalist country, a class conscious worker is accustomed, especially seamen, to grumble and agitate whenever conditions are not satisfactory. And if the boss offers to put them into a position of responsibility to correct these, we would refuse this position (usually a sectarian error, in my opinion) and in the period before the present crisis of capitalism, we attacked the S.D.s for class collaboration when they accepted positions in the Gov't.[80]

But here the people are in control & trying to organize their society. But many a class conscious worker doesn't recognize this, continues his rank & fil[e]ism (incidentally a mistaken idea of rank & fil[e]ism) agitates and condemns the leadership, especially the political, but when asked to accept a position of responsibility to help remedy weaknesses, refuses to do so. This helps fascism, and not the fight against fascism. The seamen who joined us recently have this perverted sense of rank and fil[e]ism especially bad, for it seems that they were not educated out of it at their training camp. But we'll take it out of them here.[81]

And they will have to learn they are not in the USA, nor the USSR, but in the economically backward country of Spain.

Just got word to travel with light packs, so I guess we're going to hit across some hilly country, ready for fast traveling. My summer vacation activities put me in good stead now.

So will try to write you again at first opportunity. And don't worry for I know how to take as good care as possible.

> With all my love,
> Carl

[HANDWRITTEN]

Aug. 26, 1937

My dearest Impy:

We're in the midst of our second offensive as you may have guessed from the papers. Am writing you on fascist paper and using a fascist envelope, which I obtained from a powerful fortification we captured this morning.

This offensive is much better organized in every way than the last. We rode right up to the line a few days ago in trucks, and by evening in a beautifully coordinated aerial, artillery, tanks, machine-gun and Infantry attack, we took a very powerful system of trucks & block-houses. From my position as observer, I saw the whole attack clearly. The dust & smoke was so thick from the shelling & bombing when our infantry advanced behind the tanks and stormed the enemy trenches I could hardly see them only 800 meters away. Pretty was wounded seriously in this action.

Within the next hour, the fascists had withdrawn into the church, from which they killed 2 & wounded 4 of our men as they advanced into town. And that evening we ate well on fascist food. I also obtained the symbol of the Flamas Negras, crack Italian troops & the fascist symbol.[82]

All next day the fascists held out in the church which they had made into a veritable fortress from which they constantly sniped at us. Finally some 57 persons crawled out a window, most of them kids 18 to 19 years old. They told how the officers tried to keep them from surrendering, and how the officers had killed a number who tried to surrender. The rest continued to hold out, so that we were forced to shell the church & set an end on fire to smoke them out. They had stored up plenty of munitions and supplies.

But about 1 kilometer from the town on a very high bluff, the fascists had built a beautiful system of trench works & block houses, and a number of them were in these. This morning we prepared to attack & storm these fortifications. But a few minutes before we were ready to storm it, they waved a white flag & some 600 surrendered up. Imp, you would be astounded if you saw these troops, who looked more like candidates from a Boy Scout Camp than real soldiers, and they were extremely happy when they were safely in our hands, safe from their officers & our attack.

I believe the total in prisoners taken during the past 3 days reaches between 2 & 3 thousand more than in the whole previous offensive. And our own casualties have been very light and we are quite well equipped now with fascist revolvers, clothing and equipment. For myself, I now use a fascist pair of field glasses, sheath knife, and handkerchief. & today a battalion came by with rifles, grenades, & other valuable equipment, & we are feeling fit ready to go further.

By the way, we also took a number of trucks, including 2 brand new water tanks, 5–8 inch artillery pieces, ammunition, hundreds of rifles, grenades, helmets, etc.

But here are our trucks & we are rolling on—

    With all my love,

    Carl

P.S. Enclosed is a letter form used by the fascists to send their letters. Pretty clever, eh?

Think it will pass the censor for there is no particularly important information in it, & typical of hundreds of similar letters found in the fascist trenches. [Not included.]

[HANDWRITTEN]

Aug. 29, 1937

Dear Impy:

Here is a letter I sent to Al Steele, who moved without leaving a forwarding address. The letter evidently went to the Dead Letter Office, was opened and returned to me.

Am sending it to you. Can you forward it to him or to anyone on the County Committee.[83]

Everything is going well so far. And just as soon as I finish this letter, I am going to take a nice cool swim in an irrigation ditch.

By the way, I haven't received a letter from you for about a week, so write me.

　　　　With all my love,
　　　　Carl

[HANDWRITTEN]

Aug. 31, 1937

My dear Impy—

This makes my fourth letter to you since I received your last one. Of course, at present we are in a position where mail doesn't reach us very regularly but nevertheless, I expect one soon. I am especially anxious to hear about your visit in Orrville, if you were able to stop there.

You ought to see the excellent first-aid facilities here. In the first place large numbers of ambulances. Then besides this there is an 8 car hospital train following us only several miles behind, with a well equipped operating room. And on top of that, there is an oil-electric streamlined car, which takes especially critical cases back to a hospital immediately. And this improved organization of medical service is only a reflection of the greatly improved organization of the army in every field. I can notice a great advance in the present army over that of 2 months ago. By the end of the war, Spain will be a military power to be reckoned with in Europe.

An interesting sidelight here is differences between the cultivation of the fields in fascist & loyalist territory. We are now some 12 to 15 miles in fascist territory, and the inferior cultivation of the land is quite striking.

There are many more fields of weeds, especially thistles, many more un-cultivated fields, and in general, the aspect is one of lack of attention. But there is one nice crop here, and that is alfalfa.

By the way, I am much disappointed in the way a group of 12 to 15 seamen we recently added to our company are turning out. They have such a powerful hangover from their days of fighting against the ship owners that they insist it is necessary to kick about the food even when it is good, so it will stay that way. They find it very hard to act on the principle that this is a people's army, our own army, and that we fight to overcome shortcomings by doing what we can ourselves to remedy it, rather than by protest delegations, etc. And also a number of them who pretend to be so tough, show even a subnormal amount of courage in the face of fire. But perhaps a better acquaintance with bullets will help them overcome this. I wish there were more Harry Hynes' [sic] among the seamen, or Paul Andersons. But these new seamen haven't had a real test yet, for in this offensive the fighting we participated in has not been as bitter as the last, or as severe on us physically. So far we have never lacked either food or water, which means a great deal, and our casualties for the first week are about 10% of those in the Brunette [sic] campaign.

What I miss here is news of the world. And of the U.S. The latest pa-per we have here is the D.W. of Aug. 6, 3 weeks old, and because of the limited means of transport, we don't receive any Spanish papers.[84] For instance, I am still wondering what happened to the 3 Soviet fliers forced down in the Arctic, and what is going on in China.

Say, isn't your birthday due soon. It's the 14th, if I remember cor-rectly. I am very sorry I am not there to pull your ears, but if I have any luck at all, you'll remember this one.

But I have a real surprise in store for you. Wait until you see me smoke my pipe. I am even getting to enjoy it! And I am smoking American tobacco to boot! And that isn't all. 3 days ago I found the first louse, and yesterday I found 2 lice and 2 fleas. So you see I am getting to be quite a soldier.

A few of our "Moscas" are flying overhead at the moment, our fast pursuit planes.[85] They certainly are lovely to watch. Their speed is ter-rific, and often when they come over in squadrons of 9, they fly all about twisting and turning & maneuvering about in a delightful manner. And always when our planes are about, we need have no fear of the fascist planes. It is plain that aircraft will play an increasing role in war. A squadron of 9 heavy bombers flying close formation and dropping their bombs together can practically wipe out everything in a given area, leav-ing behind them only huge columns of dust & smoke 40 to 50 feet high.

Haven't received any news from Pretty as yet about the seriousness of his wound. And as far as I know Irving is still in training. And Paul went for treatment for stomach troubles to a hospital. I doubt whether he will be back, for a number of members of the I.B. after serving four to six months are transferred to other tasks than fighting in the front line. Which reminds me, I will have been here 4 months tomorrow. I hope to take part in at least one more offensive after this one, and let us hope it will be the one that will break the back of fascism.

I believe you said you sent a box of chocolates. Anyway I am awaiting patiently for it. Just now it would suit me especially fine for we have had little sweets. Yesterday we received our first chocolate ration for about 10 days, and it was only 1 oz.

Must close & await your letter:

      With all my love

      Carl

[HANDWRITTEN]

                          Sept. 7, 1937

My dear little Impy:

I hope you haven't been worried by the lack of letters for the past week. We were again in an offensive which resulted in the taking of Belchite, a town of some 16,000 and the center of this territory. It was no easy task and cost us plenty.

I was fortunate to come through without a scratch, although our casualties were quite heavy. To give you an idea of how bitter the fight was for the town, consider the fact that on the second day we were here, the fourth that the city was besieged, we were bombed 9 times. And 2 days ago, some where between 250 to 300 planes visited us, including both ours and the fascists. On that day the fascists lost 13 planes.

At one time, when our boys went over the top to storm some buildings, in 30 seconds we poured some 4,000 rounds over their heads into the fascist ranks as cover fire. Cover fire, I might explain, is a term used to describe machine gun fire over the head of your own troops or on their flanks to force the fascists to keep their heads down while our troops advance over exposed ground.

By the way, one hot afternoon, when were engaged in several machine-gun duels, and were quite tired and dirty, I received at one time three letters from you, one from Jean H. and my first one from Al Steele.[86] Although we were so busy I didn't have time to read them until 3 hours later, they certainly were welcome and cheering. In fact, I now have a large number of letters to answer that reached me while in action.

Do you know what is the main fortification in a Spanish town? It is the church building. It is the largest, strongest & tallest building in every town. From its steeples, snipers shoot our comrades and from its lower windows comes machine-gun fire. It always has a number of subterranean passages leading to other parts of town and here is where the fascists make their last stand. Churches are very hard to take since they are very powerfully built and if you try to approach and enter it, the fascists drop grenades on your head. These things make it essential to shell all churches before storming them. Incidentally, here in Belchite, the main task assigned to our Battalion was to storm the main church. And with what heroism it was done. Sometimes one feels that our speakers exaggerate when they speak of the sacrifices and courage of the members of the I.B. but, Imp, actually it is impossible to adequately describe the I.B's courage & the sacrifices it makes for democracy & peace.

Your last letter says you are on your way back, but doesn't indicate you plan to stop in Orrville. Bennet writes me he is hoping you will stop off. Incidentally, the tone of his letters have changed greatly and is now much more sympathetic. I am anxious to hear where you plan to stay in N.Y. And am also much interested in your constant reiteration of your desire to work outside of N.Y. It's still a bit early to make any definite plans, especially if we consider all that has happened since last September.

Incidentally, several of the fellows who came here with the Lincoln boys are returning and there are various rumors about what plans are in store for us, tho there is nothing definite yet. One thing is certain, that there is no desire to see all of the members of the I.B. on the casualty list, for after all, that would mean quite a sacrifice on the part of our movement in the home countries. At the same time, the situation here is still none too favorable from the military point of view, altho greatly improved over the past. The Spanish Army is still young, and a large part of its troops are not seasoned, and can not be expected to stand up under heavy attacks, not for lack of courage, but for lack of experience and trained officer personnel. And of course the army is still very weak as far as its technical personnel is concerned, such as for the artillery, supplies, communications, etc. But one can already see more or less steady advances on all fronts, in addition to the more rapid advances where ever the offensive is staged at that particular moment. I know from my own experience how valuable actual combat is for the individual as far as his fighting qualities are concerned. And you can immediately tell when you see troops going into action whether they are veteran or new troops.

But Imp, I haven't had a chance to even wash my face for eight days and now I think I see an opportunity to get some water. I might explain until we took the town yesterday all our water had to be carried up through fire from snipers and so it was quite costly and could only be used for our machine guns and for drinking.

Dave Doran is now our brigade political commissar since Steve Nelson was wounded a few days ago.[87]

Expect to write you again tomorrow.

> With all my love,
> Carl

P.S. on back of 2nd page

P.S. Just read thru some of your old letters again, and find I haven't answered several things.

I received the soap as I wrote you, but the chocolates haven't arrived. But they may still come thru.

In regard to field glasses, we now are equipped with fascist glasses we captured. But the watch will come in handy. A number of corporals and sergeants don't have them and are always borrowing mine at night when they stand guard. By the way my rank is First Lieutenant.

And the final thing. You must not worry. It won't do any good and only hurts your efficiency. I know how to take care of myself and don't take any unnecessary chances. And with the experience I have now, there is little danger of being hit by making a mistake or thru ignorance. Although the number of wounded is quite high, the number killed is a very small per cent, in my company, it was only 5% in 14 days fighting.

And I like to feel you are not worrying and are working hard.

> With love,
> Carl

[HANDWRITTEN]

Sept. 8, 1937

Dear Brother Bennet,

Your letter was certainly very welcome and reached me just in the middle of another offensive as we were attacking Belchite. I am feeling fine now, and so far after two weeks more of battle, I haven't received a scratch.

I was much interested to hear what John and Bill and the others think of my fighting here for the Spanish government.[88] Tell them not to worry for that can't help me, but to try to get accurate information about what is happening here. Tell Bill that while there is not the concentration of artillery fire there was in the world war, the aerial bombardment and battles far exceed anything seen in the world war. One day 250 to 300 planes passed over head, and on another we were bombed 9 times. I measured a hole made by a fascist bomb—7 feet deep and 28 feet across. I believe Bill was in the medical service there. Our medical service here is excellent. Very few are ill, and quick and competent attention is given to the wounded. I believe there are over 50 ambulances already here from the States.[89]

This offensive has been even much more powerful, and much better organized than the first one. And the American boys have earned themselves a swell reputation again. The Spanish soldiers are always very happy to see us coming.

Up to the present, in the past 15 days we have taken over 3000 prisoners. And hundreds more have deserted to us, in spite of the measures used by the fascists to keep their soldiers from deserting. In Quinto, the fascist soldiers told us that the parents of any soldier who deserted was shot. Here in Belchite they made some of the soldiers fight in their bare feet so they wouldn't desert. And officers would come around to check up on where the men were firing. Several were shot because they were shooting over the heads of our soldiers

Belchite is a very important city. Do you know what the 2 main fortifications were? A seminary and a church. Many of our comrades were killed and wounded by snipers from the church steeple. The fascists also held us up a while by forcing the civilian population to withdraw to several building[s] along with them, so that we wouldn't blow those buildings to pieces. And civilians who tried to escape to us were shot. I myself saw the fascists firing on a crowd of old men, women and children who were trying to get out of town into our ranks.

And a further experience to show what "brave" men the fascist leaders are. After most of the soldiers had surrendered, we had to search the houses for those who were left, particularly officers. Three of us were searching one house.[90] I was in the lead. When I looked into the attic, of which the sloping roof on one side had been blow off, I saw a sniper sitting on a box with a rifle across his knee. The moment he saw me he stood up, raised his left hand shouting "Viva la Republica" (one of our slogans) but keeping the rifle in his right hand. Then he began to beg me not to shoot him, that he had been fighting for the Republic for 40 years and could prove it, etc. By that time the others came up. But when we felt the barrel of his rifle, it was warm, there were empty cartridges lying about, and his rifle was loaded. So we took him down to the proper authorities, he all the time insisting he was against the fascists and for us.

Last night I learned he had been identified as a leading fascist organizer and was the vice-president of the Phalangists, a fascist organization of Zaragoza. And a friend of mine who had the job of executing him told me he went to his death crying without any sign of courage. It is these kind of men that execute the parents of deserters, order the bombing of towns like Guernica, and are the dregs of humanity.[91]

By the way, we are quite well supplied with equipment now, mostly German, which we captured from the fascists. And I have the sniper's rifle, which is a beauty.

But enough of the war. What I'd like now is a quart of Smith's Better Ice Cream, or even a quart of Smith's milk.[92]

Thanks for Marie's letter. I shall write her too. And by the way are Bill and Lila going to Europe? Let me know exactly where they are going & when, if they do. You can never tell, I might meet them.[93]

I haven't heard from Sylvia yet whether she was able to stop in Orrville on her way back or not. Hope she was.

> Write me regularly. My regards to all,
> Carl

[HANDWRITTEN]

Sept. 9, 1937

My dear Impy:

Have your letter of the 25th, enclosing the print of the medal given to the sit-down strikers. It must indeed be a splendid remembrance.

At the moment we are in a reserve position, which means a few kilometers behind the front line, subject to call at any moment should the fascists succeed in breaking the lines in front of us. We'll probably be in reserve for a few more days, then go back into the line again. I am expecting Irving and some of the other comrades to arrive today or tomorrow.

Here are some interesting sidelights on the taking of Belchite.

The fascist officers took the shoes away from many of the soldiers to make it more difficult for them to desert to us. They would also observe some one about to fire a shot, and would examine to see where he was aiming. A number were shot because they were firing over our heads or in other directions where they would not harm us.

They forced the civil population to withdraw with them inside the town, and used them for a shield. When any tried to escape, the fascists shot them. In one instance our soldiers observed an old man coming towards us carrying a small child. The fascists opened up on him with a light machine gun, dropping him and leaving the child laying there exposed to their fire. Suddenly a loyalist soldier, a tall blonde fellow, darts out, grabs the child and runs back, in a hail of fascist bullets. But he never knew the answer to his question, "Is she hurt?" because he dropped dead from four bullet wounds, including 2 through his chest.

It is estimated that fascists killed some 300 soldiers & civilians during the 8 days the city was besieged, in order to maintain order.

The fascist sniper I took prisoner in the garret of a house turned out to be a leading fascist organizer, & vice president of the Phalangistas of Zaragoza. I caught him with a rifle across his knees, with the barrel still warm. He was the first prisoner to be executed of those captured in Belchite.[94] According to the comrade who executed him, he died a coward's death.

This is the first time in history that Belchite has ever been captured. Among those who failed to take it is Napoleon. It was the center of Catholic reaction for this part of Spain, dominating the country thru its Seminary, a center of brutal & corrupt religious reaction.

Yesterday our Brigade received 60 young Spanish recruits. They all wanted to join our Battalion, the Americanos. But speak with the Spaniards who have been with us for some time already and they will tell you it is nice to get American cigarettes, chocolate, soap, etc. but that we more than make up for it by the harder fighting we do, longer marches and much harder work.

There is one thing I am getting my fill of today, and that is grapes. For in this part of the country there are two principal products, grapes and olives. Everywhere you look you see olive groves and in between vineyards. Grapes are ripe now and twice a day I go on a grape-eating spree. The only other crop is a little wheat. You can also find an occasional almond tree and infrequently a fig tree. But there has been no rain for months, the grass is dead, as well as the weeds, and only grape vines & trees are green. But a mild rainy season is almost here. We have thunderclouds pass over us daily now and soon we shall have our first rain in months, in fact, since the middle of June.

Imp, I certainly appreciate your daily letters. Tell me everything that happens and all the news of New York. Is Jerry still in California? Do you ever see Herman? I have written to him several times and never received an answer. What do you plan to do with the car? Do you drive it?

By the way, Bill and Lila are planning to go to Europe this fall. Perhaps you can arrange to see them while they are in New York. But you'll have to write them at once.

I want to write to Jean & Grace yet today, so I'll close.

>   With all my love,
>   Carl

[HANDWRITTEN]

Sept. 15, 1937

Dear Herb:

Here is a nice piece of education for Spanish soldiers. It is an elementary and simple book on military tactics. You have to bear in mind that many can neither read nor write, and the majority have had only a few years of schooling. But the book itself is an excellent primer. And believe me, you have to know and practice these things if you want to live.

Am also enclosing a leaflet given to us. Pretty neat, eh?

Just now we are not fighting. But it is rumored that the fascists are bringing the Italian Black Arrows to Zaragossa.[95] They are supposed to be well trained, and we know they can run fast, especially backwards. The general opinion is that the organized Spanish fascists are better fighters than the Italian, because this is after all, their own country. But Franco is running short of native troops, especially after we took so many prisoners.

By the way, the ratio of our casualties to fascist was 1 to 10 in this offensive, due to the large number of prisoners. Usually, the attackers' losses is expected to be as heavy or heavier than the defenders. Let's hope we can keep up, or even reverse this ratio. Desertions help it, too. [Entire paragraph redacted.]

Give my regards to the Branch. I'll try to write a letter in a few days.

>   Comradely yours,
>   Carl

[HANDWRITTEN]

Sept. 15, 1937
My dear Imp,

I must apologize for not writing you for several days. Somehow in all the movement and *wind* we have had in the past few days, I didn't write a single letter, although we haven't done any fighting.

But now since I have had a bath, shave, and clean clothes, and plenty of good food, and rest inside of a building, you'll hear from me plenty.

First some answers to your letters, which I have been receiving quite regularly and are almost a daily highlight in my life.

The fellows were very interested in your account of the anti-vigilante movement, and happy to hear of the scope of the movement against it. You know here we are actually fighting against the highest development of vigilant[e]ism, fascism.

I would write to Uncle Carl in Canton, but I don't know how to reach him. I suppose he must be on labor's side there, but some accident could throw him on the other, though I hope not.

These cold nights here, I wish to be with you in front of one of your huge wood burning fireplaces. The more I think of it, the more I hate fascism and my best pal here, Ben Findley from Pennsylvania, is missing his first deer-hunting season for years. Of course, you can well imagine that our love for the out-of-doors has much to do with our friendship. And you'll have to blame him for teaching me how to smoke a pipe. I really enjoy it by this time, but the Spanish tobacco is awful. So send me some good pipe tobacco in your next package. But send it through the Friends of the Lincoln Batt.

By the way, the only package I received was the one with soap. But for a month we have been on the Aragon front where the one-way railroad is hard pressed to bring ammunition, let alone luxuries. So as soon as we return to rest, I expect quite a number of them. I am especially anxious to get a hold of those chocolates (and so are all my comrades).

I notice the letters you are answering now are those you received from me at Miraflores. Well, Imp, cheer up, for I came through this last offensive fit as a fiddle, as we say in Ohio. And I believe I feel better physically and mentally than I have ever felt since I came to Spain. For recently we over-hauled our kitchen and we are getting excellent food, well prepared & in sufficient quantity. And in addition, the experience I have gained from the Brunete campaign, and in the taking of Quinto & Belchite, make me feel a veteran soldier and capable to meet any emergency. So don't worry, and before you know it, I'll be back.

The movie "Spanish Earth" ought to be interesting.[96] And I know that if Joris Ivens could have filmed all the moving sights I have seen, it would be a most powerful piece of propaganda, and for its sheer realism & life & blood content, could only be a work of art.[97] There are many scenes in Spain I shall always remember. I wish he could have filmed the fifteen minutes of action in which we took the main fortifications before Quinto. In these 15 minutes he could have shown concentrated artillery fire, an aerial bombardment, airplanes strafing, machine gun fire from 9 or 10 guns, tank action smashing barbed wire defenses, and an advance by infantry behind tanks, climaxed by a bayonet charge all in 15 minutes. From my position as observer I was able to clearly witness the entire thing.

Or if he could have filmed that last morning in Belchite. Just at dawn, the last garrison surrendered, and some 160 soldiers and over a hundred old men, women & children marched out. Every third soldier had a bandage around his head from a head wound. Many were trying to sing the "Internationale" and the majority greeting us with raised fists. Or for scenes of horror, the roads next to the hospital piled four deep with fascist dead, or the last street we took, littered with the carcasses of dead cats, dogs, sheep, goats, mules, horses, and men, only he couldn't have photographed the awful stench. And there are many pleasant scenes, as for instance when we gave food to an old grandmother, her daughter & grand daughter, at dusk one evening, in the shadow of a huge church surrounded by the usual wall & moats. Their gratitude mixed with hysteria from their recent fear we would mistreat them and their horror at the recent execution of the male members of their family by the fascists, for they were suspected of republican sympathies. Nevertheless I want to see "Spanish Earth" when I return.

But to get back to your letters. True, I lost a good deal of weight at Brunete, but today I am heavier than I ever have been.

Irving is here with us now, not in the same Battalion, but in the same Brigade. So I see him every now and then. His rank is Sergeant and is doing quite well. He will have a lot to tell you. Paul is still at a rest home as far as I know, though I wouldn't be surprised if you met him one of these days. Pretty, by the way, died shortly after reaching the hospital. It was only a few days ago that I learned of his death from one who took him in.

I meant to write you a long letter yesterday as your Birthday present, but since I had an opportunity to get rid of my lice instead, I am doing it today. But if my plans did not go astray, you may have been reminded of your birthday yesterday, anyway.

Now a few things about what is happening here. First, the weather. It's getting very, very windy, and much colder. And a tinge of fall is in the air. I like it, especially when we're sleeping indoors. But I am afraid tonite we'll be out in an olive grove again.

Some very interesting things have happened here in the last few days. Some of our tough seamen couldn't take it, and were raising a tremendous howl. But a meeting day before yesterday & yesterday has sort of shut them up, and they may turn out all right after all. The agitator suddenly decided he was sick, and went to the hospital. I now find out these were a bunch of "problem children" with inborn "rank and file" ideas so useful in fighting the ship owners but not in our army. Anyway, all goes smoothly now.

We are due for a rest, but it may be delayed a while since the fascists are shipping the Italian "Black Arrows" into Zaragoza.[98] I'd like to meet them once. We know by this time, they are not as formidable a foe as the Spanish fascists, and they can run very fast, especially backwards.

This letter is long enough for today, so "Happy Birthday."

> With all my love,
> Carl

[HANDWRITTEN]

Sept. 17, 1937

Dear Jean:[99]

Your letter gave me both satisfaction and inspiration, especially since it is you who obviously are one of the inspirers of the new phase of the student movement dealing with the content and quality of their education. I certainly think that this development is essential to a further healthy people's front development of the student movement.

And I certainly hope you will write me regularly, and include news about your work of this character. Besides, there is only one thing a soldier pays closer attention to than his letters, that is his food. So you see, we like to receive letters.

George is now with us, for the Mac-Paps [MacKenzie-Papineau Battalion] are in the same brigade with us and so I see him almost every day. He is doing well. Give my regards to Ruth. I hear she is doing fine work in the Student [office? CG]. Irving Weisman is also here, a sergeant in the Mac-Paps, and so proud of the rifle he received the other day.

Of course, there are many things to write you about. If you see Sylvia, she can give you a lot of details of our life here, of our fighting, and what heroes the Americans are. So I think I'll write about another feature of our life here.

One of the most interesting things here is to observe the reaction of Americans to Spanish conditions, and their development in a new environment, because here they are in an army, and in Spain, a country of much lower industrial development. And I have often been surprised, although now I can see the reason for unexpected developments.

Many of our comrades in the States have been used to rank-and-file work, and here often make the mistake of thinking the way to remedy faults here is to put pressure on the "top." This leads to a certain depreciation of our command and officers as such, and to defend themselves, a certain ridicule of political work. And few are able to appreciate to what degree the backward economy of Spain causes us inconveniences. But most gradually learn this is our army, that you don't organize against the top, but that a regular apparatus exists through which we can make our needs and opinions felt. One of the groups which find this adjustment most difficult are the "tough" seamen, who have battled the ship owners so valiantly. But I want to pay my tribute to Harry Hynes, a seaman and one of the finest comrades I have ever known. And by the way, Andy did excellent work here, and as political leader for a section of seamen, solved many problems. Incidentally, it seems to me that the white collar workers make this adjustment much more easily than the others. Perhaps it is because they have a better political development, that is, those who came here.

The aversion to political work often developed is also interesting. There is not room to give you all my ideas on this, but I imagine that a great deal of it, and perhaps all of it, is due to our lack of understanding what political work in an army should consist of. If the political worker fails to get cigarettes, good food, clothing, letters, chocolate etc., he certainly will not be popular with the men. But certainly it must take in much more territory than this. And in the past, when it was often impossible to get the above things, it was the pol. worker who took it on the chin. But now, these matters are better organized, fortunately, and don't take so much time. But generally speaking, our political work is still very poor, but at least we understand it better. It must include, first of all, as thorough an explanation of what is going on, the progress of the campaign, the state of the fascist camp. And it must also include material to sharpen their anti-fascist consciousness from time to time, to help them put their life into its true perspective.

For Jean, there is nothing that is so hard as war. It is horrible, painful, exhausting, nerve-wracking, terrifying. No one who has not fought can begin to appreciate it. And men coming suddenly into it, naturally are tried severely. Some can not stand up under it, and crack up. Others become steeled, and finer human beings (though I can think of many better ways to develop men) and others only exist thru the war, lasting for a time, and then disappearing, to the hospital, sent home, or just leaving.

And in these circumstances, one needs everything possible to nourish him mentally. I almost want to say spiritually, to enable him to function as a rational human being, as an effective force in this People's Army.

Perhaps this letter won't make much sense to you, for there is much background I should fill in before giving this material. But I hope some day I will be able to discuss it with you face to face.

Give my regards to your sister Ruth. & write often,

Sincerely,

Carl

[HANDWRITTEN]

Sept. 20, 1937

My dear Impy:

Excuse me for not writing sooner, but I am again very busy. Since I wrote you I was made a lieutenant on the military side, and now two days ago, I became Assistant Pol. Commissar of our Battalion, and that means work every hour.

Now to answer the four letters I received from you since I wrote last. And I want to thank you for them.

The pictures were very welcome, especially the one of you, Tima, and your students. As soon as Steve Nelson returns from the hospital, I'll show it to him.

And I am not thin. I probably weigh as much or more than I ever have, for we are getting very good food lately. By the way, we are not in the lines now, only in a reserve position, and we hope to go out for several weeks of real rest soon.

By the way, don't entertain any ideas that I may return home soon. The way things are shaping up now indicate I will be here for some time yet.

The difference between a Battalion & a Brigade—a full battalion has from 500 to 700 men, and a Brigade from 3 to 5 Battalions. That ought to be clear now.

By the way, the world situation is more favorable to Spain than it has [been] for a long time. But there are still many internal problems and things don't look rosy in the north in spite of the Asturian & Basque heroism.[100]

Grace wrote me about her "Wild cats." I am thinking of writing them a letter.

Tell Larry S. I sympathize with him and I know it won't get *him* down. Those damn things are possible and do happen.

Your letter to Bromley was a honey. You tell her. She needs plenty of straightening out yet.

I am anxiously awaiting those chocolates and pipe tobacco. I suspect one of these days I am going to get a whole pile of packages. My mouth is watering right now. No kidding. And I can use woolen socks nicely.

No, I haven't met Dave Cook. He must be with the English. My congratulations to Tuffy.

Lewis' speech is a masterpiece, not only of the English language but also of political acumen.[101] May he continue thusly and never become a Caballero.[102]

Irving & George send you their regards.[103] We are living in the same Olive Orchard now. And the weather is not hot. It's threatened to rain every now & then, and one of these days it will.

But Imp, I have never seen such magnificent & colorful sunsets and sunrises as here. Remember the clouds are much lower than here.

Last night, the eastern clouds were the deepest & clearest Robin egg blue against a light gray sky. And the western clouds over the mountain tops were hot fiery red, and those on either side passed thru all stages of lavender. But such delicacy and depth in color have I seen nowhere as I witness morning and evening. If you were only here to enjoy it with me!

> With all my love,
> Salud,
> Carl

[HANDWRITTEN]

Sept. 29, 1937

Dear Herb:

Have anxiously awaited a further letter from you, though I have not written you for some time.

Just now we are waiting in an olive orchard for trucks to take us we know not where nor to what. But while we wait I'll write a letter to you and the Branch.

All the Comrades must be back hard at work by this time. And especially, for Spain. Are you still Spanish Director for the county? I'll try to send you material you can use for your work there. Ben Barber is only about a 100 yards from here, also awaiting a truck.[104]

How did your case make out before the NLRB? And let's have that song you composed and the one by Jack Peters. I am sending you a copy of the International Brigade Song Book.[105]

We haven't been in action now for about 3 weeks, although we have not been out at rest. Most of our time we spend training and reorganizing our Battalion. Since the war is changing from a defensive to an offensive one, where more of our fighting is done in and around cities, certain organizational changes are advisable as far as the company and section set-up is concerned.

By the way, my work now is that of Battalion Political Commissar which makes me eligible for rank of Captain.[106] But boy, it means an unlimited amount of work, and plenty of headaches. Have been so busy I didn't even write to Sylvia for almost a week.

An interesting feature of our work here is the training of our Spanish Comrades. Four hours before we went into the attack on Belchite a month ago today, 20 young Spanish recruits were brought into my company (machine-gun). They did not know how to load & fire a rifle. We taught them this before we attacked.

Today you should see them (there are 17 left). They form 2 machine-gun crews, know how to take care of their gun perfectly, are good gunners, and we are very proud of them, and they are proud of their own achievements.

> Here they come, so Salud,
> Carl

[HANDWRITTEN]

Sept. 29, 1937

Dear Impy,

Just a few words while we wait here in an olive grove for trucks to take us we know not where nor what to. But since they are not here yet, I'll give you the news.

I have taken Robinson's place who is now in our Brigade Political Commissariat, and as Battalion Political Commissar I have my hands full. Incidentally it makes me eligible for the rank of Captain.

So school begins once more. It doesn't seem as if it were almost Oct. 1 here, but soon the wind will blow and it'll rain and get cold. We have had enough rain to keep us up one night already. But now we have some tents and part of our winter clothing so we are somewhat prepared to meet colder weather.

Have received nice long letters from Grace, Sam & Ernie which I appreciated very much. I am afraid I won't be able to return more than short notes to them, for there is no rest for a Political Commissar.

Bennet writes he regrets very much that you did not stop in to see them.

The greetings from the Section Committee have never reached me, nor have any copies of the Inprecor. But I still have hopes. And when the next shipment from the "Friends" comes thru, I am planning a big picnic with all those packages. Chocolates & pipe tobacco are completely unavailable at the present time.

Do you know Abe Harris? He is heading our Brigade Intendencia now, and starting off well.[107]

Received your copy of Photo Magazine.[108] Everyone enjoyed it immensely, & I hope they bring Baltic Deputy around for us to see.[109]

Give Herman my warmest regards, and my congratulations on his closed shop.[110] I still wish he were here.

We haven't been in action for several weeks now, nor have we been at rest. But we expect to go to rest shortly. In the meantime we are reorganizing and further training our Battalion. The feeling among our comrades is excellent despite reports you may have received to the contrary.

A definite policy has been adopted that at the end of seven months service Americans may apply for repatriation, and a number have already gone after seven months service.[111]

Steve Nelson is on his way back, leaving here shortly after he came out of the hospital. I gave him the pictures including Dixen & yourself, and your address so there is a chance you might see him.

Again I must tell you of the beauty of our sunsets & cloud formations here. And last evening there was a huge unbroken rainbow with the most beautiful cloud formation in and around it, which had a beautiful symmetry. It was like a well balanced picture in this respect. And of course, these scenes invariably remind me of you.

    With all my love—Salud,

    Carl

[HANDWRITTEN]

Oct. 5, 1937

Dear Impy:

Your letter of the 12th of Sept. both alarms and pleases me. Alarms me because I see you are worrying much too much about me. I don't do any worrying at all, and neither must you, just work hard and don't worry. Pleases me because it shows your regard for me.

I hope you find it possible to take many walks thru our old haunts. I miss them very much, but since we live out of doors in mud and rain since the rainy season began, I feel a bit at home here. And this rainy weather keeps the planes away.

24 hours later—

Now I am writing under a tent for 4 men, with the sides flapping loudly in a strong cold wind, with the top gently patting me on the head. The Battalion Commander is sitting on one side of me, the Battalion Clerk is pounding on a typewriter, his fingers freezing. The weather is really becoming cold, so we have an issue of anise or coñac twice a day, morning & evening.

Have you ever lived in a tent in real windy weather. It's great stuff. About 9 last night one of the center poles snapped and down it came on our heads, but we slept peacefully on until morning.

Probably by this time you will have read a lot about some deserters being caught & court-martialed.[112] I will send you more details later, when we get the official news, but you can be certain that these rats are going to be treated as they deserve. The feeling of the men against these deserters is quite high.

Our mail service has been quite poor last few days, for the problem of transportation up in this neck of the woods is quite acute.

Our Battalion has finally acquired a canteen, selling writing paper, lighter cords, candy, pencils, etc. It gives us something to do with the money for the first time for over a month.

Perhaps you would li[k]e to know some of my headaches in a day's work as a political commissar.

The kitchen always has a problem. 2 days ago it was wood. There are few trees around here, and the houses are of stone, with only a few wood rafters. We brought some with us some 150 kilometers from the last place. Besides this it was raining more or less steadily day and night. A trip to the Town Committee gave no results. Finally, we headed in the direction of the mountains, and there, around the front lines, we cut down pines for firewood and hauled them to our kitchen.

A comrade who has not yet been to the front wants a job in the rear, where he can use his talents better, he says. The real reason is that he is afraid of the front, tho he may not admit nor even recognize it for a while. In about 15 minutes he usually decides to take a "belt" at the front, as Robbie puts it.

Then there is the comrade whose mother is dying and wants to go home. He was willing to sacrifice his own life when he left the USA, but now that he is here and trained, he wishes to leave because his mother is ill.

The work of the political commissar is to keep the aim of fighting fascism ever in the minds of the men, and not to permit it to become overshadowed by their stomach ache, lack of bread or black coffee, an ill parent, etc. And this is a 24-hour a day job.

Today I received a letter from you dated July 5, right after you reached Flint, and one of my Brother of July 3, and one of July 25 from a wounded Comrade who must already be in New York by this time, Mito Kruth, who lives near Wallingford.[113]

Your letter interests me especially because it reflects a time when we both entertained hopes of seeing each other again this fall. And now I should be greatly surprised if we meet before next year. The war is going to last a good long time yet, although no definite predictions can be made.

Am finishing this letter by candlelight. Our Battalion Commander had the great misfortune of accidentally wounding himself this morning while cleaning his revolver, the Adjutant is ill, so for the moment I am in command of the Battalion, and it keeps me plenty busy.[114] It's taken me 4 days to get your letter this far.

Your Inprecors arrived and many thanks for them. Some boxes have arrived for others, so I am expecting several any day now.

It's quite cold tonight, and I keep my fingers warm over the flames of the candle. By the end of this month it snows, and we have snow then for some 4 months I am told.

By the way, I have never received the letter from your Section Convention yet.

Haven't heard from you for several days now, so expect a letter tomorrow.

      With all my love
      Salud
      Carl

[HANDWRITTEN]

Oct. 16, 1937

Dear Impy:

Well the probable has finally happened, and I am writing you from a hospital.[115] But it is nothing really serious. I have 11 pieces of shrapnel in my left leg and foot, but they are not deep nor severe. So I ought to be back in action again in about 3 weeks.

By the way, the medical service is excellent. I was wounded at 2 in the morning, when a mortar exploded right beside me. Six hours later, I was already dressed and on a hospital train bound for the coast. And this hospital train is a beauty, and one travels in comparative comfort. In a few days I expect to be moved to Benicasim, where there is an American hospital for us.[116]

I saw the MacKenzie Papineau Battalion go into action, and I must say they went over the top without hesitation and like veterans, and did an excellent piece of work, covering a very difficult piece of territory under heavy fire. I haven't heard yet how Irving and George Watt made out. I know Dallet, the political Commissar, and Herndon's brother, Milton, were killed.[117]

Perhaps you are aware of the critical international situation of a few days before Roosevelt's speech.[118] In my own opinion, Mussolini is still planning another desperate move for open intervention. And so much depends on the American people, that they come out in firm support of a collective peace policy. Today's papers estimate that there are 200,000 Italian soldiers in Spain. And that means that the war in Spain can only be settled on the international arena, by collective action against the aggressors.

To get back to more personal things, I don't suppose I will hear from you for a few days until I get settled down and notify the post-office. But you must continue sending them every other day, and let me know what you are doing, how you like your new home, etc.

And while I am here, I shall have better opportunities to write you oftener.

> With all my love,
> Carl

[HANDWRITTEN]

Oct. 22, 1937

Dear Herb:

You can expect to hear a little bit more regularly and more in detail from me for the next several weeks. For I am now in a hospital recovering from some dozen shrapnel wounds in my left leg and foot. It's nothing serious, but a bit nasty, since there are so many of them. I acquired them one night when a trench mortar dropped down beside me.

It's been a long time since I heard from you or the branch. What's happening, anyway? I can imagine you are very busy, especially if you are still heading the work in the Bronx for Spain.

You may know more about what is happening here than I do, even though I am the political Commissar for our Battalion now. But you may be interested in a few things. First of all, Mussolini is desperately in need of at least one great victory before winter comes and slows up operations. And therefore he has already shipped 200,000 men here and plenty of war materials. The courageous resistance of Asturias is holding him up much longer than he expected, and it is possible he can't liquidate them before the heavy snows, in which case he'll have to keep a large force there.

While I doubt whether the Republican forces will take Zaragoza immediately, they are gradually closing in on it. I was wounded only a short distance from it when we were clearing away some of the approaches to it. And since then we have taken more of the mountain heights which constituted part of its defense. Since Zaragoza is the largest city the fascists hold, its loss would be a very severe loss to them. As it is, their morale is very low.

You should have seen the new American & Canadian Battalion, the McKenzie Papineau, go into action. Eight hours after they heard the first bullets whistle, they went over the top, along with us and the English, behind a bunch of tanks, but under plenty [of] heavy fire. They had to cross an open of a half mile to storm the fascist trenches, and they did it like veterans, driving the fascists out, and then making another attack a little later to help us. Of course, this kind of fighting means plenty of casualties, but they have already established a fine reputation.

Largo Caballero made a speech in Madrid a few days ago, very misleading and much of it false. All the discontented elements are taking him to their heart. The Anarchist leadership suddenly finds out he is a great man. It is not to be denied that he is tending to weaken the present government, and objectively, helps the fascists. It is certain that all semi-fascist and opposition elements will try to organize themselves around him against the government. But I don't think they'll get very far. Another good offensive would help to shut them up.

You will be interested to know the Commander of our Battalion, Capt. Philip Detro, is a member of the Democratic Party, about 25 years old, from Virginia, and a mighty fine commander. The commander of our machine-gun Company is a Brooklyn YCL'er, Milton Wolff.[119] Part of our work here is to train the Spanish comrades, so about half of our Battalion are Spaniards. And 2 of my section political delegates are Spaniards who deserted from the fascist army. And they are political leaders in our Battalion now.

I understand that a new shipment from the "Friends of the Lincoln Battalion" has arrived, so I am expecting a great number of packages. You may continue to write me at the same address, for they'll forward it to me where ever I am.

Am enclosing a peseta script issued by a Spanish Province, used due to the great shortage of change.

Give my warmest greetings to everyone,

Salud, Carl

[HANDWRITTEN]

Oct. 23, 1937

Dear Imp:

The sun is shining in the window this morning (only the Spaniards keep the shutters and windows closed so the sun and air don't get in) and it promises to be a wonderful day. I should be in the American hospital at Benicasim now, but before they got around to me last night, the train was full, so I'll have to hang around here a few more days.[120]

Several more of my comrades came in yesterday including our Third Company Commander, John Tsanakas, a Greek comrade and a fearless fighter.[121] The fascists bombed our trenches the other day, with giant bombs from their new German 4-motored Junkers. Tsanakas and several others were buried alive by the dirt thrown up by these bombs. They were dug out and sent here to recover from shell shock and a few minor injuries. However the bombing did kill several, our first casualties from aviation for over 2 months.

There are many things I could write you, especially about customs in Spanish hospitals. But I had better reserve them until I see you.

I have been trying to get some English books to read, and every one promises to get me some, but, of course they never come. There is nothing they won't promise, but you needn't expect it.

The fascists try to bomb this town almost every day, coming from Mallorca, an island now under Italian control. But during the week I have been here, they have dropped no more than a half dozen bombs, for our pursuit planes appear very quickly.

There are many interesting stories here from the front. Here is a good one, supposed to be true.

One of our telephone men was laying down a line out to one of our advanced posts one night. He ran merrily along until he heard voices and he asked, is this the 607th? A voice answered, "no, halt, you are a prisoner." A fascist officer then ordered him to come in and follow him.

A few moments later a heavy fire developed so the officer placed our comrade in a dugout and placed a sentinel over him. Where upon our comrade spoke to the guard. "Do you hear that fire? We are attacking tonight and you will have to surrender. It will be much better for you if you desert now, and I will put in a good word for you."

The guard agreed. And as they went along he called to other of his friends. By the time our comrade came back to his own line, he was followed by 40 deserters from the fascist lines.

That's got fiction beat a mile.

Here's another of a little different caliber. A Spanish soldier was so scared that he decided to mutilate himself so he would be sent out of the lines. So he carefully put his hand over the mouth of the barrel of his rifle, shut his eyes and pulled the trigger. Everything went well, except that he had an explosive bullet in the chamber, and almost tore his hand off instead of making a neat hole.

I had hoped to receive several letters from you today, for I am having them forward to Benicasim. For while I lay here there is plenty of time to wonder what you are doing, and to recall some of our happy experiences together. So write me in great detail about yourself, what you do on Sundays, etc.

Why doesn't Herman write to me? Or was he too busy organizing his shop? I have quite a few letters to answer now, including Frank, and Al and Dotty.

I still haven't heard how George Watt and Irving made out. There was a new attack on the following day, and I'm hoping they both survived it.

By the way, my leg wounds are very good, the swelling having almost disappeared. Those in my foot are also easing up but a little slower. So don't do any worrying on that score.

>With all my love,
>Carl

[HANDWRITTEN]

Oct. 26, 1937

Dear Impy:

Just a few words to let you know I am getting along all right, and am seriously considering getting up and walking, if I can get a hold of some clothes and crutches. I am still awaiting transfer to Benicasim, since there was no room for me on the last train that left. I am anxious to get there particularly because several of your letters should be awaiting me there.

Some of the misleading propaganda the people of Catalonia have been subjected to may be seen from the questions an elderly lady asked me. First, whether I was a Russian, second whether I was a volunteer or was forced to come here, and third, whether I intended to stay here or go back. She seemed very much relieved by my answers.

The Spaniards are a very promising people. Four different people have faithfully promised me that on the morrow they would bring me some English books. When I protested they might be hard to get, or it would be too much trouble they all insisted that it was no trouble at all. But the books never come. And I am very hard put to it to keep myself amused. Yesterday we had a fly-catching contest, but even that became dull. So then a young Spaniard in the bed to my right and I spent an hour preparing material for a Spanish game much like checkers. Then I beat him three straight, so he has to buy our room a bottle of anis. Are you acquainted with this drink? It's very popular among the Spaniards especially as a morning drink. It's a very sweet liquor.

I suppose the Daily [Worker] carried the story of the unearthing of Franco's military Intelligence service in Loyalist Spain. The educational part is the tremendous extent to which it was based on the POUM, which today is nothing more than a gang of criminals in the hire of fascism.[122] It's discouraging to note that the CNT organ "Solidaridad Obrera" did not print anything about it.[123]

There's a poor guy here, about 35 years old, probably was a small business man, educated, who was shot thru the throat with an explosive bullet which tore out a good sized chunk below his right jaw. But he was extraordinarily lucky for it didn't touch either his jugular or his wind pipe. He can't talk well now. But he is deadly afraid of hemorrhages, and is constantly imagining them. When ever he really has one, the nurses and doctors act quite promptly. But in order to prevent them, it is necessary that he lie quiet for a few days. A worker would do that, but he tosses constantly and groans at least 20 hours a day in all varieties of manners, greatly increasing his discomfort, so I have my doubts whether the poor bugger will pull thru or not.

A striking commentary on the cost of the war to Spain is the fact that our hospital was a school building, I would say a high school, before the fascist invasion of Spain. And this turning of schools into hospitals seems to me to illustrate so clearly what this war means for the young people of Spain.

I notice according to the Daily that the Nathan Hale branch is very busy in the campaign for the aid of Spain. It is a fitting response to Pretty's sacrifice. I still have no news of Irving & George, though I understand a number of Americans came in yesterday, but I haven't seen any of them yet.

But I have seen only one Daily in the last 2 weeks, and that one was a month old, so I hardly know what's happening in the U.S. and news in the Spanish press we get here, mainly anarchist, about the U.S. is usually limited to 50 words an issue.

Since my diet here is limited to bread & coffee with milk (I have a condition similar to diarrhea frequent among Americans in Spain, which is incomprehensible to the Spanish Doctors, and I shall have to wait until Benicasim for treatment), I spend long hours imagining what kind of a meal you are going to fix for me when I hit New York again, without olive oil or garbanzos, what I wouldn't give for a dish of Breakfast food, right now, or a good American meal.

But there are more important things to think about. In the meantime, my regards to everyone.

> With all my love,
> Carl

[HANDWRITTEN]

Oct. 27, 1937

Dear Herb:

Since your letter hasn't gone off yet due to the difficulty of getting an envelope, I'll add a few words.

First of all, I got a hold of a copy of the Daily for Sept. 24, and there I saw the 2 ads, one for a mass meeting Friday night at De Witt Clinton on Spain, and a Dance Saturday evening at American People's School, both under the auspices of the Nathan Hale Branch.[124] I could have shouted for joy, and it made me very proud of my Branch. And it is especially fitting that the Branch members should exert themselves on behalf of Spain in response to the sacrifice Pretty made. Each time we suffer a loss, it is necessary that we strike back so much the harder and in view of Pretty's popularity in the neighborhood, this should be possible.

I hope that in a few days I will receive a letter from you giving full details on the outcome of these 2 affairs.

In regard to myself, my wounds are much better, though I am still confined to bed. Yesterday they removed several pieces of shrapnel that were near the surface. The rest, it seems, will be left where they are. I am still awaiting transfer to Benicasim, where there is an American hospital, and where quite a few of my friends are. Here there is nothing to do to pass the time away. Although 4 people promised me English books, and 2 chess sets, I haven't obtained either, so all there is to do is sleep.

By the way, will you include in your next letter what has happened to the Youth Division of the ALP?[125] I haven't heard a word about it since I came to Spain, and what are Marcia, Seymour and Vinnie doing? Charlotte hasn't written me yet either.

Is the Branch doing much hiking? This is the ideal time of the year for it. I miss this very much, for where we are there are only olive trees. Hiking ought to be a major activity now.

Am hoping that when I get to Benicasim, I'll find a letter from you awaiting me. In the meantime, give my regards to the Branch.

Salud,
Carl

[HANDWRITTEN]

Oct. 28, 1937

Dear Impy:

Since I didn't have an envelope to send my last letter written 2 days ago until today, I'll include a second installment.

Probably the most interesting thing that has happened in the last 2 days is the suspension of "Solidaridad Obrera," organ of the anarchist CNT for 10 days for printing an article not approved by the censor.[126] I think it was quite a shock to the Anarchists, but in general a good thing.

Today a nurse, who has taken quite a likening [sic] for me, and is from Galicia, now in fascist hands, bought a number of things for me, writing paper and envelopes, a good dictionary, and a fair chess set. And another brought 2 Spanish novels to read including Edgar Wallace's "Daughters of the Night," so I am passing the time fairly well now.

In addition, 2 Americans came in who are at a bone hospital near here, both having been shot thru the jaw. According to them, they do first grade work there.

My own wounds are improving. Day before yesterday they removed 2 pieces of shrapnel that were near the surface, and last night they used some kind of an x-ray machine to locate the other pieces exactly. The machine doesn't make a negative, but instead the doctors can see on a screen immediately the location of the metal, at the same time they can move the foot around and examine it from all angles. I was quite agreeably surprised by the beauty of this equipment. The doctors seemed well pleased with the results, though I don't know yet whether some kind of operation may be necessary to remove one piece partly entangled in some small bones.

Am still anxiously awaiting transfer to Benicasim, more for your letters than anything else.

And in the meantime it would be my luck to miss a big celebration in Madrid in honor of the International Brigades. According to the papers, it's going to be a big thing, with a Banquet, presents, etc. and there are rumors that our Brigade is especially to be honored. They deserve it. And I'll attend thru the medium of the press.

Am also getting treatment for my diarrhea now. And part of it is a tea my grandmother used to make out of a scented weed called, as far as I can remember, Camille [chamomile]. The flowers are small with white petals and yellow center. The stalk grows from 6 to 15 inches high, and doesn't bear leaves of the customary form but more like asparagus. The tea tastes quite good. In addition they have another liquid of some 8 to 10 ingredients, and charcoal. So now I can eat better.

Today was a rainy day and a bit colder. And it makes me imagine how nice your fireplaces must be on an evening like this. Here it is not possible to read after 5 p.m., because only 1 dim blue light is permitted in a room because of the danger of fascist aviation. But I hope to enjoy the comfort of your fireplace before the winter is completely gone.

As ever, with all my love,
Carl

[HANDWRITTEN]

Oct. 29, 1937

My dear Impy:

And just think, tomorrow night is Halloween. It brings back a thousand delightful memories of life in Ohio, of mysterious tic-tacs at the window, of the ungathered cabbage crop suddenly taking up position on the farmers front porch, of gates walking off, of big corn shocks moving out on the road completely blocking it, but more especially of masquerade barn parties and dances, with corn stalks and brilliantly colored fall leaves, and cider and pumpkins and pumpkin pie and square dances. How beautiful these things become with time, especially when one is bedfast far away from them. Such traditions and customs need not die out, but in fact, can and should become more joyous than ever in the country side.

Now to get back to the present. My young Anarchist friend on my right has given me quite a shock. In the course of several discussion, he has defended the POUM, said the present government is semi-fascist, that it is suppressing the revolution which is today farther off than a year ago, etc. The inroads trotzkyist propaganda has made among the Anarchists is unhealthy. In a further conversation with him just now, he violently defended Trotsky, and slandered the USSR. Of course there are numerous contradictions in his arguments. I only wish I could speak Spanish better. Fortunately, everyone else in the room, all Catalonians side with me, and I think we are making some progress.

Today's paper carries the news the gov't is moving to Barcelona.[127] He immediately says it is sneaking closer to the border to make a quickie escape. The truth is that the Aragon front is the most vital one for the winter, Barcelona is the industrial center of Spain, and it is here that the government must be to properly organize the war, both at the front and at the rear. But I think he is a bit ashamed of his senseless and slanderous accusation now.

Have begun to read, in Spanish, "Ruins of Palmyra" by the Count of Volney, a Frenchman. It was written about 1785, after the author made a voyage thru the Near East. In it he attempts to explain the causes and laws governing the rise and fall of empires, and the sources of man's misfortunes today. He also makes a historical analysis of all the important religions.

Some of the material is surprisingly good, in that he combats the idea man's misfortunes are ordained by the Gods and do not come from his own failure to obey the laws of Nature. But of course he is far from a materialist and attributes the rise and fall of nations to man's avariciousness and ignorance, building up quite a structure around this theory more or less logical, but of course, not in accord with the facts as we know them today. However, I find the book quite enjoyable.

To make a far jump, it is my opinion that Spanish meals are the least imaginative in the world. No matter what they make, they use olive oil, and they never prepare anything in any other way than with olive oil. It wouldn't be so bad if it was good quality oil, but it isn't and that strong oily olive taste nauseates me. Everyday we have cabbage and garbanzos, a Spanish bean. The cabbage is never just cooked in water, or prepared with a little vinegar, or as slaw, but always cooked with olive oil, and likewise the beans. They even pour oil over their meats and fish. I may became accustomed to it in 20 years, but I doubt if before that time.

Of course you know, that in much of Europe, the people drink a great deal of wine with their meals, and very little water. And so naturally, the nurses would never think of leaving a bottle of water close at hand. And when you call for water, they bring you a small glassful. Fortunately, the problem has been solved for me by the fact that I have to take a number of charcoal pills a day, and the nurse, tiring of bringing me water every so often, finally conceived the brilliant idea of leaving a bottle of water within my reach.

Yesterday, several of my comrades came in to see me, who are staying at a bone hospital not far from here. Both of them carried an arm in an airplane sling, an ingenious contraption used to hold the arm in a firm position at right angles to the body, with tension at certain points to insure the proper knitting of shattered bones. According to them, the doctors do wonders there in the way of bone surgery.

By the way, George Watt received a slight shoulder wound the first day a few moments after he went over the top. I haven't seen him yet, nor have I heard anything of Irving.

Am enclosing a postcard issued by the SRI.[128] You cannot imagine the tremendous influence of the SRI in Spain. Everyone supports it and the undershirt and shorts I am wearing now are a gift of the SRI, for it seems they keep the hospitals supplied with them, as well as giving them many other things.

Every day that passes makes me more anxious to go to Benicasim so I can get your letters. It seems there was no train this week so I may have to wait another week yet. The thought doesn't please me.

But in the meantime, I hope you'll keep on writing detailed letters about what you are doing and what is happening in New York.

Give my regards to Tima and Ryah.[129]

> With all my love,
> Carl

[HANDWRITTEN]

Nov. 2, 1937

My Dear Impy:

Time passes rapidly, and I am still here, killing time as best I can, awaiting our transfer. It is now obvious there is a fracture of some of the small bones in my foot and I will be laid up longer than I thought, probably another three weeks to a month. So far they made one attempt to remove the offending piece of shrapnel, unsuccessfully and now they seem to be waiting for the swelling to subside again.

But in the meantime I am hobbling about a tiny bit on some home-made crutches a half a foot too short for me.

Both George Watt and Irving Weissman received slight wounds the first day, according to the Battalion Doctor. I haven't seen either one.

I just finished Avdyenko's "I Love." The life he describes is about as full as any you could imagine, passing through from the most degenerate to the highest forms of life. In a way, life here in Spain has a certain resemblance to that described in Soviet novels, for some of us, that uncompromising responsibility; quick changes, and desperate working. But then truly large parts of Spain have been changed only slightly yet.

The fall of the North is quite a blow for us, for it means the releasing of large amounts of troops and equipment to be thrown on the other fronts. One consolation is that this victory cost Hitler and Mussolini plenty of men and materials and any attacks they might undertake on our well-fortified positions now will likewise cost them heavily. And it is quite likely that the government will keep the offensive.

I believe I wrote you that our Brigade was in Madrid for the Celebrations in honor of the International Brigades. Undoubtedly our comrades are enjoying a well deserved rest, and gathering a little recreation for the first time in 2½ months.

The town I am in now is a beautiful one, with palm trees, flowers a beautiful walk along the sea, according to the fellows who have been outside. And the other day when an English boat was in harbor, every American who could walk went there to get a good meal. And the fellows even bring me cookies they manage to buy in town, but which are far from plentiful.

Nov. 3

There are strong rumors about that we go to Benicasim either today or tomorrow. I certainly hope so, for this place is beginning to pall on me.

The treatment they are giving me for my diarrhea is practically ineffective and I am beginning to feel it.

Yesterday's paper carried a short note concerning some plans of the U.S. Government to enroll 500,000 volunteers in 2 months in case of emergency, and to begin now to expand the National Guard to 1,500,000 men. It sounds quite alarming. There were no details given. I hope you'll furnish me with further facts on this.

The papers are now also full of news about the USSR, and a whole week has been set aside here to honor her. Both Mia[j]a and Martinez Barrio have stated more or less directly that if it had not been for the USSR, the Spanish government would no longer exist.[130]

This letter ought to reach you just a few days before Thanksgiving. And that brings to my mind those marvelous dinners you, Ernie, or Adele used to prepare on that day. Imp, I never really appreciated those meals, but believe me, from now on, no one will enjoy them more than I. But perhaps if I am at an American Hospital then we shall celebrate Thanksgiving too. Do you ever see our tall friend, Henry, from 182 & St. Nick? Give him my regards if you do. And where is Aunt Sylvia now? I want to write to her.

> Give my regards to all,
> With all my love—
> Carl

[HANDWRITTEN]

Nov. 5, 1937

Dear Impy:

Today I am very angry. It is now exactly three weeks that I have been in this hospital. On the first day the doctor informed me there was a small fracture in my foot, but that in several weeks I would be OK. And during these three weeks, not one thing more has been done except to change the bandages. Then yesterday came a chance to go to the American hospital at Benicasim. My cards were made out and I was all set to go, when the doctor arrives, says no, because I have a piece of shrapnel in my foot, which he wants to take out this morning. I could have cursed him, three weeks to do it in, and he does nothing, and now suddenly he decides to do something. I have no doubt they could do as well in Benicasim as he can here.

It wouldn't be so bad if it didn't mean staying here an unlimited time longer. For example, there have been no means of transport to Benicasim now for exactly 2 weeks. And two more weeks here would be appalling. It wouldn't be so bad if the food was halfway decent, and if I didn't have the diarrhea. But almost 3 weeks of that already, and I have to wait for Benicasim to get rid of it for they tell me they have no bismuth or Belladonna needed to treat it, to think of 2 weeks more of it is not pleasant.

The only hope is that since the others didn't leave either yesterday as planned because of some hitch in transportation, I may be able to go with them yet if they don't go for 2 or 3 days. That would be a break.

I don't know why I am writing you all this, unless it's to get it off my chest, for it'll only make you worry. But you needn't, for by the time you get this everything will have been straightened out and I'll be taking it easy and convalescing in some beautiful villa along the seashore, enjoying the warm sunshine and the swimming.

Yesterday, I wrote a long 4-page letter to Uncle John in Orrville, in which I included the state of the milk and ice cream industry here. I am a bit afraid he is slipping to the reactionary side, and I have my doubt whether he'll even answer my letter, but time will tell.

Yesterday's good news was the re-election of Mayor LaGuardia by a half-million majority.[131] The papers here printed a short dispatch from Berlin to the effect that his re-election was very disagreeable to the high Nazi circles.

There is just that slight tang in the air this morning that makes me long to get out into the woods and mountains. Imp, sometime after I get back, we are going to have to make a trip out thru the west and include a part of the Canadian Rockies. I trust, Imp, you are not losing your physical fitness for mountain climbing, or I shall have to instruct Tina and Ryah to roll you around on the floor every morning. I'll bet you aren't doing any hiking at all these days, except once in a while with your kids at school. By the way, do they know your husband is fighting in Spain?

We get a lot of sea food here. It's a shame it isn't prepared well. Yesterday for dinner we had a squid with a lot of tentacles and tubes. It didn't taste half bad. And then we get a lot of fish, but usually boiled, and served cold with olive oil.

Will close this letter and begin Leon Tolstoi's "My Confession" in Spanish which a friend just brought in.

Three weeks without seeing any of your letters, and a prospect of 2 more makes me decide that I will ask my friend at Benicasim to forward your letters here to me in case I have to stay here. So I should hear from you soon.

With all my love—Salud—
Carl

[HANDWRITTEN]

Nov. 8, 1937

Dear Impy:

Had intended to wait until I received your letters, but it may be days yet before I get them.

The rest of the boys have gone to Benicasim, so I am the only English speaking person here. And of course I am furious over being left here when I know I would receive better treatment at Benicasim than here. The rest of the boys have promised to raise hell for me there, and I have written a letter to the person in charge there, so I guess there is nothing more to do than let things take their course for a few days.

The November 7 celebrations are tremendous here. There was a whole week of it. Here the Anarchists played up a lot of so-called anarchist leaders of that time, and hailed the Kronstadt sailors who they claimed followed anarchist leadership.[132]

My young anarchist friend is now reading Proudhon's "Confessions of a Revolutionary." I have read part of it. But the false logic, shallow and clever interpretation of events, and blindness to many things, fills me with disgust. He begins with something fundamental, the first question that must be answered "What is Government?" There have been many learned answers but all miss the point for government is faith!

But the Inprecor for Oct. 16 and the British "New Statesman and Nation" have helped me pass the last 2 days. I was very agreeably surprised when my friends brought them in. And one other comfort is that the orange season is opening.

There isn't much to write, but undoubtedly, after I hear from you, there'll be more to say. Give my regards to everyone.

    With all my love—
    Carl

[HANDWRITTEN]

Nov. 11, 1937

Dear Impy:

I still haven't received your letters, but I have new things to tell you.

Last night without warning, I was moved to a nearby hospital, specializing in bone fractures. And a half hour after I arrived there, they had ex-rayed my foot and placed it in a cast, and now I am quite comfortable. The reason for placing it in a cast is to give a fractured bone, the outside one connecting the ankle with the slender bone running to the small toe. It really forms one of the bones of the arch. The doctor says he'll take off the cast in 4 to 6 weeks, but that I'll be able to walk much sooner. And even my diarrhea is letting up a bit.

The hospital pleases me very much. The doctors seem to be very capable, the food is much better, and we are on the Mediterranean. Besides 3 other Americans are in adjoining beds, 2 of them with their arms in these ingenious airplane slings used instead of plaster casts.

Yesterday it was again impressed on me how wide and horrible are the effects of the war. There were 3 girls and 2 women talking together in our room. And each one had either lost a brother or a husband in this war. One, the new nurse in our room, was one of the 12,000 evacuated from Gijon. She has three brothers still fighting in the Asturias, though she doesn't know exactly where. Will she ever see them again?

Yesterday, to amuse myself, I listed the names of the wild animals, trees, birds, I have seen in woods & fields, and flowers. I didn't do so well, 42 trees, 42 birds, 20 wild animals, and 15 flowers. I scarcely know any flowers any more it seems. It's time I was doing a little hiking with you again.

Today is Armistice Day. When I think of the usual Armistice Day activities in Orrville, I can imagine they don't celebrate it with the assurance they once did. And it seems more likely each day it was only an Armistice. But there is still reason for hope.

Give my regards to all—
With all my love—
Carl

[HANDWRITTEN]

Nov. 14, 1937

Dear Impy:

Since all of the Americans except myself are to be evacuated to Benicasim this morning, I am sending this letter along with them to be mailed from there, for I am not certain that the letters I send from here reach you.

This hospital is excellent. The food is fine, especially the fried fish which I enjoy about twice a day. And my cast on my foot fits me well. The sun shines every morning, and I can watch the fishermen haul in their nets every morning on to a beach about 500 yards a way.

My only trouble is that I am still not receiving your letters. But the boys have promised to investigate what's wrong when they get to Benicasim today. But not to hear from you for a month is quite a sacrifice. But I comfort myself when I think how happy I shall be when I receive about 15 of your letters all at once.

They really do some quite marvelous bone surgery here. One fellow who had about 4 inches of the bone between knee and ankle blown away is hav[ing] a plate put in and will have the use of his leg. Many Asturians have been brought here, some with pretty horrible wounds. But where ever it is humanly possible to save a leg or arm, they do so here.

Thru the "Daily" we read of the appeal for unity by the CIO to the AFL. And waiting for the next issues to let us know the results is many more times exciting than awaiting the next installment of any serial I have ever read. In fact, even the comparison seems a bit out of place. The tragedy is that we only get about one "Daily" out of 6 or 7, so we probably will miss the answer.

The hardest part of a letter, when you write often, is closing it, for one always seems to say the same thing. So, this time, again

with all my love—

Salud

Carl

[The last two paragraphs of the letter were written on the back side of another letter Carl mailed on Dec. 19, 1937. As he wrote in the second letter the earlier one had been "addressed improperly."]

[HANDWRITTEN]

Nov. 16, 1937

Dear Impy:

Time flies on, and still I feel isolated from the world. The only bright spot was "The Communists in the People's Front" by Browder. Can you imagine, I hadn't read it before. And as customary, reading a report of his opens one's eyes another 6 inches. And gives you greater confidence we'll stop fascism in the USA.[133]

Here everything moves along. Even my 5-week old diarrhea is a thing of the past. And I didn't cure it with medicine, but with a faja. It's nothing magical, only a woolen sleeve you wear over your stomach which keeps your abdomen at a constant temperature and prevents chill there, the cause of this type of diarrhea. So I am greatly relieved.

The weather here has been magnificent, sun shine all day, and warm. But a cold spell threatens to begin today.

At three last night the fascists finally attained part of their objectives in their frequent bombing of this neighborhood when they set fire to an oil tank, more likely a gasoline tank. But the damage is not great, and of much less value than the many bombs they have wasted here.

Yesterday I spoke at some length with an Asturian soldier. He was wounded 10 months ago, a piece of shrapnel lodging inside the bone of his upper arm, of course breaking it. Since no capable doctor was available, the shrapnel was allowed to remain there, and the bone and wound healed. But now there seems to be an infection inside the bone. So the doctor here is going to break the bone, remove the shrapnel, cure the infection, and in 2 to 3 months, his arm should be stronger than ever. And they can do this quite nicely here.

His whole family is in fascist territory. The last news of them informed him the fascists had arrested his father and brother, and he fears they have been shot. His case is typical of literally hundreds and thousands.

Yesterday a young German came in. He has been here 14 months, served on many fronts and never wounded. But the other day he injured his ankle in a soccer ball game and had to come here. Such is life.

As you can be certain, this letter must eventually turn to the topic of food. Since meat has been forbidden me, I have been eating fried fish twice a day. Always small ones four to six inches long with their heads on, and very soft and delicious. Last night it was varied by 4 fried salt sardines about 2 inches long. And in spite of the regularity of fried fish, I still look forward to it at each meal.

My hopes grow stronger each day that I shall receive a letter, or rather a handful of letters, today. And so I wait.

In the meantime, my regards to all.

> With all my love—
> Carl

[HANDWRITTEN]

Nov. 16, 1937

Dear Herb:

Since the mailman hasn't brought me a single letter from any one for over a month, I feel quite isolated from the USA. But each day I have greater hopes he'll finally find me and bring me a bushel of letters. Those last letters I sent to the post office certainly ought to have an effect.

Things haven't changed much since I wrote you some two or three weeks ago. The fascist have tried to do some counter-attacking, but without much success, and with great losses. We rather expect an offensive on their part somewhere on the Aragon front, but I am confident it will be smashed without much trouble. When they face this way it won't be like in Asturias, where the Loyalists lacked airplanes, artillery, tanks, etc. Of course, the winter will slow down the war somewhat, and make it mighty uncomfortable for the soldiers in the trenches. Now the Government is putting on a big campaign in the rear for blankets and winter clothing. And it certainly is needed. We even took up a money collection here at the hospital for this.

Just now I am at a hospital specializing in bone surgery. They certainly do wonderful work here. And if it is possible to save an arm or leg, they do it here. I came here six days ago from another hospital where I wasted three weeks. Within a half hour after I arrived, my foot had been x-rayed and placed in a plaster cast to permit a fracture of one of the bones in the arch to heal. The cast will come off about Dec. 15 if all goes well, though I ought to be able to walk about in a few days with the aid of a steel frame.

My greatest regret here is that now for once I have time to study and read, there are no books or material to read and study from. It eats my heart out. We do receive about one "Daily Worker" a week, but it hardly permits us, the three Americans who are here, to keep up with events in the USA.

As you can well imagine, I am very anxious to hear what the Branch is doing. I like to imagine that now it is the community youth center, and the liveliest organization. I still remember the thrill I got when in the Daily [Worker] I saw two ads for affairs for Spain the Branch was sponsoring. And of course, this month without mail has kept me in suspense a long time.

And what has happened to Nick, and the fellows about him? And are you back in PS 80? What are you doing to build the "Front of the Young Generation." Here you know all of Spain's youth are united behind one program something regarded as absolutely essential here. Unfortunately, a part of the Federation of Young Anarchists (Libertarian Youth of Catalonia) has refused to join it unless the unified Socialist Youth would take back their condemnation of the POUM.[134] Of course, this was turned down, and I think soon the leaders of the Anarchist Youth will be forced to change their attitude. Especially the recent exposure of the POUM as the organizer of the fascist intelligence service in Spain will force them to do that. Most of the anarchist workers and soldiers in the hospital classify the POUM very succinctly—fascists. And the Government is quite rapidly cleaning out these rats, for they commit acts of sabotage where ever possible. They already see it is impossible to build up a mass movement. Remember I told you in last letter there was a danger of the opposition elements organizing about Caballero. But the Gov't seems to have stopped that quite nicely.

The Nov. 7 celebrations here were gigantic, and for a good reason. As Miaja pointed out, were it not for the existence of the Soviet Union, Republican Spain would not exist today. For it takes more than enthusiasm to wage a modern war.

Have you seen Herman lately? And Pat? I wrote to both but haven't heard from either. Are you doing much hiking?

You probably remember Irving Weissman, the blond curly-headed chap, and George Watt, Mae's brother. Both received slight wounds on the first day they saw action.

Give my regards to all,
Salud,
Carl

[HANDWRITTEN]

Nov. 18, 1937

Dear Imp:

And still no letters! But I write plenty anyway. Just finished a 4-page letter to my youngest sister, Elsie Irene. & yesterday I wrote Sam & Ernie, and to some friends here.

Yesterday I learned some interesting facts concerning the national oppression of Catalonia. You know they have their own language, Catalán. But very few people can write it. The reason, under the monarchy all schools were forbidden to teach Catalán, and were conducted in Spanish. So while the people spoke Catalán, they read and wrote Spanish.

Now, of course, the schools are conducted in Catalán, and Spanish is also taught. The CP newspaper published in Barcelona is published in Catalán, though the Anarchist papers are printed in Spanish. Anyone who speaks Catalán and can read Spanish, has no difficulty in reading Catalán. But it is difficult to write it, for unlike Spanish, the letters are not always pronounced alike. Catalán is sort of a combination of French and Spanish. It is spoken if parts of France, and one who knows French can with some difficulty read Catalán.

Only a few days ago the government issued a statement demanding full respect for the Catalán language, calling it especially to the attention of all government departments, which are now located in Barcelona.

The UGT is now holding a national Conference.[135] Its significance lies in its work to make the trade unions more conscious of their responsibilities for winning the war. The trade union as workers' organizations must help show the people the need for certain sacrifices, and can not merely interest them selves in improving the conditions of the workers. In some places it may be necessary for the union to take the lead in lengthening hours to increase production of war materials. Let's hope the CNT unions follow the splendid example of the CGT[U] unions.[136]

But, Imp, tonite I am looking for word from you—

> With all my love,
> Carl

[HANDWRITTEN]

Nov. 21, 1937

My dear Impy:

It's Sunday morning, but in Spain the war goes on just the same on Sunday as any other day. Only on Mondays are we reminded what day of the week it is, for Mondays there are no newspapers. The printers don't work on Sundays.

Time seems to pass very slowly daily, for lack of much to do, but the weeks seem to slip by incredibly fast. It hardly seems possible I was wounded almost 6 weeks ago.

And yesterday for the first time since that day, I was outside under my own power, so to speak. With a stub support fixed to my heel, and a cane, I can navigate once more, although to only a limited extent yet. But nevertheless it feels wonderful to be able to walk about once more.

To employ my time a bit more usefully, I asked for a book of mathematics (in Spanish, of course) from our hospital library, and as fortune would have it, there was one book, Algebra, so now I am entertaining my self with extracting cube roots of binomials and dealing with imaginary figures. I find I have not forgotten as much as I feared I had.

And this morning I even worked awhile, rolling bandages. The roll bandages are washed after they are used, then re-rolled and used for wrapping and bandaging where there are no open wounds. This is quite necessary for there is by no means an oversupply of bandages and gauze.

And day before yesterday, our bread ration was cut in half. I would say that the amount we receive daily is about equal to 4 slices of Bond's.[137] Of course, for me, this is quite sufficient, but the Spaniards are accustomed to eating much more bread than we are. In Catalonia, there is produced about 100,000 tons of wheat, while the consumption, including the hundreds of thousands of refugees from fascist territory, would normally be about 500,000 tons. So bread is rationed, and the government is importing wheat in exchange for oranges and other fruits.

In my last letter I wrote you the fascists had bombarded a gasoline supply near here and successfully started a fire. But it turned out that the fire had actually been started through some sabotagers in the rear, who it seems, fired into the tanks with a rifle. The damage is considerable, and is one of those things that happens during war time.

The III Congress of the UGT of Catalonia is over, with a number of very important discussions in line with the development of the trade unions from organizations fighting the employers to organizations of the workers for winning the war, for increasing labor discipline and productivity in the factories, and for organizing and controlling the economy of the country. The prestige of the UGT, with its loyal support of the Government and its concentration on driving out the fascists from Spain, is growing steadily, while that of the CNT, is falling due to its half-hearted support of the Government, and its hollering about Revolution to hide its failure or refusal to concentrate all its energies to win the war. You can be certain few workers approve the hiding of arms in the rear practiced by certain organization under the influence of Trotskyism, when these arms are needed at the front.

There is some news about a Commercial treaty between Great Britain and the USA. As yet it is too vague to permit one to understand the full import of it. But I have a suspicion it may have quite a little importance.

But I certainly miss the Inprecor, C[ommunist]I[nternational] and Communist.[138] And of course, no letters have come yet. But one of these days I expect to be surprised.

Think I'll work a bit on my algebra before dinner. So I'll close this letter with my regards to all.

> With all my love,
> Carl

P.S. My address remains the same regardless of where I am here.

[HANDWRITTEN]

Nov. 23, 1937

Dear Impy:

Since the letter I wrote Sunday hasn't gone off yet, I shall add another page this morning.

Rumors are coming in fast now about new Government offensive, but of course there is nothing definite. And even if I did know for certain, I wouldn't include anything about it in a letter until the offensive was actually under way. I shouldn't be surprised if Franco is encountering quite a bit of difficulty, and is due for a lot more. His failure to start anything on the Aragon front, although he talked about it a great deal in the fascist press, indicates he doesn't have the men and reserves on which he can depend. And of course our slogan now is: Dig in! as soon as we take a new position, so it would be very costly for the fascists to take it back.

And strangely enough, we have been bothered very little with fascist aviation recently around here. Which of course does not make me angry.

My hopes for getting mail is going up. Yesterday, one of the three Americans here received 2 letters from the States. So here's hoping.

Yesterday I visited the hospital library, which contains some 300 volumes, including some very old ones, and very ornate and richly bound copies. I noticed some half dozen volumes on Botany and flowers. But our biggest surprise came when we found 2 English books, one huge one containing 4 novels, including "The Czar" by Tolstoi, and 2 mystery stories. Up to the present we haven't solved the problem of how 3 of us can each read a novel at a time, since all are in the same volume.

But there really isn't much to write you. And so I'll get to my Algebra.

>With all my love,
>Carl

[HANDWRITTEN]

Nov. 27, 1937

My dear Impy:

Four days have passed rapidly, aided with the Nov. 7 and Nov. 1 Sunday Workers.[139] Browder's article, "The Triumph of Democracy Thru Socialism" is another masterpiece. Reading his articles helps one understand the deep love of the people of the Soviet Union for Stalin.

Of course, we are still in the dark here regarding how many Alp [ALP] candidates were elected to the city council. But perhaps we shall know in 2 or 3 days for the I[nternational].B[rigades]. paymaster promised to bring us some "[D]aily [W]orkers" on his next trip here.

At last I received a letter, from the Political Commissar and Commander of the Lincoln Washington Battalion. They are at rest for the moment, having their ranks replenished and doing some intensive training. The commander now is Milton Wolfe [*sic*] formerly Commander of the Machine-Gun Company. You'll recall that the last 2 Political Commissars, Keller and myself, and now the Commander, come from the "Maxims."[140] We're not bragging but it is a good company. Captain Wolff, by the way was one of the leading lights of the Bensonhurst Branch of the YCL before he came here. So you see the YCL isn't doing so badly either. But Wolff and Keller are very fine examples of young men, Americans, who came here without Military Training but a strong desire to fight fascism, and in a few short months of the severest testing, have risen to the rank of Battalion Commanders.[141]

As far as my wounds are concerned, a good improvement can be reported. Have begun daily sun baths of my left leg, where the number of open wounds has been reduced to five. & my foot is making excellent progress. Yesterday, I walked over a half kilometer with the aid of a cane. And with the good food here and rest, I have returned to almost my normal weight. In 2 to 3 weeks, I hope to be discharged from the hospital, a well man once more.

Although I have written to both Irving & George Watt, I have heard from neither one. But I read in all the papers George presented an ASU [American Student Union] banner to the Student organization here, so he must be quite recovered.

The weather was marvelous today. The view from my windows reminds me of some imaginative post card portrait of some charming view. The sky this morning could not have been bluer, and this afternoon the Mediterranean was still bluer. And with the white buildings standing among the greens of evergreen trees and shrubs, reminds one of anything but war and fascism. By the way, it seems as if the landscape will be more or less green all winter long. So while we miss the brilliant fall colors, we don't have the drabness of a snowless winter.

I would write much more, but it is getting quite dark, so you'll hear from me in about 2 more days.

With all my love—
Carl

[HANDWRITTEN]

Dec. 1, 1937

Dear Brother Bennet:

Although I haven't heard from you since I last wrote you, I should write again to let you know of my continued progress. The failure to receive a letter from you is not strange for I haven't received a single letter in 7 months, the mail service seemingly sending these everywhere else than where I am.

My wounds are about healed. The cast on my leg will be off in 2 weeks or 10 days, and the wounds in my thigh are practically all closed and healed. The work and treatment I found & food at this hospital is really excellent.

I imagine that by this time Ohio is covered with a blanket of snow. And that you are doing a lot of hunting. Here along the Mediterranean, it's quite warm. The last week has been nice and warm but today it is a bit cooler. In fact, although the latitude is the same as Ohio's, along the coast the sea keeps the weather quite mild, but of course, inland, there is a different story. There heavy snow often impedes military operations.

At the moment there are no big drives underway, but I think soon there will be some large scale operations before winter really sets in. Each day that passes, of course, helps the Spanish Gov't become stronger while Franco's difficulties grow. One of the big problems of the government now is to fight speculation, especially in food. And it is taking a number of steps towards this end. Through the farmers' organizations, it is arranging for most of the products to come under the control of Government agencies, so that speculation and high prices can be cut to a minimum.

I suppose the American press has carried stories of a truce or compromise between the government and the fascists. You can be absolutely certain no such thing will ever take place. The Spanish people are determined there is only one solution, victory, and the driving out of all foreign invaders.

And you probably also read about the withdrawal of Volunteers. The Government would be heartily in favor of this, for the fascists have at least five to 8 times as many foreign soldiers as the government. But of course, Franco, Hitler & Mussolini will never agree to it, and are only discussing it now to stall for time.

Here is a fact that is very significant. In Loyalist Spain, there are now 3,000,000 refugees from fascist territory. And there would be many more if they were able to cross the lines. Reports daily show the brutal treatment given to the farmers and working people by the fascists who use terror, just as Hitler and Mussolini do, to keep the people down.

According to recent reports from our training base, quite a few more Americans have come to Spain to fight in the Lincoln-Washington Battalion. And this may make it possible for some of us who have been fighting on several different fronts already, to return to the States, to let the American people know what is actually going on here. Incidentally, the fellow in the bed right across from me comes from Toledo, Ohio. I knew him when I was still in the States, and met him here again in the hospital.

So far I have just received scanty information on the elections. But it seems to me that there were quite a few progressive candidates elected, some places on the Democratic Ticket. The victory of La Guardia in New York is a very good sign for the development of a big farmer labor middle class movement against the trusts, banks and capitalists, for democracy & peace, and better living conditions for the working people. I notice just now there is quite a drive on against the meat trust, which has jacked up prices a good deal this year. Even the retail butchers are joining in the fight against the packers. In New York, a couple days strike brought down the price five cents a pound on every article.

It's about 2 months since I heard a word of news from Orrville. So I hope you are writing regularly, and one of these days, I'll suddenly find myself with a fistful of mail. And leave a Bunny for me next year. I'll show you how to get him.

And I'm probably just in time to wish you, Grace, Leonard, a Merry Christmas and a happy New Year.

    Sincerely
    Carl

[HANDWRITTEN]

Dec. 5, 1937

My dear Impy:

It's Sunday morning again, and I can think of no better way to spend it then by writing you. Of course, none of your letters have as yet caught up with me, though this morning I did receive my second letter in seven weeks. It was from by best pal in the Battalion, Ben Findley from Turtle Creek, Pa., now our Battalion Quarter master.

Imp, last night I had a brain storm and it involves you. How about meeting me in Paris this summer, or perhaps by that time you may even be able to enter Spain? Anyway, it's something to dream about.

Frankly, I have been thinking of returning to the States soon, but in view of the likelihood of the fascists attempting a big offensive soon, it is out of the question to consider such a thing at present. Yesterday, Arnold (with whom I corresponded a long time while I was in the States, you'll recall) was here to see me.[142] And if I would have been well, he would have taken me along to work with him, which I should have liked very much. But I think it'll be some two weeks yet before I am completely well, and then a decision will be made as to my future work here in Spain.

At present, I am expecting to be moved to the American Hospital at Benicasim at any moment. It really is not necessary that I remain here longer, through I should prefer to do so because of the more capable medical treatment and better food.

I had a lot of excitement during the last few days. A comrade from the Brigade dropped in late one evening with some literature which he was distributing to the hospitals. He informed me he had taken 3 packages for me to another hospital, then returned with them to Benicasim and forwarded them here. That was two weeks ago. So then I began an intensive search for them, my mouth watering at the idea of good American Chocolates, and perhaps some American Pipe tobacco. Once I thought I was on the point of discovering them at another hospital in this area, but until today I haven't been able to lay my hands on them. But there is still hope. Of course they may not be in existence anymore. For it's very easy to rationalize "Well, the poor guy's probably dead," and some body enjoys a fine box of chocolates.

"Spain is a backward country." The trifle that impresses it on me at the moment is the way a girl, rather a woman of 24, is sweeping the floor. Of course such a thing as wet sawdust is out of the question, but it is still possible to keep much dust from flying by pulling the broom more and pushing it less. But this girl is a fast one in more ways than one, and she shows it by her little flip-up with the broom at the end of the swing. Fortunately this is a broken arm and leg ward, and not a T.B. ward. But still progress is so rapid in Spain I shouldn't be surprised if in a few months, sweeping will be done in hospitals without filling them with a dust cloud.

Excerpt from a letter received by an American comrade from his sister, not class-conscious: "Please be careful. I hear there is so much war going on in Spain. Please write me whether you are a prisoner." It hurts, but it comes from Ohio.

Our supply of literature has suddenly increased. We receive the D[aily] W[orker]s for Nov. 5, 7, 9, 11, 12 and 14. Quite a haul. And we have added a copy of "Science and Society" Summer 1937, to our library of "National Geographics" of May 1937 & May 1933. We read everything from cover to cover. In addition we made a valuable Spanish addition, Diaz's speech to the Plenum.[143] We are in an Anarchist center and it is rather difficult to get any C[ommunist].P[arty]. literature. "Frente Rojo" for example, the Party paper is not available although we are in an important city not so far from Barcelona. Diaz's speech will appear in the Daily or in the Communist, I should imagine, for it is the document of the day for us.

The hospital political Commissar is organizing some classes for illiterates, and several others by means of loudspeakers in the rooms for those who are bedridden. So far the loudspeakers are still missing, but anyway, the idea is excellent. Many are forced to spend months in a hospital, with a hand or arm in a special cast, or taking special exercises to repair the damage done to nerves in those members. And these Comrades certainly need to employ these months usefully. Of course, the constant shifting about raises problems, but need not stop the classes.

The latest "Dailies" have us right in the middle of the P.R. count, and so are Cacchione and Quill elected or not?[144] It looks as if they have a good chance, particularly Cacchione. This'll bring still more life into New York's politics.

Also it seems, the USA is entering a new depression, especially alarming is the tremendous drop in steel output, from 80 to 35. It seems to me the Party could score a homerun with a class popular statement spread as widely as possible, warning of a new crash, how the Liberty-League would make it worse, and what must be done to fight the coming depression, need for alliance of all democratic & progressive forces for a proper legislative program on taxation, relief, agriculture, etc. Such a statement could take the country by its ears. I expect to find it in the D[aily].W[orker]. any day.

Did I tell you about the louse that crawled down into my cast about four or five days ago. I was a bit worried at first, but it seems to have been a papa louse, for there is still only one there. Every evening at 5:30 he makes a trip of about four inches up the cast and back again. Of course, I have no way of telling whether it is a trip to the dining room, or just to relieve himself. I have been hoping he would get lonely and come out to look for a mate, in which case I'll have an opportunity to snag him providing he doesn't do his lovemaking while I am asleep. I could wander on and on about this topic but my letter is probably lousy enough as it is. Or if it wasn't before, it is now.

I'd wish you and all a Merry Xmas and a happy new year now, only I expect you'll get my next letter before the 25th. In case you don't, know that I wish it for you.

> With all my love
> Carl

[HANDWRITTEN]

Dec. 9, 1937

Dear Herb:

Each day I expect to receive a big pile of mail that is lying around Spain somewhere for me, with a couple of letters from you with news about the Branch. So each day I put off writing.

Still here in the hospital I am somewhat isolated from the battalion and there is not so much to write about. Although it is quite comfortable to lie in bed these cold wet days instead of freezing in a trench, and eat three square meals a day, it is much more satisfying to be in the trenches defying danger and suffering, making history instead of reading about it.

Supposedly according to the fascist press, the fascists are about to launch a big offensive to smash through our lines, probably on the Aragon front. But so far the offensive has not begun although the fascists are doing a lot of bombarding of cities in the rear. But I think the offensive can be stopped, and perhaps turned into a Guadalajara bigger than the original one where the Italian troops ran so fast.

If the fascist offensive can quickly be turned into a smashing Loyalist Counter-offensive, it may well mean the decisive turning point in the war. For it must be recognized that the government was wholly on the defensive, until last July when it staged the Brunete offensive. And the Fascists until the present have been constantly waging an offensive on one front or other. But the Army is using every minute available for improving its fortifications and better equipping and training its Army. And the morale of the soldiers is high. They are conscious of what is ahead of them, and determined that the fascists shall get a belt that will make it stagger and punch-drunk. And of course, the Washington-Lincoln and the MacKenzie-Papineau are also waiting their opportunity. Our brigade is especially equipped to be used to stop the offensive. But I'll write more of that later.

What makes me happy here is to see how the fascists and reactionaries have been set-back in the elections all over the world this fall, and not least of all in New York. If you can keep them on the run there, and if we can start them running here, it will mean fascism on a world scale will be retreating before the forces of democracy and progress. And that will mean a lot less pain and suffering for the people of the whole world.

And of course there is another reason why we rejoice in the victory of the progressive forces in every country. For to us it means more help for the fight against international fascism here. If Spain were permitted to buy the war material it needs abroad, the war would not last very long here. And the victory of the People's Front means an end to the present "non-intervention" policies.

We are watching very closely, as closely as we can with the limited information we receive, the special session of Congress. Certainly there is going to be a battle royal there. If only the people of the United States get together and make their demands felt, and give those congressmen who are progressive, plenty of support, it seems to me the movement for the People's Front can practically be established, and if in addition, this is closely linked up in the minds of the people with a struggle against the coming or threatening depression, things may move very quickly in the States. Certainly the fight against layoffs and the lowering of the standard of living must be one of the basic factors in forming the People's Front. And perhaps the loss of jobs and harder times will mean more volunteers for Spain, as well.

What is the League doing? There is very little news in the "Daily" about it. And certainly a powerful organized youth is essential today for any real progress. I hope in your letters you will give me some information about the general policies of the League.[145]

There has been a gap of 24 hours here in the letter, and in the interval I have been transferred to the International Brigade hospital at Benicasim, a splendid place where the I.B. numbers are sent to convalesce after a preliminary treatment of their wounds or sicknesses.

I suppose you have been following the work of the non-Intervention Committee, especially their latest proposal for the withdrawal of volunteers. The Spanish Government would stand to gain very much by any real mass withdrawal of volunteers. But you can bet your last bottom dollar that Franco will never agree to it though he may do some fake maneuvering on the line; pretending to accept it and using it to gain more time and bringing in more troops from Italy especially.

Here at Benicasim, I have been informed the American press is quite disheartening in regard to events in Spain. And of course, things are tough, but the Government is acting with a firmer hand every day to completely put the country on a war basis and to smash the enemies in the rear. But Herb, help for Spain today has got to be more than cigarettes and books for us. It needs to be cannons, machine guns, airplanes, etc. And first of all, an end to that disgraceful embargo or "neutrality" policy.

Some of the things the Government has done in the past few weeks and months, has been to further purge unreliable elements out of the Army command, taken firmer steps to root out Trotskyist and fascist agents, rumor mongers and defeatists, instituted military training for young people of 18 and 19 years of age, though they don't actually go to the front, taken measures to control sale of all food products so the food for the Army is guaranteed, and the food necessary for the Civilian population will be available at reasonable prices, taking steps to nationalize the railroads and other industries, etc, and a hundred and one more things. All this isn't done over night, but it is being done.

A few things about myself. My cast on my foot is due to come off any day now, and in a short time I'll be OK again.

And I got a package!! From Sylvia, a big can of pipe tobacco. And am I popular Now! And I understand there are 3 more packages, but the problem is to lay my hands on them. And I may get my mail any minute now! So then I'll have to write again.

But by the time you'll have waded thru these hieroglyphics (hen tracks), you'll be exhausted. So a Merry Christmas and a happy New Year to yourself and your mother, and to all members of the Branch.

Salud

Carl

P.S. My address is still the same.

[HANDWRITTEN]

Dec. 10, 1937

My Dear Impy:

Thanks a lot for your birthday present. I received that pound of pipe Tobacco last night and a pipe Smoker and an excellent friend of mine took one whiff of some I had placed in my tobacco pouch and exclaimed: "My God, that's Revelation." You can't imagine how popular I have become among pipe smokers.

Incidentally I was moved yesterday to Benicasim, which explains how I got your package. But the postman kindly informs me he just sent some 30 letters for me to Sabinosa yesterday, from which I had just arrived. But there's a chance they may come back. Anyway, your future letters ought to reach me here.

This is a beautiful place. Irving is here also. He wasn't wounded, being the only one out of 7 on his crew to come thru safely. But he got the Jaundice and is recovering here on a special diet. And you should see him, spending all his waking time organizing the Party, and every one remarks at his thorough knowledge of organization and ability to organize and analyze people. He really is doing an excellent job.

I see my letters to you are far from political, though there are a number of important developments recently. But it'll have to wait until the next time, for I have much to do today.

Merry Christmas & happy New Year. And thanks again for the Birthday Present.

     With all my love—Salud
     Carl

P.S. Since I moved out of Catalonia, my small change scrip is valueless, so here's a souvenir. It's nominal value is equivalent to $1/_{61}$ of a dollar.

[HANDWRITTEN]

Dec. 13, 1937

My Dear Impy:

I still haven't heard from you directly, but I did indirectly, for I am taking it for granted you must have been responsible for the cable asking why I hadn't been moved. It caused a good deal of commotion, although no action for the reason I had already been moved.

I am wondering what I wrote you to cause you such alarm, but on the other hand it also shows me how closely you follow my movements here. Undoubtedly there will be more details in your letters.

There are a myriad and one activities here for the convalescent, Library, writing room, canteen, wall newspapers and in Sports, soccer, handball, volleyball, horse shoes, hiking, swimming (it's a bit cold now) tennis, and almost anything you can think of. Of course, I am not in a position to take advantage of the sports facilities yet because of my foot, but I am getting a little reading done. And the weather here is mild, in fact I am bitten by mosquitoes every night. But because of the dampness, it gets very chilly at night, and Spanish houses, even of the richest, as these are, have absolutely no provision for heating. But when the sun shines, it is very pleasant.

I promised to include a bit more about politics in my next letters. I think I'll speak in some detail about one topic each letter.

And for this time it will be on the withdrawal of volunteers, as suggested by the NI [Non-Intervention] Committee.

The withdrawal of foreign troops is something the Spanish people desire very much, including the majority of the Spaniards in fascist territory. And certainly they would stand to gain by it, for the number of volunteers in Loyalist Spain in no way compares with the number of Italian and German troops and technicians here. In fact, Franco, without foreign troops would be hard put just to garrison the rear to prevent uprisings, let alone man the front lines. He would immediately be in a very serious position, and would certainly be eliminated very quickly from Spanish life.

And from this fact, the conclusion is clear, there will be no real withdrawal of foreign soldiers from Spanish soil. But Franco will do a little maneuvering on this issue. For instance, he has offered to permit the withdrawal of 3000 troops (I don't know whether dead, or just wounded Germans and Italians) in exchange for being granted belligerent rights, and the Loyalists withdrawing an equal number. This proposal is of course, no more than an insult. And in the meantime, he is bringing in more foreign soldiers, for his big offensive he has delayed so long. And of course, if we are realists, we won't sleep either, but more volunteers will pour into Spain. That ought to dispose of this question.

But who do you think lives in my villa? A villa by the way, is a beautiful summer house on the beach, where the rich used to idle the time away. None less than Egan Erwin Kish, the writer and the Doctor who removed my cast was his brother, Dr. Kish, chief surgeon here.[146] There are a number of other notables here, and many pass thru to visit us, and see the hospital of the I.B.

By the way, the plaster cast has been removed from my leg. And now I am trying to distinguish between the real aches and those due to using of inactive muscles not exercised for a month. It's too early yet to know whether everything is perfect or not.

Your pipe tobacco is already half gone, but I intend to make the second half last much longer than the first half. And I may even receive some of the other packages you sent me, for the mailman here remembers receiving them, but is not certain as to what happened to them.

George Watt, by the way, had only a flesh wound and is already back with the Battalion. And up to the present, I haven't been able to get a single word of information about Bernie Walsh.[147]

But this is enough for today. Give my regards to all—

With all my love—

Carl

[TYPEWRITTEN]

Dec. 19, 1937

Dear Bea,[148]

Yesterday I received your very welcome letter along with 26 others, which is the first ones I have received in 10 weeks from the States. It seems letters are afraid to come to hospitals.

But really Bea, you should not have thought I had forgotten who you are. But many thanks for the pictures, nevertheless. The one of Herman is one I value particularly, for it is so Hermanish. You cannot imagine how happy it made me to hear of the fine progress of the branch.

I certainly hope your reregistration well hits the hundred mark, which will be about 3 times last year's mark. The idea of a Neighborhood Youth Center, and the organization of a parents' group, are especially [good]. To find a big Communist Youth Center when I come back would indeed be a pleasant surprise. By the way, don't expect me back too soon, for we haven't licked the Fascists yet, although we took them over in several battles, and are making progress around Teruel just now.[149]

What's happened to P.S. 80? Is DeWitt Clinton open as a night center? And one other question. I always felt we had not yet become such an organization that young people felt that by joining the Y.C.L. they could fulfill their desires, do what they want to do, that the League would help them become whatever it was they wanted to be? And this is exactly the kind of organization the Y.C.L. should be, an organization youth can use to obtain their best and finest desires. What kind of activities is the branch sponsoring now for the young people? How do you carry on your educational work? What has happened to Nick and his gang? The more you'll write about the branch and the more branch members that write to me, the better I'll like it.

Now a few words about Spain. The Spanish people have already been fighting, on a tremendous military scale, against the Italian and German fascist invaders, and if you'll remember a bit about the World War, you'll know that conducting a war is expensive and demands many sacrifices. Bread, rice, flour, sugar, beans, fish, etc., are all national, and sometimes there is not enough. There is almost no meat for the civilian population. If I go into a town today, the only food I can buy are oranges, almonds and dried grapes, and perhaps, canned peppers. Not much of a selection.

But shortage of food is not the worst the Spanish people suffer. A few days ago the fascists hurled bombs (2500 shells) into Madrid in one day alone. They bombed [L]erida and Killed 54 school children alone. They bombed Barcelona, killing some 70 and wounding some hundreds. On one day, the fascists bombed 3 hospitals where there were Americans, Tarancons [Taracon], and Benicasines [Benicasim]. The young men from 17 to 19 are receiving military training. Those from 20 up are already in the army, and many are already killed or crippled for life. The 2 Spaniards next to me in this hospital have both [lost] an eye. I am enclosing a picture of Guernica today so you can see how some Spanish towns have been destroyed. Where do you suppose the women and children who used to live there are now? Were they killed outright or burned to death?

This is the sad part of this war. But there is also a disgraceful part. The disgraceful part is the failure of the democratic nations to help the suffering Spanish people, who are making all these sacrifices, heroically and willingly, for the peace and democracy of the world. Yes, they have sent some ambulances, medical equipment, and cigarettes. But do you know what we used to stop the fascists? Bullets, hand grenades, machine guns, tanks, cannons, airplanes, . . . And the democratic people outside of the Soviet Union and Mexico, have sent none of these. Why, the U.S. won't permit the Spanish people to buy these things in the USA.

Do you know what it means for us? We'll lick the fascists anyway, but more of us will have to die doing it than if we received the proper help. Just now after the fall of the North, the situation is plenty serious. But the Spanish people are pulling their belt up another notch, and pitching into the work and suffering, ahead of them yet. But it is high time for more real help from the American people, in military weapons, and in men, and the Y.C.L. must help the American people to understand this. And they can count on the Americans here to do their share right here.

But Bea, it's getting dark so I'll have to close soon. My foot and leg are almost healed, and soon I'll be back on duty again.

Please give my best regards to Herman and tell him to write. I haven't received his package yet but I'm expecting it daily.

Also give my regards to your sister and to all the members of the branch. I'd like to hear from more of them and I'll answer every letter I receive.

Merry Xmas and a Happy New Year if it [is] not too late.

   Salud
   Carl Geiser

[HANDWRITTEN]

Dec. 19, 1937

Dear Impy:

Yesterday I received 9 of your letters all at one time, together with 18 other letters. May I assure you I picked yours out first and read these in chronological order with the utmost joy. And many of the descriptions you give of N.Y. events are being put on our Wall Paper for the benefit of the other Americans here as well, particularly such delightful ones as the one on architectural progression, and the Nov. 7th celebration.

Am enclosing some stamps and cancellations for Maude. The cancellations are used inside the Army in place of postage stamps. I'll keep my eyes open for unusual issues.

Here is a letter you didn't get, because I had addressed it improperly, so it came back to me. [Geiser is referring to the letter he wrote on November 14, 1937.]

THIS IS

THREE

IN

ONE

....

A Story

An Invitation

A Ticket

....

                proceed

THE STORY

The Characters: Carl Geiser, his wife Sylvia,
            their family and friends.

The Scene: American, 1936-1937. Carl leaves for
        Spain to join the ABRAHAM LINCOLN
        BATTALION and fight the spread of
        fascism and help democratic Spain.
        :Carl—American farm boy—soon becomes
        a leader in this battalion, carrying
        forward the traditions of true Ameri-
        canism. What he and his comrades-in-
        arms are doing, what's happening   in
        Spain...read his "Letters to My Wife"

The Impulse: November 20 is Carl's birthday.
        Wife, family and friends decide
        to celebrate in the way he'd
        love best.....to aid the Anti-
        Fascist fight.

                  and further

Sylvia has just moved into a lovely apartment

       S c — o — o — c — o — o — o

        YOU'RE INVITED TO THE BIRTHDAY
           C E L E B R A T I O N
             . Sat. Night
             Nov. 20,   1937
                   at
                Sylvia's
               Suite 1008
              Hotel Chelsea
     23 Street, between 7 & 8 Avenues

                   and

- -

          THIS IS YOUR TICKET
               p l u s
                 50¢
        and you're in the story
        and in for a swell time
    and eligible for a swellelegant door prize
    and......SAY, COME ON UP AND FIND OUT!

Tomorrow I shall write you a much longer letter, answering some of the questions you ask.

We were visited by Italian planes from Mallorca last night, but as usual no damage except one nurse scratched her arm running for shelter.

With all my love—Salud

Carl

[HANDWRITTEN]

Dec. 22, 1937

Dear Bennet:

I received my Xmas presents about a week early, consisting of 49 letters in one batch. It included three from you, of Sept. 23, Oct. 14 and Nov. 10, for which I was very pleased.

I would very much like to hear Bill & Lila's impressions of Europe, especially Germany & Italy. And am very sorry they were unable to see Sylvia while they were in New York. They probably passed right by her hotel where she lives with several other teachers, for it is very near the boat lines. I suppose he took many pictures, which I hope to see when I return.

By the way, in regard to those guys who came here & then returned to peddle stories against the Spanish Government, you can put them down as romanticists, and adventurers, who when they got here found out what was going on was a very tough battle of the people for their rights, a battle which requires plenty of sacrifices. And they also found out war is not so much fun, as you probably know from my letters. So, not really coming here to help the Spanish people, the war & sacrifices got them down, and they have to make an excuse why they didn't stay to finish the job. If you hear a real fighter who has gone back wounded or for educational purposes, you'll hear a true & different story. About this guy Blair from Cleveland, he was supposed to be in my Battalion, but nobody here heard of him. My opinion, his story was mostly Bull.[150]

Am certainly glad to hear June & Ellen are working as nurses.[151] Can you send me their addresses, for I lost them when I was wounded. I received a very interesting letter from Marie, and shall write her. She seems to be getting along quite well.

Hope you don't mind my jumping from one topic to another for I am going through your letters and writing as I am inspired by them.

Your letter of the 14th says you are afraid I may be in danger. That was the morning I was wounded. Funny, and Don't ever think I am in danger again, or I may be killed.

The fascist propaganda that the Gov't kills innocent people is a lie — you know, I am not a bloodthirsty person, but sometimes I feel the gov't is actually too lenient with enemies of the people. And the business about killing so many if we lose a battle makes everyone smile. Bennet this is really a people's army, formed when every worker & farmer got down his shotgun & went out on the street to fight for his rights. With such an Army you can't do anything the people feel is not right.

Dec. 23, 1937

Excuse the pencil, for someone borrowed my pen and hasn't returned it.

In regard to the weather here, most of Spain is a high plateau, and is plenty cold in winter. On some fronts at present there is 6 to 7 feet of snow, which slows down fighting a bit. But of course on the Mediterranean coast where I am at present, it doesn't even snow, the houses have no provisions for heating, and flowers are blooming in our formal gardens in front of our villa 3 days before Xmas. So the weather depends entirely on where you are.

Am glad to hear the power line is being extended out to the farming districts, for evidently the effort of the private utilities to prevent this has been defeated.

So Ross Bartchy & Bill Cayer are on the Ohio State football squad. That makes a good name for Orrville. It doesn't seem so long ago I was their Sunday School teacher.

By the way, don't get the idea that we don't try or want to kill the fascist soldiers, when we are at the front. This war is much different than the World War, where it is true the soldiers had nothing against each other, when it was a war between two imperialist blocs for their own interests, and not that of the people. But here it is different. The Spanish people are fighting for their freedom and to drive out the Italian & German armies, and for democracy. Every loyalist soldier is in dead earnest and knows why he is fighting. Of course it is true many of the fascist soldiers don't want to fight & many desert to us. And every time when we have taken prisoners, I was surprised by how happy the soldiers were to be our prisoners, free from the fascist army.

I am glad you liked Pres. Roosevelt's Speech.[152] As you say, what is necessary is for everyone who doesn't want war to stand together, and the fascists won't dare to start anything. But as long as the United States stands alone, doesn't act together with England, France & the USSR, the fascists will take advantage of it. Japan will continue her war on China, [and] Mussolini & Hitler will continue to send troops to Spain.

Thanks very much for the picture of Leonard. He certainly is a husky youngster. When I think how proud I am of him, I can imagine what a proud father you are.

My foot is almost well. The last wound is closing and I can walk around quite well. There is no danger of a limp, & I will be as sound as ever.

Say, aren't we getting old already. Nevertheless, greetings on your 26th Birthday, & may you celebrate many more. My regards to Grace & Leonard.

Salud,

Carl

[HANDWRITTEN]

Dec. 23, 1937

My dear Impy:

The 18 letters I received from you during the last 5 days make an excellent Xmas gift. Only I am afraid you won't receive more than 1 or 2 letters from me, & that won't make much of a gift.

Since I received 31 other letters at the same time, you can imagine I have plenty of work. I enjoy Sam's letters especially. Among those who wrote me are Herman (at last), Steifberg, Marie, Bennet, Grace, Herb, who told me how glad he was to meet you at Clinton, & Jean. I wish you could read some of them, for they are of all types, Bennet's & Marie's especially have some unique notions. Marie for instance writes:

"According to the Reader's Digest the war in Spain is secondarily to give Germany & Italy a chance to experiment with new war mechanisms. However since they can find no successful new weapons, perhaps they will let the war come to an end."

And Bennet wants to know if I don't think war is barbarious [sic]? But at least he approved Pres. Roosevelt's peace speech.

Will now try to answer a few of your letters, in chronological order.

Sept. 24—I am quite proud of you in your H.S. work. Al Steele writes:

A yaller haired gal who teaches in—I think you remember her. Well, we finally got her for H.S. director for the Bx [Bronx]. So what happens. Like being awakened from a dream she is stolen from us. Our hands were buttered, and from our very grasp she was taken away and now she's the property of the District. Tragedies—oh tragedy!!

Your description of the Apt. is interesting. I remember the building well. You say $33. This is a month a piece, for it certainly can't be anything else.

Sept. 27—Sorry I frightened you with that wall board article on Milton Rappaport.[153]

The news about the activities of the Nathan Hale branch is certainly very heartening to me. If the branch would have fallen apart after I left, I would have been sorely disappointed, and it would have been a bad reflection on my work. I understand the county considers it one of their best branches. Hope they are successful in obtaining a headquarters for the youth of the community.

Your answer to Herman is the only correct one & his letter to me makes me feel good for it indicates he is looking for a way to contribute his share. You must keep close touch with him.

& your report on your conversation with Marie indicates you are ever becoming more skillful at selecting the vital point which will best clear up a problem, and bring out the real issue at stake which is a trait of great value.

I have received your pictures, and value them very much. I am planning to go to a large town nearby and there I may have my picture taken. I haven't had an opportunity to do so up to date. Films you know are none too plentiful. My picture has often been taken in groups, but I have never seen the proofs of any of them.

Sept. 27—From Paul Wendorf who is now working on a history of the I.B., I heard you are not looking so well. Imp, if it is because of worry over me, you should be reprimanded, for it doesn't help me nor you in the slightest. But then the pictures you send me show you to be your own impish self—so I don't worry.

Right, believe very little of what you read in the capitalist press. For instance now the fascists are supposed to be on the offensive—but instead we are taking Teruel, the first provincial capital we ever took, and doing it very, very neatly.

Pretty, as I believed I told you, was wounded as we maneuvered into position to attack Quinto on Aug. 27, I believe was the date. We advanced through artillery fire, taking up a position behind a small hill, which was being grazed by rifle & machine gun fire. I remember bullets were flying all around me while I was on the crest observing the enemy positions.

Pretty was wounded just before we began the attack, by this fire. He received an abdominal wound and died on the way to the hospital. I saw him just a little before he was hit, and he was reacting very courageously to his first taste of fire. To be killed in the first few minutes of his first battle certainly was a tough break. Herb wrote they were planning a memorial meeting, but I haven't had any further report on it yet.

Sept. 29—You write you are about to see Dave White, but your next letter is dated Oct. 3 and doesn't mention it so one letter must still be on its way. I am anxious to hear your impression of Dave, for he was one of my best friends here.[154]

How about more details about your union local, who's heading it, and what are you doing to draw in the Catholic teachers. Certainly this old division of Catholic & non-Catholic must be overcome today.

If I answer four letters every other day, I ought to catch up soon.

My foot is coming along satisfactorily but not as speedily as I had hoped. Regards from Irving W.

> With all my love—
> Carl

[HANDWRITTEN]

Dec. 24, 1937

My dear Impy:

To continue answering your letters.

Oct. 3—Am glad you are pleased with the ring. You can keep the other as a historical memento, for companion with the new one.

Also am very glad you got those magazines, especially when you turn these into so much cold cash. Have been looking for more, but haven't seen anything more than these ILD [International Labor Defense] (SRI) cards.

Your leaflet for the Chinese meeting is on our wall board, and likewise most of the clippings you sent are occupying a prominent place is the picture of Kent[?], Browder & [Elizabeth Gurley]Flynn.[155]

Oct. 6—Your description of "My Day" satisfies me. I think you're working hard enough you won't get fat even if you don't go on hikes—but watch those headaches.

The NYT clipping of the clergyman's statement on Catholic Spanish propaganda was excellent. When it's finished its service here on the Wall board, it's going to Bennet.

Irving received some awful letters from home—but the fight against fascism comes first, and it's too bad his parents don't appreciate his activity, instead of making themselves ill over it.

Oct. 8—The stationery tells me your Tima & Ryah are now "at home" and in quite a historic building & apartment.[156]

You congratulate me on my epistilarian [sic] efforts. But Imp, anyone who experiences these things and merely sets down what he can observe, can do the same. You will note my letters are best when I am in action—but you don't say anything on the legibility of my handwriting.

Am really sorry you didn't get to see Lila & Bill when they were in New York. I am a bit afraid they are moving to the right, which would be unfortunate.

Oct. 10—Your descriptions of your apt. are really making me anxious to see it. You'd understand this better if you knew better the "Apts" I live in now. Tho it is very nice to sleep on a bed, in spite of the mosquitoes & lice. There is a big battle here against them, and the louse casualties are high, nevertheless a few always manage to slip thru.

Your logic for making the house warming my birthday party instead of yours is irresistible. I regret it very much that I found myself unable to attend.

The weather here at Benicasim is really quite warm. Flowers are growing in the formal gardens in front of our villa, there are palm trees, and a hundred yards away is an orange grove loaded with ripe red oranges.

But 150 miles away there is 6 to 7 feet of snow on the front. Most of Spain is a high plateau—and there the weather is as cold as that of New York. But along the seacoast, it's quite mild, and houses are built without any heating arrangements.

Oct. 11—About my coming home—you know the I.B. is now a regular part of the Spanish Army—and we have enlisted for the duration of the war. Only under special circumstances, such as being unfit for further action, for educational purposes, can anyone leave. And besides we came over here to wipe out fascism. Of all those who write me, Sam is the only one who does not suggest my return, for he appreciates this is a fight that needs to be finished.

And now that Teruel has been returned to Spain, we are all very anxious to follow it up with more smashing blows to put Franco definitely on the run. Teruel is our biggest victory yet—for more and greater victories.

Oct. 12—Your record for writing is excellent—one every two days, at least.

The news about the closed shop in the BMT, the Columbus Day Celebration, are very welcome.[157]

Your clippings on fascist reactions to Roosevelt's Speech is on the board for everyone's entertainment.

Oct. 16—Give my congratulations to Ruth W. for her excellent work. I vividly remember my first contact with her one night when she helped me fill in and write in good English an article by Sue Young when I was already much impressed by her excellent good sense. George is doing good work here also.[158]

Oct. 19—I am anxiously awaiting that Fruit cake—yesterday we were informed that our Christmas packages would arrive after Christmas, and I am expecting several packages.

Your clipping on Everett Hobbs was the first news I had had of him since he had dinner with us one year ago tonight.[159] Am glad you sent protests to Franco.

The picture of yourself in the laboratory is excellent, for it looks every bit like you—& you still do your hair the same way, I see.

Oct. 22—Marshall's statement on education indicates it may be possible to really work towards making the educational program of the public schools more suited to the majority of students and to take up the problems facing the American people. Hope you keep me informed of everything the Party and your union does in this direction.

Oct. 29—Here you are worrying about me when I was perfectly comfortable & safe and out of danger—so you see it was wasted worrying, as if all worrying wasn't wasted.

Your understanding of the Soviets position in regard to the withdrawal of troops is one of the most lucid I have found & you know we never need worry about whether the Soviets' position is correct or not, considering who is directing it.

Your description of historical progression in Architecture is a gem.

Nov. 1—I received your letter without a stamp on it, and didn't have to pay for it. Nice!

You haven't sent me Aunt Sylvia's address yet, so I can write to her.

Your letters progressively express more concern over my health. You'll have to cut that out, young lady, or it'll affect your health and work, neither of which is permissible.

Your invitations to my party are indeed original. Everyone admires it. But the rest of your letters must wait.

Tomorrow's Christmas, so we are throwing a party for the 75 war orphans here at our hospital. Some time I'll write you more about them.

We're having some kind of a Grab-bag ourselves, and I shouldn't be surprised, if something special to eat.

Italian planes are around bombing Castillon three to four times a day, in retaliation for our taking of Teruel. But they haven't been able to do a great deal of damage because of the anti-aircraft guns.

I see Dave White is Chairman of our friends [Friends of Abraham Lincoln Brigade]—an excellent choice.

Am enclosing some sample local paper money used to facilitate change. It'll be replaced by metal currency in a few days.

  With all my love—
  Carl

      [HANDWRITTEN]

             Dec. 27, 1937

Dear Impy:

On Christmas Day I received two more letters from you, and one from Bennet & one from Ellen. Besides the English Speaking Volunteers here had a Xmas party & in the evening I was a guest at the dinner & dance arranged by the Transport workers of the Hospital which was quite sumptuous for Spain today. Enclosed you will find my place Card.

Your packages are awaiting transportation from Albacete to here, so I expect them any day.

Now to answer more of your letters.

Nov. 5—those lunch counter stools at the breakfast nook fascinate me. Do you eat in a hurry like you do at a lunch counter? I'll bet you do in the morning.

My account of the work of a political commissar, I am afraid, only spoke of his myriad minor duties without a basic statement of his tasks. Besides, each day I learn a bit more about this work. In my opinion, it is the hardest job in the Army.

Nov. 11—I was somewhat curious to note your reaction to my being wounded, and I am glad to see you took it so calmly. But you should have believed me about the state of my wounds—for you know I would not deceive you.

Your union meeting for Spain and China must have been well organized. Of course, Bates alone could make a meeting—and I really imagine Dave White can keep the attention of the audience. Give him my warmest regards the next time you see him.

Your article on the new form of organization of H.S. work interests me, and the work certainly must interest you.

Your opening is very fine, for it quickly gives the main problem in such a manner that the students immediately understand the basic issue involved—the old form of organization is no longer adequate, and we have to build a new form.

Of course, I can see that you still have many problems to solve—one of which undoubtedly will be the old one of leadership—whether the system of counselors will do it I don't know. At any rate, some kind of counselor organization seems necessary to me.

Then also the interests of the youth not going to school are not exactly the same as the students. And these branches won't hold together on educational projects alone. But you are undoubtedly aware of all this, and working out plans to take care of them.

I shall expect to be kept in close contact with the development of this form of organization.

But Imp, you don't go on hikes because I am not there. This will never do, for I want to come back and find a tough girl awaiting me.

Nov. 14—Your description of the meeting celebrating the XX Anniversary [twentieth anniversary of the Bolshevik Revolution] is also being used for our wall board—I certainly appreciate a detailed description of such events.

I believe I told you here a whole week was set aside for the Celebration—and with very good reason.

Nov. 21—Quite a gap. You must be very busy preparing for the party. Sorry I was absent. Give my thanks to Sam, Ernie, Uncle Sam & Adele, Grace, Tima and Ryah for their fine work.[160]

So you're down to 115 [pounds]. How do you account for it? I'm hoping it is hard work & not worrying.

Seems to me 90–100 people are enough for a party in an apt. But after all it's a 2-story apt. and what a view you evidently have—am looking forward to watching a sunset with you. I have written you before of some of Spain's glorious sunsets, and sunrises. Tell Mrs. [Edith] Lubell I regret I can['t] finish that work in her book immediately, but that I shall be very happy to do so as soon as I return.[161]

I hate to spoil your pride in my taste, but you see the Government takes care of that—it was all I could get. And since Art Front does get to Spain, I shall watch for Ryah's article.[162]

Nov. 23—that's better. Jerry's letter shows he has hit the right road, too. I should think Uncle Sam & Aunt Adele should be quite proud of him—and to think, my letters are being used, coast-to-coast.

About my opening my mouth and "pounding my fist on the table" you see every little jar hurt my wounds, so if I would have pounded the table?

But really, your scolding is well taken, though I bear in mind I am here quite safely.

Your letters are getting quite bad, in fact I am surprised the censor lets them pass—you must know fascism isn't licked yet. And how important every one is here then. But I believe when you know I am well you will worry less, and not write me to come back—when it is time for me to return, you can be certain I should do so. So in the meantime keep your chin up, and let our friends admire you for your fortitude. And blame our separation on fascism.

Which reminds me of a little scene here—a young Spaniard, now convalescing was walking up and down our dormitory: "All the blame falls on the fascists: that's why I am here in a hospital, and have only to look forward to more war, instead of going home to my girl & work." Imp, the Spanish people really hate fascism.

Nov. 19—This is the latest letter from you. No, it isn't, but I had it on the bottom of the pile.

I received a number of letters from Bennet recently, and he asks me for advice on "opening up a business" of course, I shall advise him against it.

Your story about the Trotskyists at CCNY was a darb.[163] Here we can treat them even more fittingly, but it appears that you are not letting up on the battle against them in the States.

You know of our great victory at Teruel. But you may not know how the fascists try to retaliate. Yesterday morning I was awakened by the shattering of glass due to the concussion from shells fired from 4 battle ships standing some 10 miles out to sea. They were firing quite a ways over to our right, but the noise was heavy enough. They didn't shell the hospital, but there is no guarantee they won't. Of course, we have shelter prepared in case they do. In addition to this, they have been doing a lot of bombing—but this won't save Teruel for them.

This morning I ate the most gigantic orange I have ever seen—and it was of high quality.

I had hoped to get some time to read, but to my surprise I find I am always pressed for time to do some necessary political & organizational work here, and to answer all those letters I received. So the time passes swiftly.

So, Imp, salud—
With all my love—
Carl

[HANDWRITTEN]

Dec. 31

Dear Sylvia,[164]

I am taking this opportunity to get acquainted with you before another year rolls around. From all I have heard I am more than convinced that Carl is correct when he says you are one in more than many millions. So who am I to pass up a chance to become acquainted?

I have been writing the last few letters of the year, and just finished writing to Carl so I know of no one [more] appropriate to write to now.

Carl wrote me yesterday that his foot is doing pretty well, and that we can expect him about very soon. Everybody here will be more than glad to see him back again. His absence has been felt daily by all the comrades that knew him.

Carl was more than a capable & efficient P.C. to me: he was & is a comrade, a damn good egg if ever there was one so I am anxious to have him back with us.

There have been a number of changes in out battalion since Carl was hurt. We have a couple of new units now, and some changes of different kinds so that a comrade like Carl is always welcome in smoothing out the rough spots. Just now we could use his voice at the piano.

Which reminds me that I should mention that the Link-Wash. kitchen is temporarily the proud possessor of a piano. One of those "so many pesetas down you get the piano back when we go into the lines" deal. We have had it now for over a week. It made possible several "kindergarten" dances with the kids around here.

It is becoming a bit difficult to continue this letter: piano playing to the right of me, poker playing behind me, a big fire burning to the left of me (the Left is always the warmest direction), and the candle in front of me is about done so that means an end to this first attempt. But I hope it receives a grade high enough to get an answer: if it doesn't I'm afraid I'll forget what a U.S. postman looks like.

Best wishes for an Anti-fascist New Year to you, and all the gang Carl has told me bout.

So long,
Ben Findley

Lincoln-Washington Bat.
No. 17.1
Albacete, Spain

[HANDWRITTEN]

Jan. 1, 1937[8]

My dear Impy:

The New Year begins with a most violent storm, with much rain and wind. So I shall brighten up the day a bit by writing to you. Besides you will undoubtedly agree this is a good way to begin the New Year.

I have your letter of Nov. 30, in which you "bubble over with enthusiasm" for the League Convention, and with good reason. It's good to know the League is progressing rapidly—but these days even the greatest speed is hardly fast enough. I would appreciate very much any material you can send me on such conventions.

Willy Stone hasn't changed, I see, and I am glad of it. I don't have his address, so it gives me some kind of an excuse for not writing to him. And by the way, I received a telegram from Nathan Hale with Birthday greetings and pledges of solidarity, which move me very much. Steif promised me a report on the Conference as well.

I received another letter from Marie. She is marrying the Minister, and her letter is much concerned with my belief in God, for those who do believe die so much easier. Just now they are very much interested in "Cooperatives and Folk Games." Both Marie's & Bennet's letters give me much enjoyment, especially Marie's where she writes "as you go forth daily to Battle." But I can read in the letters from both of them certain positive results from my letters.

Irving Weissman has gone back to the front after doing some fine work here during his convalescence. And I met a Danish seaman who knew Andy yesterday.

Today's papers report five foreign correspondents whom Franco was sending to Teruel killed by our artillery fire. This should improve the proper dissemination of truth from fascist territory, for it certainly will make the foreign newspapermen a bit more suspicious of Franco's statements in the future.

Also it is evident now that the battles around Teruel may prove to be more decisive than we thought at first, for the fascists are throwing all of their best troops available to try to retake Teruel—and if we can kill off a number of divisions of these, it will weaken Franco still more.

Put me down for "Ickes for President" to smash the 70 families and save the American people.[165] He seems to be a real democrat, now just so he gets straightened out on the role of the Communists, and the USSR as far as democracy is concerned.

Incidentally we had a nice New Year's eve celebration here—with roast pork, no less—and a pudding of bread crumbs and marmalade that was delicious. Excuse the emphasis on food—but as you know these items are somewhat rare in Spain today.

Are you still mailing me Inprecors? They haven't reached me for a long time now. And for some reason, there are none to be found hereabouts—am reading "from Bryant to Stalin"—I didn't know how much I didn't know about labor history before.[166]

You may get a picture yet. Now we are waiting for paper to print the negatives.

   With all my love—
   Carl

[HANDWRITTEN]

             Jan. 6, 1938

Dear Impy:

Just a few words to let you know I am well, and sending you an envelope with 2 SRI Calendars you'll be able to use, and several post cards painting the "Life of a Soldier."

The fine treatment one gets here can be seen in the fact they are giving my foot several days of massaging before letting me return to the Battalion. The foot is no longer sore, is completely flexible, but the muscles which were unused for 2 months are weak. I think that even without any further treatment, the foot would be perfectly strong shortly. As it is, I can already walk without a limp unless I take very long steps or walk too long. By the way, they have a Japanese Masseur here who knows his work thoroughly.

I have your letter of Dec. 6. You hint at some information that would be very valuable for me, that is that concerning European Volunteers to help the North during the Civil War. I would certainly appreciate very much any information you can send me of international solidarity with the North.

Roosevelt's Speech was very warmly welcomed here and stimulated all kinds of rumors of huge numbers of American Volunteers coming here. We are waiting for his organizational proposals for collective security, by strengthening League of Nations, or some grouping headed by USA, Great Britain, France & USSR. Certainly there must be a situation in the States now very favorable for building progressive opinion for peace and democracy.

Am receiving letters from Sam quite regularly. And I treasure these next to yours. His own war experience makes him able to appreciate much more accurately life here, and this is reflected in his letters.

But, Imp, believe it or not, I have a lot of work here, so I must close. But first I must insist again you are not to worry, nor become melancholy for my return too soon.

     With all my love—

     Carl

[HANDWRITTEN]

Jan. 16, 1937[8]

My Dear Impy:

I haven't written to you for a whole week, so I have a few things to tell you.

First of all I have been discharged from the Hospital, and am now making plans for a political commissars school which I may direct. Paul Wendorf may work with me on it. This is a very tough job, and would mean I wouldn't return to the front for at least 2 more months. Frankly, I would much prefer to go back to the Brigade, but my foot won't let me yet, so I'll do this first. And it is absolutely essential that such a school should be conducted.

Yesterday I was overwhelmed. 7 packages from home. Congratulate Aunt Adele on her fruit cake; it arrived in perfect condition. Among other things I received was 12 large cakes of *good* soap, 4 pairs of woolen sox (it is impossible to buy them now here and these are invaluable) a can of pipe tobacco & 6½ lb bars of cocoa chocolate, all from Herman, 2 lbs of Page & Shaw candy & a can of pipe tobacco from Frank, and several pipes & chess sets from Herb Prince. But everyone was disappointed that there were no cigarettes, except myself. And also 2 lbs of chocolates from you. Many, many thanks. And I suppose there will be more in the Christmas shipment that just arrived.

Poor Paul told everyone he might come home, so he is [not] getting any packages. Imp, so we won't be mixed up, I will not be home before fascism is licked here, & won't see you until then unless you come to Europe this summer. So in your next package, enclose a pair of gloves. There cannot be bought here either. And a pocket size note book with plenty of paper.

I have to make plans for the school in the next 3 hours, so I'll have to close.

     With all my love

     Carl

[HANDWRITTEN]

Wednesday Eve.[167]

Dear Impy:

Will add a few words on my status here, especially since a certain reorganization is taking place now.

As you know while in action last Sept. & Oct. I was a Battalion Commissar, which is equivalent to the rank of Comandante (between a Captain and a Major). Since I have been released from the hospital, I have been assigned to direct a political Commissar's school, supposed with the rank of Battalion Commissar. But since most of the students will be Spaniards, a Spanish Comrade may become Director and I his assistant, or

[Missing page(s)?]

unexpected place.

Paul Wendorf was in the Hospital for a few days with the Grippe & an ear complication, but is well again. He doesn't know what he is going to do here yet.

Don't forget your promise to write often. Your letters are always a bracer for me.

    Salud y love
    Carl

[HANDWRITTEN]

Jan. 18, 1938

Dear Herb:

I received your package, of pipes and the chess set, for which you get many thanks not only from me, but also three other fellow who are enjoying the pipes you sent. And since I received 2 lbs of pipe tobacco at the same time we have some good tobacco to smoke in them, instead of the Spanish Anti-tank. (so-called because of its great strength)

Was discharged from the Hospital several days ago, and my present assignment is to organize and direct a political commissars school for the next two months. This is a rather difficult job, but such a school is very essential.

Judging from some letters I receive, many think I may be coming home soon. So I want to make it clear that I came here to smash fascism and I don't intend to leave until the job is well-done.

For this is a war that no true anti-fascist can leave unless he is crippled and no longer useful here, or some extraordinary situation demands his presence in the USA.

Our battalion has been stopping some of the counter attacks at Teruel, at least all that came in their direction. The wounded comrades who come to Benicasim Hospital were bragging about the fine fighting the Lincoln-Washington Battalion is doing. The fascists made four attacks on one day alone. Our casualties, none killed & 4 wounded. Fascist casualties must have been well over a hundred. And our artillery is doing the finest work so far, firing much more accurately than the fascist guns.

But it is plenty cold. They are living out in the open, with snow & wind & temperatures down to zero—without hot food. It's frozen by the time it is carried a couple of miles into the mountains. But they got cold chisels to dig holes into the rocky side of the mountain & are making some kind of protection for themselves.

Christmas packages arrived today, but there were not enough to go around, so I didn't take any, in view of the number I received a few days ago from you, Herman, Sylvia & Frank, who works on the I.R.T. The boys are certainly glad to get them.

You asked me what I need here. Well, here goes—a pair of gloves, copies of Inprecor & C.I., & of the latest books, especially on Spain & the People's Front, and then anything to eat in the way of Candies, tinned ham or fish, sugar or *coffee*, etc. And a good pocket-size loose leaf note-book—that ought to keep you busy a while.

I am ashamed to admit that I haven't prepared the letter-lecture I promised—but I do have the outline drawn up. So you may expect it soon. I am sending it direct to the County office.

Some here are predicting when the fascists will be driven out of Spain (I don't put my foot in my mouth) some say within 6 months. They are pretty optimistic, for that would mean getting a lot more help from the Democratic Countries. But at least, Teruel has proved victory will be ours to even most reactionary circles—but in their desperation, they are likely to give Franco a lot of help. So it means we cannot let up on our help to Spain until the last battle is won.

Give my regards to all Comrades
& Thanks again for the packages
   Comradely
   Carl Geiser
P.S. Several packages of material are on their way to you also.

[HANDWRITTEN]

Jan. 19, 1938

Dear Herb—

It has just been called to my attention that many comrades here receive letters from comrades in the States asking or suggesting they come home, that they have done enough, etc. This is very bad for the weaker elements are very much affected by it.

Our comrades should write letters praising them for what they are doing, urging them to continue & put in a lick for them too. There should be no suggestion of their returning before fascism is smashed here.

Whatever you can do to improve this will certainly be very valuable. Perhaps you can even speak with the County Buro about it also.

    Comradely
    Carl

[TYPEWRITTEN]

Jan. 25, 1938

My dear Impy:

I still hope to meet you in France this summer, in spite of your gentle scoffing at the idea, and in spite of what Gil may have told you. And it will be "wonderful" as you put it.[168]

There are many reasons for my not coming soon. One which doesn't admit of any arguments that the term of service in the IB by government decree is for the duration of the war. In addition to that, you know the fascists are not licked yet, and so my job isn't done yet. Of course I have learned much during the last 8 months (You'd be surprised at how much) but do you know, I am learning faster now than I ever did and the longer I stay here the more capable I become. As you should realize, this military experience is just what is needed to iron out some of my weak spots.

The present assignment, to organize and direct company commissars school, and since I have now been informed that if all goes properly, I shall be expected to work through two of them, that will take me into the middle of May, of good hard organizational and educational work, with heavy responsibilities. Just now I am going back to the Brigade for a week to become familiar with the latest experiences and problems, and to get Dave's opinions and directives on the School. Already I have made the first outlines and gotten the work under way. Paul will probably help me prepare some of the material, and perhaps attend the school.

So you see, this is very useful work, and one which suits me particularly, since I still limp a bit and this gives me a chance to do something while my ankle grows completely well again. So, Impy, for your own well-being, start thinking in terms of my coming home when the war is over, and of coming to France this summer if possible.

My battalion has been doing some splendid fighting, with very few casualties and inflicting heavy punishment on the fascists. I have never seen the boys in such good spirits after an action as they are today.

George Watt is also here, having just graduated from the Officers Training School here at our Base. He's doing very well.

I might just add a few words on the whole problem of repatriation, for you should be informed on this question. After Brunete there was a good deal of desire on the part of some to return to the States. Unfortunately, our political leaders gave in to this feeling, and promised the men that they would be eligible for repatriation after seven months. This was a very serious error, for it caused our comrades to forget about the reason they came here, and when they had only a month of two to go any more, they became more interested in saving their own skin than in fighting the fascists. And such a morale greatly lowers the fighting capacity of any military unit. The War Ministry, a little more experienced in these matters, immediately fixed the term of service for the length of the war when they heard of these proposals. And now, our comrades have a better perspective and are better fighters. Believe me, this unfortunate policy has created many problems for us, but most of them have been overcome. Of course, there is still some repatriation, on the following basis, I believe: 1) those who are unfit for further service, or need medical treatment which is not readily available here, 2) those who have some personal problem, such as seriously ill wife or parent, if it was a matter which could not be foreseen when they left the States, and 3) Those who are needed in the States for political work, such as Steve Nelson or Dave White, who are doing such fine work for Spain now.

But many of our comrades are still receiving letters from people in the States imploring them to return home. And this is absolutely wrong. All of our comrades ought to receive letters praising them for their work here, and expressing their hope to see them back WHEN THE WAR IS OVER. I think the Party should carry on a little campaign to that effect, and it would help some of our weaker comrades a great deal. And Imp, I might suggest that you begin with yourself (but come to see me this summer).

It's midnight and time to go to bed, for our rising hour is 6:30 here.

　　With all my love,

　　Carl

P.S. Sorry I don't have any more lice to write to you about. I drowned them all a couple of days ago.

[FIRST THREE PARAGRAPHS TYPEWRITTEN; THE REST HANDWRITTEN]

Feb. 5, 1936[8]

My Dear Impy:

I am going to take a few minutes rest and get some much needed inspiration by writing you a few lines.

You probably wonder why you didn't receive any letters from me for such a long time. The reason was that I was traveling, visiting the Brigade, and several other places, gathering material for the political commissars school. But now I am back in one place for a few days, so you'll hear from me occasionally.

Received two letters from you, one a very old one, which was placed by mistake in the censors office into a letter for professor in the Mc-Paps [MacKenzie-Papineau] battalion, but he deduced since the program of the ASU conference had your name on it, that it was for me, so today I received it. I saw him in the trenches only a few days ago, not more than a hundred yards from the fascists, where he told me about it. His name is Sydney Cohen, I believe.[169]

Anyway, I am quite proud that my wife is doing such fine things.

This month, the capitalist press must have given you a few lessons regarding its accuracy. The boys in the Brigade are writing home that the reports "of my death are greatly exaggerated." In fact, our Brigade has never come thru an action as well as we did in this one. Ask the fascists how they came thru?

I spent several days in Teruel, and believe me, Imp, the fascists will never take it, in spite of all Hitler & Mussolini may do. Incidentally it's interesting to note, Franco is not using Italian troops to make attacks, for it seems he doesn't have very much faith in them.

I have some samples of Pre-war German marks (valueless now) which the fascists used in Teruel on the ignorant soldiers & peasants. It fits right hand in hand with their demagogy. I saw a beautiful poster, showing a lovely young mother holding a baby over head, with the slogan, "for a free & happy Spain" signed by the Falangistas. Others give a combination of Gen. Mola, Jesus Christ, & Gen. Franco. A weekly review of the church is entitled "the Bread of the Poor." You see their lying propaganda every where. But it did not save Teruel, and will not save them in the end.

We are changing the plans for the school by including Spanish students, instead of having a separate school for them. This makes it more difficult since everything must be translated. I am suggesting that some one with a better command of Spanish than I have should direct the school, but I don't know whether such a person is available. My Spanish enables me to get along in the Battalion, carry on conversations in Spanish, but to deliver lengthy lectures in Spanish is a bit more difficult.

One of our main political tasks is to improve our relations with the Spanish Comrades. All enemies of the I.B. & the Communists, attack the I.B. internally by trying to create friction, and by agitating to make the I.B. only foreigners, to be used as shock troops. & Externally, they try to influence the people against us. Of course, they haven't had much success in this. But the struggle against chauvinism on our part is a continuous one, and we are really only beginning to appreciate the scope of this struggle.

But, Imp, let's hear more about what you do every day, at work & for recreation & never a word of Tima or Ryah.

I want to again acknowledge receipt of your packages and am anxiously awaiting the next.

And are you coming to France this summer? I hope you find it possible to do so, for I doubt whether this war is going to be over by summer.

With all my love,
Carl

[TYPEWRITTEN]

Feb. 9, 1937[8]

My dear Impy:

Your letters of Dec. 21 and 29, and the Round Robin of Dec. 12 are here. And while waiting for a meeting here, I shall write you again.

Your comments on Maverick (apropos the Tom Mooney Garden meeting) interest me, particularly that he understands the need for a People's Front in America.[170] After my experiences here, it galls me when I read of some half-baked socialist or liberal saying the People's Front may be good in Spain at times in France, but. . . . The only possible way to defeat fascism and war, to have democracy and peace today, is through the People's Front. There is absolutely nothing more important than building this Front, for if we don't build it, we shall pay dearly. In planning the course for the Commissars school, we are laying a great deal of stress on the People's Front, why it is so vital, and what it means in practice for us. Hurrah for Maverick!

The many descriptions of "People of France" make me anxious to see it. But when are we going to put out something like it in the States, and make use still more of the movies. Incidentally I haven't seen a movie since the end of Sept. Too many of the movies being shown here are still of the old type of trash from the USA. Much more, could be done in using the motion pictures for winning the war here, than has been done to the present.

Yes, I received the copy of the New Masses' Literary Supplement you sent me, as well as the cable, and the packages, which I believe I acknowledged before.[171] The present set-up in regard to packages is such that we are pretty well guaranteed we will get anything sent to us thru the friends of the Abraham Lincoln Brigade.

Incidentally, if anyone is at a loss about what to send me, here are some suggestions. Sugar, Coffee, powdered milk, adhesive bandages and vaporub, Chocolates, Inprecors and books. It is well to bear in mind that as the war goes along, less and less things can be bought here. All foods are rationed, and it is impossible to buy chocolate, sugar, milk, or any edible luxury whatever.

By the way, you may see Bernie Walsh pretty soon, anyway I gave him your address. But I am still waiting to hear about your plans for the summer.

The ASU is getting quite swanky, taking over a college such as Vassar.[172] Convention facilities there certainly should be quite lovely. I see they even furnished stationary. And I see your role was quite different in this one than at the one in Chicago in 1932, when I didn't even see you about, you cook. And now you lead one of the panels! And I am sorry I missed the ice skating with you. Here I hadn't even thought about it until I read your letter.

That M[a]cCracken is head of the Committee for the World Youth Congress is good.[173] He always [was] some kind of a liberal, though somewhat limited by his job. (and perhaps by his understanding of what is going on in the world too.) This World Youth Congress, considering the time and possible events in which it will meet, can mean a lot for all humanity.

Has Negrin's speech to the Cortes been published in the USA yet?[174] It is very important, and if I have to hang around here much longer I'll translate it into English. The Speech is very heartening for it indicates that the heads of the Government are really doing their job, and doing it well. The Negrin government has the Caballero government beat a million ways.[175] Hans Amlie's letter to the Socialist Call was a good one.[176] Baron won't make another trip to Spain, especially since they are tightening up the department of justice, and apparatus for dealing with enemies of the Republic.[177]

There are still plenty of Leftists today, even among us. In a characterization of the Revolution in Spain today for the Commissars school, I have: The Government of the People's Front is an alliance of all those who oppose fascism and national enslavement, of all who want a free and democratic Spain. The task of the Revolution today is to deepen this alliance in the administration of the Country for the victorious ending of the war, and for strengthening the economic and political power of the new type of democratic, republican parliamentary government.

And anyone who says that task of the Revolution is something else than this is not living in reality, and probably a couple of jumps ahead of himself, or at least of the Revolution. One can do a lot of speculating about what there will be in Spain when the war is won, but our main problem now is winning the war as quickly as possible, and that means enlisting as many as possible on our side against the fascists, native and foreign. And Imp, from what I have seen of the Soldiers of the People's Republican Army, I can assure you we need never fear a swing to the right against the interests of the people in Spain. And from the forms of economic organization (nationalization, government control) being imposed by the need to win the war, we know that the economic base of fascism is being wiped out in Republican Spain.

But Imp, a little more help from the states, especially in the way of arms, and of sanctions against Mussolini and Hitler, would be very welcome. Mussolini is threatening to send over another hundred thousand troops, and while this won't be enough to ensure a fascist victory, it certainly will make the war drag out longer.

Am enclosing some more stamps you may be able to use. Have you received the packages of art work, magazine, etc, which I sent you.

> With all my love,
> Carl

[TYPEWRITTEN]

Feb. 9, 1938

Dear Brother Bennet:

Have received two letters from you since I wrote you the last time. And the one with clippings from the Courier I enjoyed particularly, for it gave all the news about Orrville in a hurry. And I also find all of my old high school mates have gotten married.

Am quite well again, even did a little running with my feet the other day when I had to cover a short space under fire from the fascists, and it went pretty well, at least I crossed through it unscathed.

You probably got a few lessons on the truthfulness of American newspapers during the past few days. I understand they claimed the fascists had retaken Teruel on January 2, and even printed the telegram of thanks the liberated prisoners sent to Franco. Of course, it was all a lie. You see, the Yanks were holding that part of the line, and you know the fascists will never break thru them.

And at the end of January the papers had us wiped out. When I told the fellows about their being wiped out, they were very much amused and claimed the "news of their death had been greatly exaggerated." In fact, the casualties among the Americans have been about one-fourth of that we have had in each previous campaign. And believe me, Bennet, with the officers we have now, and the trained men, you need have no fear of our ever being wiped out no matter how many times the paper prints it. But why do you suppose the papers cannot learn that the news they get from fascists is only a bunch of lies?

Did I tell you I got seven packages from the States? They certainly were welcome, for they had woolen socks, soap, pipe tobacco, chocolates, etc. I especially like chocolates. But if you send anything to me, don't send it direct, but send it to me, care of the Friends of the Abraham Lincoln Brigade, 122 West 45th St., New York, and then they'll send it to me. The American post office isn't so reliable in sending material to Spain, and often times they won't even accept packages for fellows over here.

There are rumors here that there is a depression started back in the States. So Bennet, when you run out of a job, come and join me. But seriously, reports indicate quite an increase in unemployment, and that the CIO is one organization that is trying to do something about it. I hope Americans won't take unemployment laying down like they did in 1929 and 30. Now's the time to bring out that slogan some rich guys were using about every one has the right to work. I'll bet they don't say a word about that right now.

By the way, you have heard of the new American Battalion, MacKenzie-Papineau, made up of Americans and Canadians. They were holding a hill, or rather a part of one company of this battalion was holding it. The fascists concentrated all their artillery on it for two days trying to drive them off of it. And our boys stood there and took it, even though over half had to be carried out. It was some shelling, lowering the hill 16 inches (I saw the place, and never saw anything like it). Modesto, the head of our army corps came around later, saw what the boys had done, and then right on the spot made Cecil Smith, the commander of the Battalion a Major (he was a captain before) and promoted two other fellows.[178] It certainly was a swell illustration and example to everyone how to fight, and to hold your position until you get orders to withdraw or move.

All in all, the fighting around Teruel has shown some very nice work on our part, that is of the Republican Army. Today's news indicates that the fascists have given up their attacks in that sector, and that they want to bash in their heads a bit more there.

But I have a meeting scheduled now, so I'll sign off. Keep up that steady stream of letters, for they are most welcome. Give my warmest regards to everyone, especially Leonard and Grandmother.

> Sincerely,
> Carl

P.S. I picked up some German marks in Teruel. It's all pre-war stuff, and worthless, but the fascists used it to pay the soldiers and peasants who didn't know it was worthless. So that's a new way the fascists have figured out to fool the people. I want to use it for an exhibition here, then I'll send you a sample of it so you can see for yourself.

[TYPEWRITTEN]

Feb. 12, 1938

My dear Impy:

Just a few words to let you know I am very well, and to enclose this very charming letter from my sister Irene. I know you will like it very much. I have written her quite a long reply.

I have two more letters from you, of December 15, and January 5. In regard to that louse in my cast, I completely forgot about him when the cast was removed due to the difficulty in cutting the cast off. But I am afraid he starved to death for there was very little to eat in that cast after I got thru with it. The other day I picked up a whole gang of lice, some twenty-five of them, when I slept in a barn in Teruel. But fortunately, I am wearing fleece-lined underwear and since there is no place for the lice to hide in them it is a very simple matter to pick them off and toast them.

Am very glad to hear that Joe Lash made such an excellent report at the student convention.[179] But certainly the matter of collective security is something that must not be discussed much longer, but needs to be acted upon pretty soon. But how large is the ASU now and how many schools and colleges does it reach? Is Celeste still working with the ASU?[180]

I wrote you that I visited Teruel, and found the Brigade in very good shape. Franco made a decided mistake there. If he would have been wise, when he saw that he couldn't retake it about Dec. 22 or 23, he should have let us have it, but continue with his plans for an offensive, conduct the next battle wherever he wanted too, and thus might have kept the upper hand. As it is, he permitted his whole plan for the offensive to be broken up, using his reserves and men in a useless attempt to regain Teruel, a place where the geography and the conditions made it a much more suitable place for us to fight than for him. Now I believe that we shall be able to make the next move where we want it, and keep the upper had from now on.

But it is necessary to realize that Teruel did not break Franco's back, but only gives us a much better position for future battles, the decisive ones needed to break his back. Of course, he is asking Mussolini for another hundred thousand troops (which won't be enough to win the war for him but certainly can prolong it a good deal) and it seems he is getting 50,000 at once. Franco should be licked in a fairly short period of time if we could prevent him from getting all this help from Hitler and Mussolini. And part of that is the job of the people of the USA, demanding that the government take firmer steps against the aggressors.

Yesterday I received a letter from Edith Lubell, from Nice, France. It was a very pleasant letter, and I shall answer it immediately.

I hear from Sam quite regularly, and I enjoy his letters a great deal. His letters indicate that he has a good appreciation of what war is like.

Believe it or not, I have Vol. 8 of Lenin's Selected Works, and I am doing a little reading in it every evening. There is nothing better to keep one on his toes and his spirits high.

Let's hear from you regularly, Imp.

   With all my love,
   Carl

[TYPED IN RED INK]

Feb. 12, 1938

Dear Sister Irene:

The red ribbon is plainer so I'll use it instead of the black.

I received your letter of Jan. 17, and it pleased me very, very much. You sound so grown-up, with such a fine sense of humor, and how well you express yourself. Few letters have given me as much pleasure to read as yours.

And Sarah's letter was also a particularly pleasant surprise, for some reason or other, I was under the impression that she was dead, and so you can imagine how happy I was to see her letter. Please give Aunt Sarah and Uncle Noah my warmest regards.

Your description of life and work on the farm makes me almost homesick for it again. Perhaps what appeals most to me about it now is its peacefulness. It would be quite a contrast to my present life, and many times much peacefuler, and quieter.

So you are five foot seven and mischievous. That makes it just about right. Now quilting quilts doesn't sound very mischievous to me, in fact it sounds like very serious planning. But still your picture tends to make me believe you might be a bit mischievous. I can imagine what a time the four of you must have had on that trip to Virginia. But I do know the beauty of Skyline Drive. Sylvia and I hitch-hiked along there once. We drove along part of it in a driving rainstorm, with Sylvia so tired she slept most of the time, and missed some really beautiful sights. But we didn't have time to visit the many caves.

I see we both enjoy the out of doors.

Perhaps some time you'll be able to accompany Sylvia and myself on a long hike, like the 200 mile one we took two years ago through the Adirondack Mountains. I do quite a bit of hiking here, much of it in mountains, but too often the shells falling around and the machine guns rattling rather prohibit one from enjoying the scenery fully. However, I have enjoyed some magnificent sunsets and sunrises here. Since we are usually up pretty high, the clouds are much lower, and with the clear air, one gets exceptionally bright and deep colors. And they change very quickly, so it is like a glorified and magnified movie.

So you'd like to have a pet monkey. I wish I could bring you a burro. You could have a lot of fun with it. It's in between a pony and a mule in size and shape, and seems to be the favorite farm animal here. A five-burro team pulling a big Spanish covered wagon is a sight to see. They are all lined up in front of one another, the smallest one out in front. I must get a picture of one to send you.

But here my letter is half written and I haven't really told you anything about Spain yet or what I am doing here. As regards my wound, I have been out of the hospital already a month, and my foot is practically well again. I can't run very fast yet, but it'll be all right in a short time.

You know, Irene, there are about two to three thousand Americans here, and hundreds more coming here. Perhaps I can best explain to you what is happening here by telling you what kind of people these Americans are. First of all, there is not one single banker among them, no business men, no rich men. But they are all farmers, or people from factories. Protestants, Catholics, Irish, Negro, descendants of the Mayflower, in fact from every section of America that has to work for a living. And here we are in a Spanish Army together with the same kind of people from 51 other countries in the world. But still we are only a small part of the whole Spanish Army, which is made up mostly of farmers, and doesn't have any rich people in it either.

And what are all of us fighting for, and many of us dying for. The Spanish people are fighting first of all to defend their government, a government which has given the land to the farmers (before most of the farmers did not have land and worked for rich land-owners) which has raised the wages of the working people so they can live more decently, which has set up schools for the people (before 45% of the people could neither read nor write), and for a government which is democratic like our government in the United States. And now on top of that the Spanish people are fighting for their national independence, to drive out the Italian and German armies that are in fascist Spain (at least 150,000 Italian and German soldiers are here).

Who are we fighting against? Well, there are some Spanish fascist soldiers, sons of the landlords and rich of Spain. Then there are a lot of Spanish soldiers who don't want to fight us. When we took some five hundred prisoners at Quinto, mostly young soldiers, you should have seen how happy they were to get out of the fascist Army and be our prisoners. In fact many of the Spaniards that are fighting at our side were once in the Spanish fascist army. Many of these are afraid to desert to us because they are told we will kill them, which is completely false. Also the fascists make a practice of killing the parents or wives of those soldiers who do desert to us. Then there are besides the 120,000 Italian soldiers. There were some wounded Italian soldiers brought to the same hospital where I was taken, and there they explained to us how they had been fooled into coming to Spain, that they did not want to fight against the Spanish people. But in Italy there is little work, so they join the Army, and then suddenly find themselves ordered to Spain. The Italian troops have proved to be very good runners, especially in retreating. While you see the soldiers on our side are fighting for their own interests, to defend their family and home, the Italian soldier has no real reason to fight here, so they don't fight nearly as hard.

But why have all these farmers and working people from every country in the world come to help the Spanish people? For one thing because they hate fascism, which takes away all their rights and means suffering for the great majority of the people so the rich can grow richer. And secondly, they realize in every country of the world, that if fascism wins in Spain, if Hitler and Mussolini are able to conquer Spain, then these two countries will be much better prepared to start a new world war that will involve their own countries. Hitler and Mussolini make no secret that they are organizing and preparing their countries for a world war, and that taking Spain is part of their preparation. So all the working people who understand this, and are free to leave their own country for a while come here to help the Spanish people smash fascism. And those who cannot come, send money, food, clothing, etc. The United States has sent over 50 ambulances, over 300,000,000 Francs ($15,000,000) were collected last year in different countries to help the Spanish people.

So you see, Irene, the whole thing may seem very complicated, but actually it is the practice of the brotherhood of man among all people who work for [a] living. I am certain that if Jesus were alive today, he would take the side of the working people of Spain against the rich fascists. And if I remember right, when the money changers were in the temple, he didn't just ask them to leave, but drove them out.

Incidentally, you will be glad to know that the Americans fighting here have a very fine record for bravery and for being good soldiers. In fact, one American battalion did so well at Teruel, holding their lines under terrific artillery fire that they were especially commended by the head of our Army corp. We here try to be worthy representatives of the people of the United States, and I believe we have done a good job so far.

But if and when I come back, I shall be very glad to tell you much more about Spain, about my experiences here in the war, and even about Switzerland. You are right, Switzerland is a very beautiful country. I too would like to see the pictures Uncle Bill took when he was there.

But in the meantime write often to me, and I shall answer every letter.
Very sincerely,
Your Brother
Carl

My address
Carl Geiser
Soccorro-Rojo 270
Albacete
Spain

[HANDWRITTEN]

Feb. 13, 1938

Dear Mrs. Lubell:

I received your letter yesterday when I returned from Teruel. And it certainly was a very welcome surprise. I recall you and your husband quite well, and Sylvia spoke of you several times. I wish I could speak to you about your trip thru the U.S.S.R, for I know it has changed much from the country I saw in 1932, when the Russian people had tightened their belt to the last notch, in order to ensure the success of the first Five-Year Plan.

I was discharged from the Hospital a month ago today, and am quite well now, although running is still a bit difficult.

Teruel is a great victory for us, especially due to the fact that Franco, instead of letting us have Teruel and continuing with his plans for a "great" offensive, used his reserves of men and material in a vain attempt to retake Teruel, thus permitting us to disorganize all his plans. And I believe that from now on the fighting will be where we want it and on our initiation, which means half the battle.

Of course, a severe handicap for the Republic is lack of adequate arms. A little help from England and France here would help to shorten the war considerably. As it is, the 50,000 Italian troops entering Spain now under cover of the Non-Intervention Committee means more fighting and suffering for the Spanish people. If only people outside of Spain could realize the tremendous suffering and sacrifices the Spanish people are bearing for the sake of world peace and democracy as well as their own, they would give them much, much more aid.

The Americans did some brave and excellent fighting at Teruel, and received special praise from the Commander of the Army Corps. They were greatly amused at the reports of their annihilation, and are writing home that the "report of my lamentable death is grossly exaggerated." In fact the losses of our Brigade were exceptionally low in this campaign.

Your offer to send me some packages makes me very happy. Today all you can buy in the way of food in this region are—you would never guess—hazel nuts and oranges. Of course we receive good plain meals in the Army. But there is a decided shortage of cigarettes, and chocolate is a great luxury here. I would greatly appreciate if you could send me some bar chocolate. All packages come through very well now. And reading matter is always very welcome.

[CG:] [The following continues the above letter. It was written on one quarto of a 12" x 16" newsprint folded twice. All but one of the eight sides contain photographs or text of the activities at the training base for English-speaking troops, leaving a page for correspondence.]

This is my address for the next 2 months → Carl Geiser
Socorro Rojo Internacional
Plaza del Altozano, 270
ALBACETE

                                        1938 [month and day missing]
This will give you some idea of our base where I am now. My present task is to organize and direct a school for company political leaders here. And it keeps me quite occupied.

Many Americans are arriving here now, in fact more than ever before. And our XV Brigade, made up of Americans & English, is one of the strongest in the Army.

There is just a bare chance that Sylvia may come to France this summer and I may get leave to see her, but all this is still quite uncertain.

My warmest regards to you and your Husband—
    Salud,
    Carl Geiser

[HANDWRITTEN]

Feb. 14, 1938

My dear Impy:

Isn't this rather luxurious stationery? It's all that is available at the moment, and is quite expensive. But since I am writing to you, it will do.

I am enclosing a folder put out here, which will give you a very inadequate idea of our Base. This is where the school will be conducted, and where I expect to be for several months, perhaps two.

Did I write you about the large numbers of Americans coming in now? It is evident that the return of Steve Nelson and Bill Lawrence have done a good job.[181] But we can use every possible man here, in order to shorten the war as much as possible.

This evening I am to speak to a company of recruits, and I think it shall be very interesting. Incidentally, we find the majority know[s] very little about Spain itself, and one of the tasks of the political workers is to help them become acquainted with the Spanish people and their problems, which of course, become our problems too. And attendance at Spanish classes is compulsory for all new men.

Some, or most of the comrades here, have very interesting histories. One man spent 3 years surveying in Patagonia, Argentina, several years in Spitzbergen (Norway) and in upper Canada among the Eskimos, 4 years in the World War, etc, and has had innumerable narrow escapes from death. He is quite old, from a military point of view, but is now doing very useful work here.[182]

Remember I wrote to you some time ago, about the Party raising the need for sending more encouraging letters to comrades here, paying more attention to the families left behind, and to counter act the desire for repatriation among some of the weaker comrades. Has any thing been done on this score yet? Of course I can see from the men coming here that much more is being done to aid Spain than a few months ago, but this a phase of aid which would help as well.

George Watt read your account of the ASU convention. It was the first real account he had of it, everyone else who wrote assumed everyone else had informed him of it in detail.

Give my regards to Tima and Ryah.

With all my love
Carl

[CG:] [The following was included with the preceding letter. It was written on a 12" x 16" newsprint broadsheet identical as the one sent to Mrs. Lubell above—except for the message of course.]

Feb. 14, 1938

Some views of the Base and of our comrades, issued for our anniversary Celebration, Feb. 12.

The blue folder is put out by the I.S.U. Tima can probably read it.

Herman Engert (see inside [I pointed out the picture of him]) was a machine-gunner in the German Army during the World War, trained me here, and was commander of our Company at Brunete, (I was commissar) where he received a chest wound. He has again returned to the Front, still plenty tough.

The town will live long in the memories of the Americans who came to Spain.

[CG:] [Also included with this package (note the date, i.e., Valentine's Day) was the flyer following: "Comrades be careful . . . Beware of deadly kisses." See following . . .]

COMRADES

BE

CAREFUL

In the rear-guard as at the Front

You use a helmet...
You wash your face and hands to prevent an epidemic in the trenches—that is all well—but also take special care of the dangers in the rear-guard.

If after you have escaped fascist bullets you are incapacitated by syphilis it is sad, stupid and injurious to our cause.

In the city a minute's satisfaction may cause you a whole life time of suffering. Be careful!

BEWARE

OF

DEADLY

KISSES

COMMISSAR OF THE INTERNATIONAL BRIGADES

SOCORRO ROJO INTERNACIONAL

Plaza del Altozano, 278

ALBACETE

1938

Feb. 14,

Some views of the Base and of
our comrades, issued for our
anniversary celebration, Feb. 12.

The blue folder is put out by
the I.S.U. Tino can probably
read it

Herman Engert - (see inside) was
a machine - gunner in the German Army
during the World War, trained me here
and was recommended for our company
at Brunete, (I was commissar) where
he received a chest wound. He has
again returned to the Front still
plenty tough.

This town will live long in the
memories of the Americans who came to Spain

[HANDWRITTEN]

Feb. 15, 1938

My dear Impy:

Just received your letter of the 24 of January. And I detect just a little note of sadness in it, because I asked you to write me cheering letters to stay rather than to come home. And I want to abolish that note of sadness by stating very clearly that I want to see you very much, and only my understanding of why I must see this war out to its end made me write you that. And some times, my desire to see you comes dangerously equal to my understanding of why I must stay. And perhaps this summer you really should continue your work of last summer, though I can not help hoping I shall meet you in France.

Today's mail also brought me a copy of the "Ohio Yearbook" entitled "Ohio Marches toward peace & Progress," beautifully done, and brings me news of many of my old comrades.[183] And the book itself, and it is a good sized one, is another indication of the rapid advance our Party must be making in the States.

It is quite cold today, and snowing. And that makes me hungry for sweets, say a big bar of chocolate, but a big one. But I still have some of the "Revelation" you sent me, and it'll have to do.

About my safety, you need not worry, at present I am in as safe a place as there is in Spain (I have my fingers crossed).

Last night I spoke to 100 new recruits. I am becoming so much a soldier that I automatically use the military term for new men instead of the term "volunteer." They are a very fine bunch of men, and full of questions. They will have an opportunity to take part in the battle to begin to really drive Franco's forces back. There is still plenty for them to do, for over half of Spain is still fascist.

It seems Hitler may try something desperate in Austria soon, but in the long run it will probably help us here by forcing the hands of the non-fascist countries.

Am enclosing a few more cards for your collection.

      With all my love,
      Carl

Brr, this cold weather makes me wonder whether you ever succeeded in lighting those two big logs in your fireplace.

[HANDWRITTEN]

[no date, first folio missing]

[Dear Impy,]

must sleep less, eat less, and work more. The ovation he received indicated this will be done.

The last few days the fascist Army, or rather the fascist planes, have made a large advance below Zaragossa. It is not Franco's army that is driving them back but his aerial bombs. [five lines redacted] But it seems our resistance is stiffening now. The fascists undoubtedly undertook the operation because they feared we would take Zaragossa, and perhaps, taking a leaf out of our book, trying to break up our offensive flow. You can be sure our General Staff know how to meet the situation, and will deal with it.

But, Impy, I haven't heard from you for some days. So write, and don't worry, but work hard.

> My regards to all,
> With all my love,
> Carl

[HANDWRITTEN]

Feb. 18, 1938

My dear Impy:

Today I received your letters of Jan. 9 & 13th. Am sorry to hear Irving's parents react so badly to his being here. They only make it harder for themselves.

Now I understand the business of the cable. I am pleased by your solicitous care of me, but Imp, I'm still alive & well after 9 months in Spain, so you should have confidence in me that I can take care of myself.

Your description of your day dream, complete even to my admiring the big brass knocker on your door, amused me very much. I hope it will really come true some day.

But what is this wife's curiosity you speak about? And Imp, you should be most proud of me when I am at the Front. But where did Mrs. Merriman get the idea I am doing non-combatants work at Albacete?[184] I have already written you I am working on a political school at our training base, which will keep me busy 2 months, and then I expect to return to the front, for that is where our real work lies. And when you write me about rats such as Stolberg, I enjoy front line service where I can wreak all the physical violence I am capable of, on people like him and his agents.[185]

If I remember correctly, you have a fireplace. Well you should see mine, with a little fire blazing away, and me right next to it. For Spanish houses are not intended to prevent free and unlimited circulation of air, and so they get very, very cold. But this little fire reminds me of the Adirondacks. Now if I only had a bit of sugar or sweetened condensed milk, I'd make some nice cocoa with the chocolate Herman sent me. But unfortunately, these things are exceedingly difficult to obtain.

But I see I haven't been writing you very much about Spain. The best news today is that the UGT & the CNT are meeting together to form a joint plan of action. In my opinion it is a shame, and very costly for us, that this has not been done before.

Prieto, the Minister of National Defense has issued an order removing all ranks and pay from company political leaders. It won't make our work any easier. But it will tend to bring extra-fine people into these positions, for many would not accept this additional work & responsibility without any reward. And undoubtedly it will raise the number of Communist political leaders still higher. This decree makes the need for training political leaders still more important, for their work is more difficult now, and higher capabilities will be demanded of them.

My fire has died down, and it is time for supper.

> With all my love,
> Carl

[TYPEWRITTEN]

> Socorro Rojo Internacional
> del Plaza Altozano, 270
> ALBACETE
> Feb. 19, 1938

Dear Dave:[186]

Just a few words to let you know I am well and working again, just now organizing a political workers' school which is to open in 2 days here at the Base. My foot is practically well, although it complains a bit yet when I run or jump.

I visited the boys at Teruel at the end of January, and also met Matthews there when he came up to check up on the AP report we were wiped out.[187] The boys were greatly amused over it. You probably have heard of the great work they did there, and actually with fewer losses than ever before.

Herman Engert has gone up to the Front again, along with Suni, Bushka,

Connors (who attended the Officers Training School) and several other old timers.[188] If you were to return today, you'd recognize more of the fellows in the line than you would have a few months ago. Max Schwartzberg is here in a "convalescent" home, unfit for front service because of those 19 pieces of shrapnel, so he has made out an application for repatriation. Frank "Bat" Buturla is here in the armory, unfit because of an oversized artery above the heart.[189] The Brigade is much more powerful than it ever has been, both in numbers and ability. And we saw and knew nothing of fortifications until Teruel. Now they speak about bomb and shell proof dugouts in all frontline trenches, to say nothing about other places. And it is necessary.

Prieto has just issued a decree abolishing the rank and pay of company political leaders. No explanation has been forthcoming yet. Of course they will continue their work just the same, but it becomes a bit more difficult, so this training will come in handy. It is interesting to note that the day the decree came out, Diaz had an article published emphasizing three fundamental tasks in order to win the war in the shortest possible time, and one of them was the intensification of political work at the front and in the rear.

It would be good if you could send some samples of your propaganda material here.

Salud,
Carl Geiser

[HANDWRITTEN]

Sunday, Feb. 20, 1938

My dear Impy:

This Sunday afternoon reminds me of one of my last memories of my mother, when I spoke with her on a Sunday afternoon at her bedside. And she trying to amuse or interest me, told me of the story she was reading of a little boy who hated Sundays, because on Sundays there was nothing he could do. I was only 7 at the time, but it so fitted in with my opinion of Sundays at that time that I never forgot it. And today I have no prescribed tasks to perform, not any urgently pressing work, and I almost sympathize again with the boy in the story.

This Sunday is being spent in the following manner. Reading several chapters of Bates' "The Olive Field," writing you a long letter, taking a walk, reading several articles from Vol VIII of Lenin's Selected Works, and a few hours work at the office taking care of some comrades who have arrived for the school.

We had hoped to open the school Tomorrow, but there is still no sign of the students from the Brigade, so it may be delayed 3 or 4 days or even 2 weeks.

This morning I explored the house in which I am sleeping. I am the only one in it now. It will be the Quarters of the school. It is near the center of town, white (as are all Spanish buildings I have seen) of one-story and an attic. Houses here are built with a single front wall the whole length of the street. It looks like one building a block wide from the street, with a number of small doors for people and some larger ones for burros & carts. But the buildings do not actually adjoin each other, for behind this solid wall you find patios. In fact you never know when you enter a door from a street whether you will step into a room, or a patio, or a driveway to a vulgarized patio in the rear, which leads to the stables, rabbit warren, out house, tool shed, etc.

These houses are often five to six hundred years old, always of stone and mortar, covered with a very wicked white wash with a remarkable preference for your overcoat over the wall. The only wood is in doors, windows, and rafters. Floors are either concrete or tile. The rafters are covered with a layer of slender canes, similar to bamboo, fastened together with mortar and covered with red tile. But always red. Of course after the first hundreds of years, they may become a bit moss-covered.

The rooms inside are seldom all at the same level, which makes traveling about at night very disconcerting. Of the 6 rooms on the first floor, one can be heated—by an open fire-place—but the drafts get you then!

Water is obtained from a well dug below the wall separating us from our neighbor. And both of us can draw water from it, though we can't see each other. You use a pail, rope & pulley. The water is about 25 feet down.

There is electric light, but the wiring breaks every known fire regulation. But there is no danger for I doubt whether these houses would burn.

But the interesting part is the Wine Rooms. There are 15 huge clay vases, some 8 to 10 feet high, perhaps 6 feet across, with a capacity of 100 to 125 gallons. And then you see a steep stairway downwards. You have to use a candle, some 8 feet down there is one notch on each side, in which rests about a 50 gallon vase. Some 10–12 feet further down you come broadside win to a large H like this ⟶ . And here are about a dozen more huge clay vases, taller than your head. Why are they put 20 feet under ground? The Temperature is more even there. It's always quite cold.

Of course, they are all empty, but I can imagine they once held a fine stock of liquors & wines.

But these wine cellars are very valuable now, as dugouts during air raids.

Monday Morning

Dear Impy:

This is a bright splendid Spanish morning, with the sun streaming into the patio this first day of Spring as if to give a warning that in summer time it's going to be hot. But the sunshine, the invigorating freshness of the air, and the noisiness of the sparrows, make me want to put my pack on the shoulder and hit the trail. Imp, I doubt whether I shall ever really be satisfied in my work unless it is connected with the great out-of-doors, and with its wild-life. But I don't see any chance of really doing such work.

But these nights here remind me very much of our hike through Suffern to West Mountain one Easter vacation, especially of that one cold night we slept in a lean to. Sleeping is like that here, for at night it gets very cold, and the only advantage of being inside is that you escape any air that might be about, and you don't collect as much frost. But by 10 in the morning you can take a delightful sunbath.

Have I written you about Prieto's decree abolishing the rank and pay of company Commissars. No explanation has been forthcoming from any source of why such a decree. The Company Commissars will continue to function as political leaders, but of course this does not make their work any easier. Previously they held same rank & pay as the Military Commander. This new move makes training the Company political leaders more imperative than ever before.

It was interesting to see that day before the decree was made public, the press carried an article by Jose Diaz, giving three tasks as fundamental for winning the war in the shortest possible time. 1) Creation of more reserves of men; 2) Organization of war Industry; and 3) Intensification of political work in the Army and in the rear.

All this has raised in my mind what is the proper role of the Commissar today. The role of commissar originated in the Paris Commune, where the commune assigned trusted political workers to each military leader or commander who was trained in the old order, to control and guide his actions. It was necessary to use those military men because the new class did not have able and well-trained military leaders. The same was true in Russia in 1917, and also here in Spain, where the political parties and trade unions appointed special delegates responsible politically, for the work of the early columns.

Today the commissars are responsible directly to the People's Front Government, thru the Minister of National Defense. They are not representatives of the soldiers, but representatives of the Government.

I am informed that in the Red Army today there are only Commissars where the military commander is not a Party member. Where he is a Party member, there exists a Political Dept. but no one called a commissar. I do not know for certain whether this is true, nor have I been able to find a detailed account of the work of the Commissars and Political Depts. in the Red Army.

In the past the Commissar, Company as well as Battalion, have been responsible for the functioning of the services, such as Intendencia, Kitchen, Armory, first-aid, etc. But I should not be surprised if this becomes an ever lesser part of their work, and their work become[s] more [like] that of a political dept. You might put it this way, they will work to develop and maintain a good morale less by what they put in the stomach and more by what they put in the mind.

The work of the Company political leader, it seems to me, will be concerned with the mental & cultural and recreational needs of the men. As for example, news about what is happening in Spain and abroad, translating where ever necessary, supplying such material as will aid the men to develop and maintain their anti-fascist consciousness, providing them with cultural facilities, and organizing recreation. But the problem of improving discipline, of creating a desire for better mastery of military science, of developing a high fighting morale, seems to me to be one of developing a strong anti-fascist consciousness, and of showing the relation between discipline, military training, etc. and the fight against fascism. In other words again, the work of company political leaders will have to be much more of an educator than in the past. Now I suppose you'll have the idea you could make a good company political leader and come to think of it, you probably would.

One weakness I have noted in the work of company political leaders, including my own, is the failure to always know what the men are thinking about, what is bothering them, what they want. And this is more than just a matter of living among them, for often, at least occasionally the political leader is amazed and surprised by some development in his company because he did not enjoy the confidence of the men, nor know what they were thinking about. For when he came around, they promptly discussed something else.

The rumor of the morning is that the British Cabinet met 3 times last night. Why? No one knows. When I read it in the papers I'll believe it.

But of course these things make you feel maybe something big is happening, such as Hitler marching into Austria, and that may mean a little more spine in England & France's attitude towards the war in Spain.

There has been a particularly strong turn during the past 2 or 3 months towards fortifications on the front line. Trenches are now much deeper, much more zig-zagged (for protection against aerial strafing, tank machine guns, shrapnel from artillery & mortars, much better firing pits are built, and now the drive is for deep underground dugouts for protection against bombing and heavy artillery. In fact, this need for solid defen[s] es to protect the soldier from artillery barrage & aerial bombing may lead to the establishment of a series of camouflaged fortified posts rather than a continuous system of trenches. As it is now, if the enemy wants to dislodge you from a trench, it can do so by laying down an artillery barrage on it which will destroy every living thing in it. And then they march up and occupy it. Of course that requires a lot of artillery, but the fascists have a lot of artillery.

Well, Imp, this letter is long enough so I'll close it. Just one word, don't let our separation get you down, the less you think about my returning & the more about what I am doing here, the happier you'll be and the better work you'll do.

> With all my love,
> Carl

[TYPEWRITTEN]

Feb. 24, 1938

Dear Impy:

Today I received your letter of January 16. Although it seems to have come directly here, it is taking a long time for your letters to reach me.

Imp, your description of your class, in which you describe your study of Soviet Democracy, makes me feel that you'll be away far ahead of me in regard to understanding Marxist Theory. I certainly am glad to know that you are continuing your study. Here our opportunities for that kind of study are a bit limited, but I do manage to get some reading accomplished.

There have been rumors here that the League was going to pay more attention to the wives and sweethearts left behind, and now I see you were invited to a dinner and dance sponsored by the National Council. Excellent. But I don't understand your remarks about my not going to the front. As long as I am here in Spain, I intend to go where I am sent and where I can be most useful. Dave Doran has been up on the front for many months now, doing well, so.

I have already written to Jerry. That is nice to know that he was able and did use my letters. And the clippings you sent me, particularly the one by Matthews are beauties. Just as I was reading, in walked Joe Sameres, one of the fellows Matthews mentioned as being wounded in the back, and so I gave him the clipping, with his name and all, only it was written George Samores.[190]

The government reported yesterday that we had evacuated Teruel due to the danger of its being surrounded. The fascist must have suffered very heavy losses in making these attacks. Now we are back where we started from over two months ago, with this difference. At that time Franco was threatening to begin a powerful offensive, we knew not where. But by the Republican strategy, Franco used all these forces he had prepared for this offensive at Teruel where the fighting was to our advantage. And so today we don't face the danger of a big fascist offensive, and Franco has had much greater losses than we did.

But the fall of Teruel was in large part due to the superiority in Aviation and Artillery that the rebels enjoy thanks to Hitler, Mussolini and the Non-Intervention Committee, and the U.S. Neutrality Act. I hear the Herald Tribune has come out for aid to Republican Spain against the Neutrality act. Can it be true?

It has also taught us the importance of much better fortifications. As it is now, either side can by concentrating artillery and Aviation at one point, break through the other's defenses without much trouble. But if we learn to build bomb and shell proof dugouts on the front lines, it won't be so easy. And that is what we must learn to do now.

I am enclosing the latest Volunteer for Liberty, so you'll have plenty to read.

> With all my love,
> Carl

[TYPEWRITTEN]

March 1, 1938

Dear Impy:

I don't know whether you are receiving copies of the Volunteer regularly or not, but since you don't write about it, I imagine you don't get it. So am enclosing the latest issue.

I saw Paul two days ago. He has some trouble with an ear, but it is much improved now. He does not yet know what he is going to do in the future.

There was great rejoicing in the camp yesterday. One comrade received a box from home with three boxes of Nestles chocolate, 24 bars in a box, and 20 tins of fifties of cigarettes. I rated a whole Nestle bar.

I received a letter from Tillie Weinman, with much pleasure. Also a long letter from Grace and two from Sam. He is doing almost as well as you.

Since you will read my letter to Grace, in which I deal at some length with our present problems, I won't repeat them here. A few days ago I attended a Party military conference, which gave me much interesting and valuable information. While we have many weaknesses in our work, nevertheless we are moving. It is when you attend such a conference that you really know fascism can never be victorious here, that you realize the tremendous strength and powerful forces we have.

The political situation in this town is quite interesting. The man who became mayor immediately after the uprising, was forced out of office by a maneuver of the local Caballero people. And the development of the Caballero followers is very interesting. Immediately following the uprising, popular enthusiasm to fight fascism was very great and the half-hearted did not dare raise their heads. But some who were never poor found that the war was profitable, that higher prices can be gotten for their produce, that speculation is possible. And these people looking out for their own interests craftily supported and worked in with the Caballero opposition to the government, not exactly an open opposition, but one taking advantage of the war rather than doing everything possible to win the war.

So quite typical of their work is their present decision to build a public park today. Of course, we want to be far-sighted, and we want parks. But the town has not water-works, the water-supply being in private hands, and so for 10 days we haven't had water. Many streets are in very bad condition and need to be prepared. Very much needs to be done to improve the sewage system. Education should be undertaken for adults, and a library established. But instead, the Caballero administration has decided to build a park, and use the people's money and the limited labor supply for this. You can be sure that the residents of this town would welcome an election. Undoubtedly, elections would do much to reinvigorate the whole governmental apparatus, to mobilize the people for the war.

The political school has not yet begun because the students have not yet arrived from the Brigade. They may arrive at any time, though I am hoping for a few days warning. Personally I am feeling very fit, and my foot is completely well now. So you needn't worry about me.

With all my love,

Carl

[TYPEWRITTEN]

March 3, 1938

Dear Impy:

This is to acknowledge your very intriguing valentine, and the package of 6 Inprecors. I hope you will continue to send me Inprecors for they are quite hard to obtain here and I need them for the school.

Today it is a problem to know what to write you. As far as my own work is concerned there is nothing much new. I am putting on the finishing touches on the preparation for the school, although as yet I have no word from the Brigade when students will arrive for it. And on the side I am speaking to one or other company each day. Yesterday I spoke to No.1 on the wherefore of Italian and German intervention in Spain. One guy fainted after fifteen minutes, but the rest stood it in fine shape. At the end of the discussion when I asked them whether Hitler and Mussolini would withdraw their troops from Spain, there was a resounding "No," so they must have understood my talk.

This afternoon I spoke to [one or two lines redacted] political meeting, and I think they got started off properly, and they are not worried about the fall of Teruel. I have the impression that the volunteers who arrive today adopt and acquire the necessary discipline much quicker than when we arrived here.

Today's news briefs are very interesting. The American Naval Maneuvers have been called off because of the discovery of an espionage ring. Perhaps it will result in a firmer attitude towards Germany and Japan. And [Anthony] Eden is being named Ambassador to the USA, to get him out of England. I hope that the British labor movement can utilize Eden to organize a struggle against the reactionary group in power now.

The big news in Spain continues to be the mobilization of the people for carrying out the necessary tasks to win the war quickly. Numerous meetings are being held in spite of a ban on public meetings sometime ago, and enthusiastic crowds adopt resolutions supporting the proposals of the [Communist] Party. March 1 headline in Verdad, organ of the Valencia Party says: Let the firing squads function to exterminate the speculators and hoarders. It gives you an idea of how much of a crime it is today to speculate and hoard food, for that is one of the way[s] to sabotage the war, and every honest person must help to win it.

The Party Polburo Resolution of Feb. 25 has an interesting statement on the Commissariat. Quote: "A number of actions of our Army has shown that the political work in its ranks has been weakened, this causing some cracking of the morale observed in some units. There is no doubt that the obsession of reducing or increasing the "positions" of one or other Party without bearing in mind the merits of war, an obsession which has inspired the work of the Commissariat in recent times, has not served to awaken the enthusiasm and strengthen the unity, but at times has created a state of discontent which does not in any way favor the development of the morale and fighting ability of our soldiers. Therefore, we ask that there be applied a new spirit to the leadership of the work of the Commissariat, inspired only in the interest of unity, of the war and of the revolution."

I hope that this results in some healthy changes, and that things like the Commissars bulletin appear again, and that we receive more directives from above. Now we are pretty much on our own, and not knowing what is what officially.

A number of young men left this town who were called to the colors. Of course, we gave them a send-off. And soon we will receive a number of Spanish recruits to train with us. Of course, many of the conscripts do not understand very well what the war is about, for many of them are illiterate, and some come from elements that are not exactly suffering from the war. But the healthy instincts of the great majority will make it possible to train very fine soldiers out of them.

Stalin's letter to Ivanov was very welcome here.[191] I should not be surprised if it were no accident that such a letter was made public at this time. Certain countries need a warning. And action from all democratic peoples is essential today to check these desperate madmen before they cause the world a lot of suffering.

We have had very delightful surprises in the way of food in the last few days. One day there was ham and eggs, which almost bowled us over. And the next day we received omelets. And today breaded veal. We are totally at a loss to explain it, but does it taste good. Of course after two weeks of rice and garbanzos, these dishes are extremely welcome.

Am enclosing a block of fascist stamps. My hatred of fascism half tempts me to burn them, but since the stamps are not to blame, I will send them to you as a curiosity.

Give my regards to Tima and Ryah.
    With all my love
    Carl
Thanks again for the Valentine. Everyone is admiring it.

[HANDWRITTEN]
                                        March 4, 1938
Dear Herb:

Here are the resolutions adopted 2 weeks ago in Barcelona by the Anti fascist Youth Alliance. This organization is made up of every national youth organization in Loyalist Spain, including the Anarchist Youth. The Trotskyites have to hide their face for it is very dangerous for them to appear in public, and they are of course not in such an alliance.

You will notice a lot about Revolution but nothing about Socialism. That's because the revolution here is not a socialist Revolution but rather a democratic revolution connected with a bitter struggle for national independence.

You will also notice the main idea running through the resolutions is to win the war, and to prepare the Youth to help win by giving everything they are capable of giving with the proper training and opportunity.

"Alerta" is a mass movement of Youth, boys under military age and girls, for physical education & sports. And it really is a mass movement.

The principal organizations supporting the AYA are the Unified Socialist Youth, the Union of Muchachas (Girls) and the Student organization. I soon hope to have an English copy of the latest resolution of the ISU, and then I shall send you one.

Our political school is prepared and all set to go as soon as the students for it arrive from the Brigade. I am quite well, and busy. Yesterday I spoke to some new volunteers and it was good to see them.

Let's hear from you a little oftener. My warmest greetings to the Branch.
    Salud, Carl

[TYPEWRITTEN]

March 5, 1938

Dear Brother Bennet:

Your letter of Feb. 5 reached me today, just exactly four weeks after you sent it. Thanks a lot for straightening me out on my age. Somehow I had the idea I was a year older than I really am. That suits me fine.

Your remark about the [aid] Mussolini [is] giving the rebels hits the nail on the head, for after we took Teruel, he sent over a tremendous amount of artillery and planes, and tens of thousands of men. They are using some new modern weapons, which are better than anything they have used so far. And this plus the help Hitler gave, made it possible for Franco to retake Teruel after 2 months of hard fighting, in which he had to send terrific amounts of material and men. In fact, the military organ of the General Staff of the German Army raised the question whether Teruel was worth as much as it was costing Franco. But I think that perhaps in a few weeks we shall catch up with Franco again as far as armaments are concerned, and since we have much better infantry and more of them, we ought to be able to make a nice little drive. The only thing is that Hitler and Mussolini may get quite desperate, and throw in everything they can, and that would make it pretty hard on us.

Incidentally, the Nazi victory in Austria, the uncovering of the espionage ring in the United States, ought to sort of make the American people realize here is fire they had better help Europe control before it gets out of hand and burns them too. And believe me, if the USA has to go through anything like Spain is going through today, it will be a real shame, and cost us all very dearly. From the northern to the southern border, a double line of trenches, sometimes 3 and 4 deep, with all the towns along these trenches uninhabitable, and often destroyed. And the whole economy of the country has to be geared to produce war material that is spent to cause more destruction. Now the two next classes are being called to the color, those of 19 and 31 years old, for an Army at war has to be fed a constant stream of men. And just to think with a little effort, a few words from the USA, Great Britain, France and Soviet Union acting together, could stop Mussolini and Hitler from sending in more war material and men to Franco, and the war would be over in a few months. Otherwise it may easily drag on another year.

Today I talked with two Englishmen, who were taken prisoner by the fascists on Feb. 12 last year, kept in jail for three and one-half months, then turned loose for publicity value. The experiences they have to relate make your blood boil. Shortly after they were captured (they were captured when a group of moors approached them singing the International as if they were planning to desert to our side, and then when they got close threw hand grenades and captured some 20 men) one fellow asked permission to light a cigarette. When he reached into his pocket to take one out, they shot him, the bullet passing through him and killing the fellow behind him as well. A little later they executed one of them, a Communist. He died with the Republican salute and a "Salud, Comrades." One of the fellows who was telling me about this said before that he was afraid to die, but that this gave him such courage that he felt he could face anything. Incidentally this fellow is only 23, but looks more like 33 after those several months in Francoland.

They described the execution pits. Those who are to be shot are made to stand on the edge of it, so they tumble in when they are hit. The pits were 90 feet long by 30 feet wide and 10 deep. One was already full and the other partly filled. The conditions of the prisoners was very, very revolting, extremely crowded, very bad food. While they were there, several times one or two of their group were taken away, without any explanation. They also saw women being taken out to be executed as well as men. Finally they were brought to trial. The defense lawyer made a 2-minute speech and they were condemned to be shot. Fortunately Franco thought of a bright idea. He gave them all private rooms in a hotel, clean clothes, a good meal and called in the movie cameramen, and then sent them back to England. Now most of them are back here again in the Republican Army. And no one hates the fascists more than they do.

The way Franco treats his prisoners and the way we treat them is as different as day and night. I remember both at Quinto and Belchite, where we took several thousand prisoners all told, and how glad they were to be captured, and get out of the fascist army. Quite a number of the Spaniards in the Washington-Lincoln battalion have been fascist soldiers before, but who have deserted to us or had been captured. It is just one more proof that the people are on our side.

But you should see the surprise on many of the faces of the people in towns we capture and of the prisoners, when they see that we are not Russians. For the fascists tell them that they are fighting Russians who want to enslave the Spanish People. And the number of Russians I have seen here I could count on my two hands, while from the USA. there are well over 3,000. And I am sure no one thinks that we are here to conquer Spain for the USA.

The fascists are continuing to bomb defenseless cities in the rear. Yesterday they bombed Barcelona again, killing some 40 I believe. Great Britain and France are supposed to be negotiating to have both sides agree not to bomb defenseless cities. We are not bombing them now waiting for the results of the negotiations. Personally, my opinion is that the fascists will not quit bombing these cities until we prove to them that we can do more damage than they can, and then they'll be glad to quit. But this is a very unpleasant way of making them stop, and I hope very much the negotiations will be successful.

I am quite well, prepared to open the school the moment the soldiers arrive for it. We have a very thorough course on the history of Spain, its present problems, and the duties of a political worker in the Army. In the meantime I am responsible for training the political workers here at the base, functioning now in the training battalion. I don't believe I have ever told you what the functions of political commissars and delegates are. I shall do that in my next letter.

But now it is getting late, so I shall close.

> Very sincerely
> Carl

[TYPEWRITTEN]

March 5, 1938

Dear little Impy:

Today was a red letter day with two letters from you, one from Bennet, and one from Phil Ressine. Which has been on its way here since October 16. I am enclosing two envelopes. One is a curiosity, the one from Phil, which traveled all over Spain until someone finally recognized the name, and forwarded it to me. The second is proof why you must mark all letters to me "Via France" in order to avoid their passing through countries like Greece, and their possible censorship.

Your two letters are dated Jan. 30 and Feb. 11. And I am relieved to know that you received the calendars, postcards, etc. But I didn't mean to suggest you should start knitting. I couldn't imagine you doing that. It would look very funny.

Your quotation from Marx on the Civil War in the United States makes me anxious to see the new book containing his writings, which I understand has now come out. It hasn't reached here yet, but perhaps it will before long. Though actually we are woefully short of good books of that nature, and long on fiction and romances of all kind, some of which we had to burn for its anti-democratic and anti-peoples sentiments. Time is too valuable here to waste on that sort of trash.

You must answer Ben's letters as regularly as mine. By the way, he is one of the very few, perhaps two or three, that have been with the Washington ever since it was formed, without being wounded or ill or away for some other reason. I saw him a good deal when I was in Teruel. And it shall be extremely pleasant if some day after we are through here, the three of us can reminisce around a fine meal (notice how my mind runs to food) about how fascism was defeated in Spain.

Your letter indicates you are really quite busy, studying, preparing reports and programs, and even don't have time enough time to sleep. Probably you shall have changed as much as I have during the past year, and both for the better I hope. And it's not so bad if you wish me to come home, as long as you don't wish too hard.

Yes I knew Amlie quite well. I first knew him one afternoon when he took us out to drill in close order formation last May, and then he has been with the battalion ever since except when he was in hospital. His article should be read by all readers of the Post, for they are well done.

Everything here is going along well, except that the students from the school have not arrived yet, and time is passing. Of course in the meantime, we are improving the lesson plans, gathering together more material, doing a good deal of translating. Monday morning we begin instruction of the political workers here at the base. I am responsible for the organization and content of this instruction as well.

Today I spoke with two English Comrades, who were among a group of 29 Englishmen taken prisoner on Feb. 12, 1937, held in Franco's jails for three and one-half months, then sent back to England, and are now back here to fight fascism again.

The account of their experiences in Francoland is ghastly. Shortly after they were taken prisoner, one asked for permission to roll a cigarette. But when he reached for his pocket, they shot him, the same bullet killing the man behind him as well. Then they executed one of their number, a Communist, in front of them. He died with a proletarian salute and "Salud, Comrades." The young fellow who was telling me this said that previous to this (he was not a Communist) he would have been afraid to die, but after witnessing this, he could have borne up under anything. And the executioners pit. 90 feet by 30 feet, ten feet deep, two of them, one filled with dead bodies and the other partly filled.

They were taken out several times to be shot. They saw girls being taken out to be executed, and can tell horrible tales about the fascist prison regime.

Franco finally decided to release them several weeks after as fake a trial as ever occurred, in which they were condemned to death. He gave them each a private room, clean clothes, a good meal and called in the movie photographers. And most of these men are now back in the Republican Army, fighting against fascism, and an inspiration to all of us.

Very interesting material is being unearthed by the trials in the Soviet Union, bringing many things to light. To think that Lenin, Gorki, and others might still be alive if it were not for those filthy deeds. It must teach us to be careful, particularly with those who at critical moments oppose us. Incidentally, it would be very unwise for Mr. Norman Thomas to show his face around the front anywhere.[192] He has no followers here.

Which reminds me of your question about my lice. They are neither big nor small, in fact they aren't at all. At present, I believe there are very few lice in the base, a steady battle against them with disinfecting and hot showers, etc., has put them on the run.

As I wrote you before, I have received all the packages you sent me, plus the Inprecors, for which I thank your very much.

> With all my love—
> Carl

P.S.

The cook's difficulties here: the water is so hard it won't soften the rice or garbanzos regardless of the hours of soaking. It's so hard they start cooking the Garbanzos at 3 in the morning, and they are still hard at noon, 9 hours later.

So we are looking for some soft water, so we don't have to eat hard rice and garbanzos.

The problem is, is this a soluble or insoluble problem.

> Nada mas,
> Carl

[TYPEWRITTEN ON THE BACK OF A PROPAGANDA LEAFLET TITLED "XV BRIGADA: UN AÑO DE LUCHA POR LA DEMOCRACIA"]

March 9, 1938

Dear Mrs. Lubell:

I was greatly surprised, and very agreeably so, when your packages arrived today, two at once, with the cigarettes and chocolate. I could scarcely believe that you were able to send them so quickly. And the cigarettes arrived just in the midst of a tobacco shortage, which makes me immensely popular. And you would be surprised at great appreciation for chocolate for it is a great luxury here. And a few pieces distributed among the children of this town go a long ways towards deepening still further the love of the civilian population for the volunteers.

Are you corresponding with Sylvia? She is writing me of many interesting things happening in School indicating the growth of progressive thinking among your co-workers, and the much firmer unity among all teachers. Sylvia herself seems to be growing also to judge from her letters. Since I wrote you the last time, we have lost Teruel, due to the superiority of aviation and artillery enjoyed by the rebels, of course thanks to Hitler and Mussolini. But I am quite certain that we shall be able to overcome this superiority shortly. Negrin has said that this war can be ended in several months, if the democratic nations would make it possible for the Government to obtain arms to put it on an equal footing with the rebels.

Our Brigade carried out a splendid night attack several weeks ago, in which they climbed over a mountain one pitch black night, with occasional snow flurries, to attack the rebels from the rear at dawn. They took nearly 200 prisoners and plenty of material. Such events are very demoralizing for the fascist forces. As well as our successful attack on the fascist fleet two days ago. The confidence of the Spanish people today is very high, and with the proper help from the democracies, we could be victorious in a short time.

My sincerest thanks for the chocolates & cigarettes. Salud,

Carl Geiser

March 9, 1938

Dear Mrs. Lubell:

I was greatly surprised, and very agreeably so, when your packages arrived today, two at once, with the cigarettes and chocolate. I could scarcely believe that you were able to send them so quickly. And the cigarrettes arrived just in the midst of a tobacco shortage, which makes me immensely popular. And you would be surprised at great appreciation for chocolate for it is a great luxury here. And a few pieces distributed among the children of this town go a long ways towards deepening still further the love of the civilian population for the volunteers.

Are you corresponding with Sylvia? She is writing me of many interesting things happening in School indicating the growth of progressive thinking among your co-workers, and the much firmer unity among all teachers. Sylvia herself seems to be growing also to judge from her letters. Since I wrote you the last time, we have lost Teruel, due to the superiority of aviation and artillery enjoyed by the rebels, of course thanks to Hitler and Mussolini. But I am quite certain that we shall be able to overcome this superiority shortly. Negrin has said that this war can be ended in several months, if the democratic nations would make it possible for the Government to obtain arms to put it on an equal footing with the rebels.

Our Brigade carried out a splendid night attack several weeks ago, in which they climber over a mountain one pitch black night, with occassional snow flurries, to attack the rebels from the rear at dawn. They took nearly 200 prisoners and plenty of material. Such events are very demoralizing for the fascist forces. As well as our successful attack on the fascist fleet two days ago. The confidence of the Spanish people today is very high, and with the proper help from the democracies, we could be victorious in a short time.

[HANDWRITTEN]

Sunday, March 13

My dear Impy:

I wish I could adequately describe the atmosphere here today, and our reaction to the open seizure of Austria by German fascism.[193]

This plus the French Cabinet crisis (was it engineered to take place at this moment?) makes a very real threat. Mussolini may decide to launch an attack from the sea, probably between Castellón and Barcelona to cut Loyalist Spain in two. You can be certain we are completely mobilized for such an eventuality. Even the latest recruits are being given a quick instruction in use of a rifle yet today.

Within a few hours, I hope to know what my work will be for next few weeks. It is quite possible that the present emergency will entail some postponement of our political school. And I may even be on my way to a front before the next 12 hours pass.

Just as I wrote the last line an order came "Everyone confined to Barracks."

It is very difficult to predict at the moment what may happen. Perhaps this war may be over much sooner than we expected. Surely it will not drag on another year under these conditions. But the one thing I can predict is that for the next few weeks we are going to work at top speed. Today one does not spare himself. No matter how much one does, it is not enough.

There has been no news from England or France for some 36 hours. But I know the Party is mobilizing, not only its own members, but the whole people, to fight the danger of fascism. There must be literally thousands of meetings today in England, France and the USA. Awakening the people [to] the danger confronting us today.

If I were given my choice of where I could be today, I think I should pick the People's Army of Spain. When in a large powerful military body such as this you feel our power, and can be confident victory shall be ours. You know what you have to do, and you do it, with all your might, with the knowledge that by doing so, we can win.

I wish you could have been here with me at a Party last night, or a meeting just a few minutes ago . . . Last night the non-commissioned officers school held a "party" celebrating the first week's work. As I looked around at these very fine young men, heard their whole-hearted singing, watched the entertainment they put on, men from their own ranks, one playing a violin, others singing, pantomime, etc. I felt proud and happy of our Army, of its cultured men. Then Major Johnson spoke.[194] In short, friendly but firm sentences. The Nazi invasion of Austria means a grave danger for Spain.

[five lines redacted]

You have done well in the school, but I am not satisfied. No matter how much you do, I shall ask more. This is my revolutionary duty, for today we cannot spare ourselves. For the next period of time we [end of page; the rest of letter is missing]

[HANDWRITTEN]

March 17, 1938

Dear Herb—

Just a word to you and to the Nathan Hale branch to double your efforts on the side [of] the Spanish Republic.

The fascist offensive which reached to Alcaniz yesterday is commanded by Italians, consists of motorized Italian Divisions, and is aided by many German technicians and a huge German and Italian air fleet. You know they have already taken a great deal of territory.

This plus the fact that news indicates Hitler & Mussolini have decided to send over enough men and material to Spain to ensure Franco's victory immediately—for possession of Spain is essential to them to begin a new world war. It makes the situation here more critical than it has ever been. We are working very hard,

[twelve lines redacted and snipped out from letter]

How we are working here can be illustrated by a remark made by [three-fourths of a line redacted] Commander, at a party 10 days ago of our non-commissioned officers school. The school had done good work, better than any previous one. But [a few words redacted] told them, "I am not satisfied. If you did twice as much, I would still demand more of you. If I did not, I would not be doing my revolutionary duty. Today we can not spare ourselves or each other. Today I demand everything you have from you."

Comrades, we are already late. Let everyone double his work, and not spare himself. It is essential if we are to win.

I am well, and working as Adjutant to the Base Commissar of our Training Camp.[195]

Salud y Victoria
Carl Geiser

[HANDWRITTEN]

Socorro Rojo Internacional
Plaza del Altozano 17.1
Barcelona
(*Don't* use French address)
June 16[, 1938]

Dear Sylvia:[196]

I got your letter of March 6 just a few days ago. So much happened since you wrote it, the moving of the I.B. Base into Catalonia, and my own moving around from place to place. I got back to the Battalion a month and a half ago, and my mail has just about caught up. The Battalion today changed to a different [?] aspect. There is a minority of our men who have been through a number of actions, most of them embittered by what has happened to them and their comrades, and a majority of young Spanish recruits many of whom have little idea of what the war is about and still less of what they are going up against. The last 2 months have been spent training in reserve positions. The recruits have learned the rudiments of their job, and we hope they'll be all right.

News these days isn't so good. Castellón has just been evacuated and the 43rd Division, which had been defending the Pyrenees border, has been forced to cross the frontier. Our chief hope right now is from France—but hell knows when they are going to really do something about the situation they know has been threatening them for a year and a half. Reality is such a senseless nightmare that sometimes a person must stop himself from thinking about things too much. Ever since I've been in Spain I've heard fellows say, "Well, I think something that nobody expects is going to happen to save Spain." You sometimes like to think like that. It's the reverse side of the gloomy picture of the immediate reality—reality which some political writers qualify by some word like "superficial" or "temporary," but which is very real in the front lines. We need a hell of a lot more than a trade union resolution to make up for the quick-firing artillery which can uproot every inch of ground on the hill you're on within a few hours. I hear that some people are "inspired" by the stand that the men in the Republican army have put up against machines. We over here are quite uninterested in reading the fulsome praise showered on us. Human nerves are fragile, even the strongest of them. It hasn't been inspiring to us to go through these experiences, and see a vista of more experiences like them. The only thing it brings to our minds is the consciousness of how few familiar faces are left around us. One of the saddest days of my life was last summer, after Brunete when we received 250 reinforcements that was for the already merged Lincoln-Washington Battalion. I'd look around whenever we were gathered for meals, and turn all around, and all around me were strange faces. I felt that either they didn't belong to my outfit, or I didn't belong to theirs. Of course, the feeling was just sentimental—if I may be pardoned for using such a word about the feeling one has for comrades who are lost or wounded.

Maybe I'm getting sunk in a sea of gloom. What I am trying to say, is that we, whether Internationals or Spaniards, can't be expected to keep carrying this burden forever. In a few days we will be going up to the lines again. Maybe it will be a move to relieve the seacoast South of the line. "Relieving another front" by an attack on a more distant front is a technical maneuver which means that troops are thrown in as a sacrifice to save the lives and the units of forces suffering a concentration of enemy forces. We don't know just where our point of attack may be—an attempt to slash through the fascist arm to the sea, or a stand to defend the French border area. Whatever it is, we know it will be a similar story, an attempt to make up for equipment by daring, quickness, and the capacity of men to face superior odds. We know that we've gotten new stuff in the last couple of months; the interesting question is how it compares to what the fascists have gotten.

I am not writing much about Carl in this letter. Few people around here remember him as he returned to the Battalion just a couple of days before the affair on Batea-Gandesa road. You have probably been more [illegible 6 or 7 words] could give you. My information is that he was captured without a struggle—a scouting party walked into a fascist nest and were taken before they realized what was happening. I last saw him on March 24th, when he left Tarazona for the Brigade. He was quite recovered from his limp and seemed to be in good shape. A group of men were talking about going home. Carl remarked in his quiet way that he wouldn't be able to face his friends if he went home at such a time. It was said in the way that made me respect him so much when we were working together years ago, the statement of a personal will which had made up its own mind, in the sure way of a Communist.
Please continue to write me.
      Paul

[CG:] My note penned in later at the bottom of Paul's letter:

Stuck it out to the last & killed on last day of fighting on the Ebro

POSTSCRIPT

The sun was rising in a cloudless sky on a fresh and lovely spring morning.[197] Bushes and small trees along the ridge provided cover as we advanced rapidly. In less than ten minutes we came to a dip in the ridge. A faint odor of wood fires alerted me. I halted when I saw ahead of us several hundred soldiers preparing their breakfasts on a slope facing us. They seemed protected from fascist observation and fire by the ridge behind them.

An officer came alone to greet us, calling out in good English: "Come on over. Don't be afraid. We are your friends."

I thought, we got to our positions after dark last night, and the fascists would not know that we spoke English, but the 11th Brigade would expect us on their left flank. I was overjoyed, as was the rest of the patrol. We hurried forward happily to greet the officer. Less than fifty feet from him, I saw "23 de Marzo" on his jacket, the name of an Italian division.

I stopped. For the first time, I noticed crews behind three light machine guns on tripods in the background zeroed in on us. I carried a liberated Luger, for which I had been unable to obtain ammunition, and a hand grenade.

I looked back. Everyone had stopped. Hodge, carrying the light machine gun, had it resting in the crook of his arm. The riflemen were not prepared to fire. All were watching for my signal. It was painfully obvious that since we were out in the open we would all be shot down before we could open fire.

The officer, now identifiable as a captain, after motioning to a squad of soldiers to come out, came up in jubilant mood. "Welcome! Welcome, men of the 15th! Glad to see you! You won't be needing your guns, so my men will take care of them.

I was wearing a new officer's jacket, my first one, so new that I had not sewn on insignia. The captain, observing my jacket and seeing that I carried only a side arm, came directly up to me and with a smile asked: "May I take your pistol?"

Without answering, I allowed him to take it. Something caused him to break it open. He looked at me in astonishment. "Where's the ammo?"

"Sorry, I don't have any."

Recognizing it as a German Luger, he joked, "Oh, that's all right, I'll be able to get some."

Next he unhooked my grenade and gave it to a member of his squad, the rest of who were disarming my comrades. "Now, let's see your military identification." My heart sank. I handed over the card showing my rank as battalion political commissar.

The captain's eyes lit up. "You're just the man I need. Step over there and call those men up here." He pointed toward the soldiers in the valley. They had halted, sensing trouble.

When I made no move to obey, he pulled out his pistol. "This one's got ammo in it. Now turn around!" Pushing the end of the barrel hard against my back, he ordered, "Forward march!"

Thirty steps brought us to a fifty-foot cliff, overlooking Cane's men. "Now, Commissar, call those men up here!"

Fall forward with a bullet in my back, or backward with a bullet in my chest? Since I could see that my comrades were already taking cover, I decided to face the captain. I turned slowly and told him, "As an officer, I will not call them up."

Scarcely had I finished when bullets started to whistle past our ears. Sergeant Cane had ordered the group in the valley to open fire as close to us as possible without hitting me.

The captain and I looked each other in the eye as bullets sang in our ears. If he pulled the trigger, those bullets would be directed at him. Motioning with his pistol, he quietly remarked, "OK, let's get out of here. You first!"

This time I obeyed willingly, and we soon joined the others in a slight hollow. Italian troops began to fire down on Cane's men to prevent them from coming to our rescue.

The captain's staff congratulated him on the way he had fooled us. I asked him where he had learned his English.

"Brooklyn. Lived there quite a few years. Sure came in handy, didn't it?"

"You speak it perfectly. But how did you know we spoke English?

"Oh, a little pigeon told me."

This, plus the fact that we were not being questioned about our military strength, made me suspect that the fascist officers already know how thin our line was.

The captain detailed a squad of six soldiers to escort us, and four MacPaps captured earlier, to the rear. He did not give my identification booklet to the sergeant in charge.

We climbed a hundred yards through masses of troops to the top of the ridge. The view on the other side, to the right and left, was sickening: it was filled with troops preparing for battle. At the next ridge, the scene was repeated. After picking our way to the left through troops for about ten minutes, we reached the road to Calaceite, much to my surprise.

We had to walk on the side of the road; it was filled with troops coming toward us. Long curving stretches below us on the road's descent to the Algas River were filled with military units. We passed battalion after battalion of infantry in close-order formation. We saw only regular Italian Army units. Between the infantry battalions were machine gun companies, their gun carriages strapped on mules, a luxury we did not enjoy. Whippet tanks noisily climbed the road, along with batteries of antitank guns. Always more infantry, all on foot. And only the MacPaps and 59th were standing in their way.

The foot soldiers we met paid no attention to us as they toiled up the steep hill, sweating under the burden of their packs and rifles. At the bottom of the hill we saw to our left a walled enclosure with several one-story buildings. There our escorts directed us into an alley that led into a large courtyard, where they turned us over to another Italian squad.

The ten of us immediately gathered together in the center of the courtyard to decide on what we should say. We agreed that we would give our names and nationality and identify ourselves as part of the Mackenzie-Papineau Battalion. We would know nothing about the number of men, tanks, or amount of artillery.

EPILOGUE

General Franco ordered the execution of any International Brigader taken prisoner, a policy largely followed through the war. Geiser, along with the other soldiers captured with him, expected to face a firing squad. When told to assemble in front of a wall, they steadied themselves, ready to sing "The Internationale" as a last act of defiance against their executioners. But the moment was lucky. Under pressure from Mussolini, who wanted to have prisoners to exchange for captured Italians held by the Spanish Republic, Franco permitted a cessation of killing International Brigaders on April 1, 1938; the order remained in force for ten days. Instead of being summarily shot, Geiser and about 150 other International Brigaders were transported to a prisoner of war camp at San Pedro de Cardeña in northern Spain. There they joined an international mixture of more than six hundred prisoners of war from thirty-eight countries.

Conditions at San Pedro were harsh, the food meager, sanitation poor, and beatings common. An experienced organizer, Geiser recognized the importance of bolstering morale. Relying on the varieties of the prisoners' interests, he created a lecture series and even spoke on one of his favorite pastimes, hiking in the Adirondacks. On Decoration Day (Memorial Day), he recited Lincoln's Gettysburg Address and discussed its importance. In the autumn, the prisoners organized an Institute of Higher Learning and offered a spate of classes to educate each other. Eventually, they also produced a newspaper called the *Jaily News*.

Back at home, the Friends of the Abraham Lincoln Brigade had begun to pressure the State Department for the release of the U.S. prisoners. Washington officials refused to intervene, insisting that the volunteers had violated neutrality laws and lacked protection. But as journalists reported the fate of the prisoners and the International Red Cross visited San Pedro, negotiations for prisoner exchanges began. Fourteen prisoners were released in October 1938; three months later, a contingent of thirty-seven British prisoners were exchanged. Not until April 1939 was Geiser among a group of seventy-one prisoners allowed to leave Spain. The last U.S. prisoners did not find a way home until April 1940.

By then, Franco had marched into Madrid on March 31, 1939, claiming victory in the Spanish Civil War, and installed a dictatorship that would last until his death in November 1975. By then, too, world affairs had moved to the precipice of world war. In January 1939, President Franklin D. Roosevelt admitted at a cabinet meeting that the U.S. refusal to assist Spain's elected government had been a grave mistake. Two months later, in March 1939, German troops completed the Nazi occupation of Czechoslovakia, and Adolf Hitler began making demands against Poland. Great Britain and France warned they would respond to an attack on Poland by declaring war on Germany. On September 1, 1939, Germany invaded Poland and, as most historians assert, World War II began in Europe. The Spanish Civil War, where the European allies had an opportunity to confront fascist aggression and instead allowed Hitler and Mussolini to help overthrow an elected government, proved the failure of "appeasement" of the dictators. In fact, some historians consider Spain the first battleground of the European war.

Soon after landing in New York, Geiser began to work with the Friends of the Abraham Lincoln Brigade (FALB), pressing the U.S. government to repatriate remaining prisoners of war. The FALB dissolved at the end of 1939 and was replaced by the Veterans of the Abraham Lincoln Brigade (VALB), which continued the political agenda. High among its priorities was assistance and rescue of Spanish republican refugees who had fled the victorious Franco armies into France and now were interned in concentration camps. However, U.S. policy remained anti-Republic and provided little assistance to the trapped Spaniards. Indeed, when World War II broke out, the VALB expressed its anger at U.S. policy toward Spain by opposing U.S. intervention in the war. Many veterans adopted the Communist party slogan, "The Yanks Are Not Coming!" Only after Hitler's invasion of the Soviet Union in June 1941 did the VALB endorse U.S. involvement. After the Japanese attack on Pearl Harbor, four hundred Lincoln veterans joined the U.S. armed forces and merchant marine and went on to win a disproportionate number of combat medals.

Geiser, meanwhile, resumed his familiar role of political and union organizing. While helping the United Electrical Radio Machine workers organize a union, he was offered a job as a machinist in 1939 (concealing his college education so he would not appear different from his coworkers). His work focused on inventing and developing fuel gauges that were used in the burgeoning aircraft industry. This national defense work kept Geiser out of the military, and he used his time to promote unionization. Geiser moved on to an engineering job and invented improvements in the fuel gauge area. After the war, Carl and Sylvia ("Impy") were divorced. She remained a school teacher until the red scare of the 1950s forced her to leave that career and later remarried.

Carl also remarried to a New Yorker named Doris Rieck. They shared an interest in the outdoors, hiking, and skiing. While Carl and the Communist Party parted ways during the 1950s, he remained involved in left-wing politics, but he also found a new intellectual focus. While working in quality control for various manufacturing firms, he enrolled at Columbia University, earning a bachelor's degree in psychology (Phi Beta Kappa) in 1962.

These changes later in life could not diminish the importance of the Spanish Civil War for Geiser's mature identity. He remained active in veterans' affairs, particularly efforts to assist political prisoners held by the Franco regime and opposing U.S. support for the dictatorship. As he entered retirement in the 1970s, moreover, Geiser undertook a major project that had been deferred for forty years: writing a history of Spanish Republican prisoners of war. Geiser's professional career as an engineer/inventor depended on thoroughness and attention to detail. He brought those skills to his historical research, uncovering numerous archival collections not only in U.S. State Department records but also from many European archives. His book, *Prisoners of the Good Fight*, published in 1986, told a story that had been deliberately concealed by government secrecy. Besides chronicling the experiences of the diverse prisoners held by Franco, Geiser discovered that Roosevelt's Secretary of State, Cordell Hull, had approved illegal transactions between U.S. corporations and Franco's rebels and had blocked efforts to assist the POWs.

"When we went to Spain fifty years ago," Geiser concluded, "our goal was to stop fascism before it could spread further and threaten our country. We failed to do so." He went on to say that younger generations faced "an infinitely more serious situation." He referred to the possible extinction of life on the planet. In his later years, Geiser remained a political activist, participating with other veterans of the Abraham Lincoln Brigade in demonstrations for nuclear disarmament, raising funds for humanitarian aid for Nicaragua, Cuba, and South Africa, and advocating for environmental protection. He visited Spain for the last time in 2008. He died the next year in Oregon.

NOTES

1. Carl Geiser's unpublished biography, 8.

2. Joe Dallet, *Letters from Spain,* New York: Workers Library Publishers, 1938; *From a Hospital in Spain: Letters from American Nurses,* New York: n.p., 1937; *From the Cradle of Liberty . . . to the Tomb of Fascism,* Philadelphia: Communist Party of Eastern Pennsylvania, 1938; *Let Freedom Ring,* Los Angeles: Friends of the Abraham Lincoln Brigade, n.d.; *Letters from Spain,* San Francisco: Friends of the Abraham Lincoln Brigade, 1937; and *Letters from the Trenches from Our Boys in Spain,* New York: Workers Alliance of New York, n.d. *From Spanish Trenches: Recent Letters from Spain,* New York: Modern Age Books, 1937 edited by Marcel Acier, contains letters by volunteers from many countries. Letters were also included in publications devoted to specific individuals or small groups of volunteers, including *Ben Leider: American Hero,* New York: Ben Leider Memorial Fund, n.d.; *WPA Teachers in Spain,* New York: WPA Teachers Union Chapter of the Friends of the Abraham Lincoln Battalion, 1938; *A Negro Nurse in Republican Spain,* New York: Negro Committee to Aid Spain, n.d.; Joseph Starobin, *The Life and Death of an American Hero,* New York: New Age, 1938; *Somebody Had to Do Something,* Los Angeles: The James Lardner Memorial Fund, 1939; and *Let My People Know: The Story of Wilfred Mendelson,* New York: published by his friends, 1942.

3. Cary Nelson and Jefferson Hendricks, *Madrid 1937: Letters of the Abraham Lincoln Brigade from the Spanish Civil War,* New York: Routledge, 1996; and Peter N. Carroll, Michael Nash and Melvin Small, *The Good Fight Continues: World War II Letters from the Abraham Lincoln Brigade,* New York: New York University Press, 2006.

4. The Hamburg American Line was a transatlantic shipping company that provided regular passenger service between Hoboken, N.J., and ports in Europe.

5. This is a reference to Geiser's earlier trip to Europe when, on his way to Moscow, he visited family members in Switzerland.

6. [CG:] These fellows were undercover—just like I was—on their way to Spain. [Editors: After January 1937, when the United States Congress banned travel to Spain, many volunteers applied for U.S. passports by concealing their ultimate destination.]

7. [CG:] Cobh (pronounced "cove") is the Irish name, of course.

8. The RMS *Berengaria* was an ocean liner of the British Cunard Line.

9. [CG:] Bennet is Carl's younger brother by a year, and Grace is Bennet's wife.

10. General José Sanjurjo died when his plane crashed on takeoff on July 20, 1936. He was attempting to return to Spain to join the military rebellion from his exile in Portugal.

11. On April 26, 1937, planes of the German "Condor Legion" and the Italian "Aviazione Legionaria" bombed the town of Guernica in the Basque region of northern Spain. The attack caused great destruction and significant loss of life; it also became the subject of Pablo Picasso's famous painting.

12. [CG:] Sister, uncle, and an aunt who married Gus back in Ohio.

13. [CG:] Socorro Rojo Internacional (SRI), International Red Aid, took the place of the Red Cross in Republican Spain. The Red Cross was regarded as too reactionary. Oftentimes when we got paid we had nowhere to spend the money so we gave it over to the Socorro Rojo.

14. [CG:] The United Auto Workers was one of the more militant labor unions of the time. It was a member of the Committee for Industrial Organization (CIO) before the amalgamation of the AF of L/CIO.

15. [CG:] Andy's full name was Paul Anderson. I first met Andy when he was working his way aboard the ship I sailed in to the South American Conference Against War and Fascism. Paul Wendorf was a big guy, a good friend of ours and a member of our Nathan Hale Branch of the Young Communist League (YCL) in the Bronx.

16. From May 3 to 7, 1937, bloody fratricidal fighting erupted between Catalan government forces supported by the Communists against anarchists and the dissident communist Workers Party of Marxist Unity (POUM) in the streets of Barcelona. As a result of these so-called "May days," the central Republican government assumed control of public order and of the defense of Catalonia suspending the core dispositions of the Autonomy Statute granted to the region in 1932.

17. [CG:] When not in action, every company's commissar arranged to have a "wall board" or "wall paper" put up for the men to keep informed and boost morale. Wall paper is put up on wall boards but they mean the same thing: a display of announcements, information, news, clippings, questions, jokes, etc.

18. [CG:] Herman Engert; he was wounded four *times,* actually.

19. [CG:] U.S.-based support group, the Friends of the Abraham Lincoln Battalion (FALB), also known unofficially as the Friends of the Lincoln Battalion or the F of L.B.

20. [CG:] Almeria is a port on the Mediterranean Sea. In retaliation for a Loyalist air attack on one of their battleships, the Nazis bombarded the town and killed many civilians.

21. [CG:] Irving Weisman and Pretty were also from our Nathan Hale Branch of the YCL. Irving was Sylvia's nephew. He and I had been hiking when we heard about Franco's insurgency. "Pretty" was a nickname Mel Purdy picked up in the neighborhood—a play on words. He wasn't ugly, anyway. They were both good guys.

22. The "branch" was the basic neighborhood Communist organization that covered electoral district lines.

23. Tom Mooney (1882–1942) was a labor leader in San Francisco. At the time he was serving a life sentence in California falsely accused of bombing a Preparedness Parade during World War I. A cause célèbre for radicals in the 1930s, Mooney was pardoned in 1938.

24. [CG:] My sister Ellen.

25. The Congress of Industrial Organizations (CIO), founded in 1935, is a consortium of industrial labor unions (as opposed to the more narrow trade unions of

the American Federation of Labor [AFL]). It achieved great success in organizing sit-down strikes *inside* the factories that were struck.

26. Paul Wendorf, a graduate of Columbia University, served in Spain from February 1937 through August 1938 when he was killed in action.

27. Founded in 1905 the Industrial Workers of the World (IWW) was a revolutionary syndicalist organization. The volunteer Geiser mentions is probably Patrick Reade, an Irish American from Chicago.

28. [CG:] Herman Engert; see letter #88 below for more on Herman the German.

29. After some discussion the "3rd American Battalion" was called Mackenzie-Papineau after two nineteenth-century Canadian nationalists and consisted of volunteers both from Canada and the United States. Typically, international volunteers were incorporated into separate units divided according to nationality. Named after Communist icons or national heroes, such as John Brown, James Connolly, Giuseppe Garibaldi, Abraham Lincoln, and George Washington, such groups served to overcome linguistic differences while affirming the distinctly national yet universal character of the struggle against fascism.

30. "Andy" is Geiser's nickname for the volunteer Paul Anderson, a friend from New York, who was later killed in Spain.

31. The Battle of Jarama in February 1937 was an attempt by General Franco's rebel army to isolate Madrid from the rest of Republican Spain by occupying the Jarama river valley southeast of the city. After days of fighting, Republican forces were able to thwart Franco's plan and save the capital. Volunteers of the newly formed Abraham Lincoln Battalion first saw action at Jarama.

32. Based on the example of the Soviet Red Army, each level of command of the Spanish Republican army — section, company, battalion, brigade, and division — was assigned a political commissar. Responsible for explaining the political significance of military tactics and for ensuring morale, the position was usually reserved for members of the Communist Party.

33. [CG:] Walter Garland: one of the first African American officers to command ranks of mixed American soldiers.

34. The Friends of the Abraham Lincoln Brigade was founded in New York City in 1937. With chapters in over a dozen cities across the country, the FALB held fund-raisers and other public events to raise money to send care packages to the volunteers, provide medical assistance to wounded veterans, and generally support the Spanish Republican cause. When the war ended, having served its purpose, the organization disbanded and its activities were taken over by the Veterans of the Abraham Lincoln Brigade (VALB).

35. [CG:] The C.I. (Communist International) was a regularly published report of the Comintern.

36. Geiser was referring to "Popular Front Committees" but used the Anglicized term of "People's Front." In Spain these organizations were run by local anti-fascist groups to ensure the support of the home front for the war effort.

37. [CG:] Ralph Bates, British novelist, first editor for *The Volunteer For Liberty,* weekly paper of the XVth Brigade.

38. In 1937, as Franco's troops advanced toward Bilbao, almost 4,000 children were evacuated from the Basque region to Britain. Since the British government refused to provide financial assistance, funds to support the children were raised through individual donations.

39. In early spring 1937 rebel armies under the command of Gen. Emilio Mola launched a major offensive against the Basque country. After fierce and protracted fighting, Nationalist troops entered Bilbao on July 19.

40. [CG:] John Little worked his way high up in the New York Communist Party. Via research for my book, *Prisoners of the Good Fight,* I discovered that he had been an agent of the FBI for many years.

41. [CG:] A reactionary organization notorious among leftists. [Eds.: In 1934, a number of conservative businessmen and anti-Roosevelt Democrats founded the American Liberty League, which became the center of conservative opposition to the New Deal within both parties.]

42. [CG:] Two of my four sisters.

43. In 1928, the Sixth Congress of the Communist International determined that the world's economy had entered a period distinguished by an increase in industrial output due to rapid technological expansion and by the incapacity of markets to expand accordingly. The Communist International predicted that a global crisis of unprecedented magnitude would arise from these contradictory economic conditions.

44. [CG:] Bennet has been a life-long, devout Mennonite, who prays four times a day.

45. Leonard "Les" Grumet (1908–59) was originally from Turtle Creek, Pennsylvania. He worked in the Cleveland area before going to Spain; [CG:] NSL: National Student League.

46. During the course of the Spanish Civil War, the Italian dictator Benito Mussolini dispatched over 60,000 troops along with a significant amount of material to support General Franco's Nationalist forces.

47. Geiser refers to the Brunete offensive, launched on July 6, to drive the fascists back from Madrid and, by forcing the enemy to shift troops, relieve pressure on the Basque front in the north of Spain.

48. [CG:] Dimitrov Battalion was composed of volunteers mostly from countries of the Balkan region.

49. [CG:] Herbert took over as leader of my YCL branch after I left for Spain.

50. [CG:] Arnold was a member of the Branch.

51. [CG:] Branch members.

52. Mirko Markovics (1907–75), a Serbian American, briefly commanded the Lincoln-Washington Battalion at Brunete; Steve Nelson (1903–93), a long-time Communist Party organizer, served as battalion commissar until wounded at Belchite. Extremely popular among the rank-and-file, Nelson rose to the upper ranks of the Communist Party during the 1940s. Sydney Levine (1911–99), one of the original Lincoln volunteers, known for his skill and courage, commanded a machine gun company.

53. [CG:] Inprecor: *International Press Correspondence* newsletter put out in several languages by the Comintern (Communist International).

54. This letter is in ALBA #4, box I, folder 13, "Geiser Sylvia: Incoming correspondence from Ben Findley, Paul Wendorf, Unidentified, 1937–1938."

55. [CG:] This letter was from Sylvia's nephew, Irving [Eds.: Weissman], who I have mentioned in previous letters.

56. Weissman, like many other volunteers, kept his whereabouts in the Spanish Civil War a secret from his family, so as not to worry them. Often, parents found out anyway.

57. Weissman refers here to a remarkable confrontation between Joe Dallet, the authoritarian commissar of the Mackenzie-Papineau Battalion, and rank-and-file soldiers who challenged his severe and threatening discipline. After an all-night meeting behind the lines just before going into combat, Dallet acknowledged his errors. According to Weissman's later recollections, "It demonstrated that the [Communist] party was a self-correcting organism. That was my immediate feeling. . . . I felt it as a

cleansing, perhaps even a purification." See Peter N. Carroll, *The Odyssey of the Abraham Lincoln Brigade* (Stanford, 1994), 160–62.

58. [CG:] Alvarez del Vayo, chief of the Spanish War Commissariat and Republican Spain's last Foreign Minister.

59. The official newspaper of the Communist Party of the United States.

60. [CG:] Golubiev, Soviet correspondent and military commentator.

61. [CG:] All outgoing correspondence passed through the International Brigades military censor. The censor redacted sensitive material by smearing it over with an inked swab that left sections blacked out. For an example, see the letter dated September 15, 1937, to Herb.

62. [CG:] Bennet's son.

63. During the Spanish Civil War, the U.S. Communist Party (CPUSA) equated the objectives of the Spanish Popular Front government with the principles of the American Revolution. While Franco and his generals were compared to Tories who had relied on foreign mercenaries, the international volunteers who fought for the Spanish Republic were likened to Thaddeus Kosciusko, Casimir Pulaski, Baron von Steuben and were also referred to as "American Lafayettes."

64. [CG:] My sister Irene.

65. Bernard Ades (1903–86), a graduate of Johns Hopkins University and of the University of Maryland Law School, served as a commissar in the Washington and Lincoln-Washington Battalions.

66. [CG:] From Sylvia's nephew Irving [Weissman].

67. [CG:] *The Volunteer for Liberty* was "the organ of the International Brigades" as it declared on its masthead. *The Volunteer* was published in Spain by the Commissariat of, by, and for the International Brigades. The English-language weekly newspaper's first issue came out on 24 May 1937 and ceased with 7 November 1938, volume II, issue number 35.

68. Benjamin Franklin Findley (b. 1908) served in the machine gun company and later with the medical services.

69. [CG:] John Quigley Robinson was known as "Robbie." He lived around 7th or 8th Street in Manhattan. [Eds.: John Quigley Robinson (1897–1995), Irish-born, a veteran of the British army in World War I, and a seaman, was Geiser's immediate superior office. After the battle of Belchite in September 1937, Robinson was sent to the Soviet Union to present a firsthand report on the problems of using of tanks with infantry. Geiser then replaced him as battalion commissar.]

70. [CG:] Herbert L. Matthews was the *New York Times* correspondent assigned to cover the Republican side of the war. William P. Carney reported for the fascist Franco's side, with a pronounced bias in favor of his subject.

71. Harry Hynes, a British-born but New York-based seaman, served as a company commissar in the Washington Battalion and was killed in action at Brunete.

72. [CG:] A New York City subway line.

73. *La Prensa* and *La Voz* were two Spanish-language dailies published in New York in the late 1930s. During the Spanish Civil War, *La Prensa* assumed a cautious position and equivocated in its support, but *La Voz* (whose masthead read *Diario Democrático Avanzado*) was specifically founded to cover the war and to mobilize support for the Republic.

74. The Battle of Guadalajara (March 8–23, 1937) saw a decisive victory of the Republican army, with the participation of Italian, Slav, and German volunteers, against efforts by Italian Fascist troops to encircle Madrid.

75. [CG:] Led by Jay Lovestone who broke off from the U.S. Communist Party to oppose them. [Eds.: Jay Lovestone (1897–1990) was among the founders of the Communist movement in the United States. In 1927 he became the Party's national secretary but was expelled two years later for defying Stalin. During the 1930s he led non-orthodox communist organizations.]

76. From August 1936 to mid-1938 the Soviet Union was rocked by a series of trials that led to the execution of thousands of members of the Communist Party. The accusations, all of which were fabricated, were quite fantastic and ranged from planning terrorist attacks and assassinations of party leaders to conspiracy with Germany and Japan to overthrow the Soviet government. Because of their faith in the Soviet Party, many Communists, including Geiser, subscribed to the official version of the trials provided by Moscow.

77. *Mundo Obrero* (Workers World) was the official newspaper of the Spanish Communist Party; José Maria Gil-Robles was a Spanish conservative politician who supported the military revolt; the Spanish Communist Party falsely accused the POUM of being a pro-Franco organization. The Republican government dissolved the POUM in June 1937.

78. Followers of the Russian revolutionary leader Leon Trotsky.

79. In August 1937, the Washington-Lincoln and Mackenzie-Papineau Battalions were moved to the Aragon region to participate in an offensive aimed at capturing the town of Zaragoza. North American volunteers captured the town of Quinto on August 24 and moved against Belchite three days later. Belchite was taken on September 6. A subsequent attack on Fuentes de Ebro on October 1 proved disastrous, stalling the offensive.

80. [CG:] Social Democrats.

81. Geiser's complaint referred to the seaman's section of the machine gun company composed of class-conscious men who objected to saluting officers or accepting orders they didn't understand. Years later, while transcribing his letters, Geiser added the following footnote to his remarks, quoting a letter he had written to Lincoln vet Alvah Bessie: "Alvah, not only was I rather optimistic here [about the remark "we'll take it out of them here"], but I was yet to learn that grumble they might, but most would also fight under tough conditions."

86. "Fiamme Nere" (Black Flames), was the name of one of the three Divisions sent by Mussolini to Spain.

83. [CG:] When I was the Education Director in the Bronx YCL, Al Steele was the head of the Bronx County YCL.

84. [CG:] *Daily Worker,* U.S. Communist Party newspaper.

85. "Mosca" (Housefly) was the nickname coined by Republican forces to identify the Soviet-made Polikarpov I-16 fighter plane.

86. Carl Geiser is probably referring to Jean Horie one of the leaders of the American Youth Congress; see letter of September 17, 1937.

87. David Doran (1910–38) was a prominent Communist Party organizer in the trade union section before going to Spain. He rose through the ranks to become commissar of the Fifteenth Brigade. He was captured and killed during the retreats of March 1938.

88. [CG:] My uncles.

89. During the Spanish Civil War tens of thousands of Americans offered their time, money, and talents to provide direct aid to the embattled Republic. Millions of dollars were raised to provide tons of clothing and food — mainly powdered milk

for children, wheat, rice, and beans—to Spain's beleaguered population. Among the Republic's top needs were medical supplies and equipment, including mobile hospitals and ambulances. A broad range of organizations, individuals, and community groups set up funds to purchase ambulances for Spain. Several dozen fully equipped ambulances were sent from the United States, each displaying the name of the donors, such as the Negro Committee to Aid Spanish Democracy, East Harlem's Club Obrero Español, the International Workers Order, the Theatre Committee for Aid to Spanish Democracy, Fredric March, Ernest Hemingway, Paul Muni, or the Popular Front Committee of Ybor City, Florida.

90. [CG:] Ben Findley, Ralph Thornton, and I. Ralph was an African American, like Walter Garland mentioned above. I only mention that because American Blacks had to wait until long after World War II for segregation to end in the U.S. Armed Forces. For us in the International Brigades, solidarity meant humanity in all respects.[Eds.: Ralph Thornton (1902–84), an African American from Pittsburgh, fought with distinction at Quinto and was transferred to the Brigade staff.]

91. [CG:] *Guernica,* title of a historic painting by Pablo Picasso—one of his most memorable—was a Basque town carpet-bombed by fascist planes but first blamed on "the Reds."

92. [CG:] As a teenager I made and delivered ice cream for my Uncle John, owner of Smith's Dairy in Orrville, Ohio.

93. [CG:] Uncle and Aunt.

94. Geiser's description of the execution of prisoners during the Aragon offensive reflected an unusually tense moment in the war. The Spanish Republican Army, unlike Franco's Nationalist policy, explicitly forbade the mistreatment of prisoners of war. But after taking Quinto, brigade leaders ordered the execution of selected fascist officers. The arduous house-by-house combat at Belchite had delayed the offensive and cost many lives. The shooting of a brigade doctor prompted Cdr. Vladimir Copic to order the execution of fascist officers by firing squad. Geiser shared the belief that fascist officers, unlike their conscripts, were beyond rehabilitation. The Franco side felt the same way about Republican officers and International Brigaders, as Geiser would soon learn.

95. The "Frecce Nere" ("Flechas Negras") was a mixed brigade composed of Spanish and Italian troops.

96. [CG:] A great propaganda movie that utilized the talents of Ernest Hemingway, Orson Welles, John Dos Passos, Lillian Hellman, Archibald MacLeish, John Ferno, Helen van Dongen, Marc Blitzstein, Virgil Thomson, etc.

97. Joris Ivens was a Dutch documentary filmmaker, who recruited a team of American writers to make a propaganda movie to gain support for the Spanish Republic. *The Spanish Earth* (1937) enjoyed a private screening at the White House in July 1937. During the showing, President Franklin D. Roosevelt indicated his personal sympathies, remarking "Spain is a vicarious sacrifice for all of us." But he refrained from endorsing the movie and lacked the political support to alter U.S. neutrality.

98. [CG:] I spelled the name of this ancient city a few different ways: Saragossa to Zaragozza. Depending on where you are, the spelling changes, like Rome and Roma, or London and Londres, etc.

99. [CG:] Jean Horie, head of the American Student Union. [More likely of the American Youth Congress.]

100. At the end of March 1938, following the defeat at Guadalajara and the failure to capture Madrid, the Nationalist army shifted its campaign north against

the Basque regions and Asturias. Following the fall of Bilbao, Nationalists troops entered the Asturian city of Gijon at the end of October bringing the north of Spain under Franco's control.

101. [CG:] John L. Lewis, president of the United Mine Workers union (UMW), was head of the CIO at that time. What a terrific speaker!

102. [CG:] Francisco Largo Caballero [1869–1946]—timid, phlegmatic, uninspirational Socialist Party Premier of the Spanish Republic—told people not to disturb him for any reason after he retired for the evening at 8:00 p.m. [In September 1936, a few months into the Civil War, Francisco Largo Caballero was chosen Prime Minister and Minister of War of the Spanish Republican government. As the conflict progressed, growing dissatisfaction with his conduct of the war along with Communist criticism of Caballero's unwillingness to prosecute POUM leaders after the May events in Barcelona forced his resignation on May 17, 1937.]

103. Most likely a reference to George Watt (1913–94). Watt studied at Brooklyn College and Cooper Union in New York and was an officer of the American Student Union, before volunteering for Spain where he served as commissar of the Lincoln Battalion. He wrote about his World War II experiences in *The Comet Connection* (1990).

104. Ben Barber appears to be a pseudonym.

105. [CG:] NLRB: National Labor Relations Board, a New Deal arbitration bureau; Jack Peters was the author of "Song of the Lincoln Battalion," published by the Friends of the Abraham Lincoln Brigade in 1937; printed in Barcelona in 1938 and edited by the German volunteer, Ernst Busch, *Canciones de las Brigadas Internacionales* was a collection of Spanish Republican and revolutionary songs in a dozen languages.

106. Geiser's promotion followed John Q. Robinson's assignment to Moscow to explain to Soviet military leaders the problems encountered in coordinating the use of tanks with infantry at Belchite.

107. Abe Harris was in charge of supplies and provisions of the brigade. He also served with the John Brown artillery battery;. [CG:] The Intendencia performed the same function as a quartermaster.

108. Geiser is probably referring to *Photo-History.* A short-lived *Life*-size quarterly, the journal devoted each issue to photographs on a current subject. The first issue focused on images of the Spanish Civil War.

109. A 1937 Soviet film based on the life of Russian scientist, Klement Timiriazev.

110. A "closed shop" is a labor agreement that requires the employer to hire only union members and for employees to remain members of the union.

111. High casualty rates at Brunete and the Aragon front created pressure for the repatriation of International Brigaders. Mental and physical exhaustion mixed with the trauma of war (what today might be called post-traumatic stress) understandably led some soldiers to request repatriation. At the same time, Communist leaders in Spain and the United States realized that the war was taking away some of their best people. Some wounded volunteers were sent home to recuperate; others, who were considered influential among the general public, were repatriated to build support for the Republic. On the other hand, the leadership did not want to undermine the strength of the brigade. Geiser's description of a "definite policy" put an end to rumors that men would automatically go home after a specific time of service. But even this policy did not last long. In the face of military shortages, Brigade leaders announced that all soldiers were expected to serve for the duration of the war. Some accepted this responsibility as part of their personal commitment

to anti-fascism; others felt that they had been tricked into extended service. The issue remained a divisive factor with the brigades.

112. As part of an all-volunteer army, motivated primarily by the ideology of anti-fascism, brigade leaders understood that discipline depended on the morale of the soldiers. Nonetheless, some volunteers had second thoughts about their obligations and commitments, especially just before, during, and after battle. In sum, approximately one hundred American volunteers left the ranks without permission, sometimes more than once. Several managed to reach a port city, stow away on a ship, and leave the country. Some went directly to U.S. consul offices to seek repatriation. But American officials typically refused any assistance, and many would-be deserters returned to the ranks. In cases where deserters were caught or returned voluntarily, brigade policy was to accept them back, sometimes with a pep talk, sometimes with a minor penalty (such as digging trenches). The case that Geiser discusses here was exceptional: a group of deserters had fled in the midst of battle in a stolen ambulance that might have saved the wounded. To set an example, the commissars organized a two-day court-martial with a jury of the rank-and-file. Two deserters were sentenced to death. But in the end, brigade leaders had second thoughts about the effect on world opinion of executing volunteers and, therefore, the convictions were remanded. In a few other cases, however, deserters were executed, some without official consent. Whatever the circumstances, the issues were closely linked to the urgencies of war, battlefield fear and fatigue, and the vaguely understood psychology of traumatic stress.

113. [CG:] As a serious activist Sylvia volunteered support work for the great Sitdown Strike of 1937; Mito Kruth was born in Finland in 1899 and lived in Brooklyn, New York, before enlisting in the Lincoln Brigade. After returning from Spain with a leg wound, he worked as a Communist Party organizer in the midwest and New York; [CG:] Wallingford Riegger has been called "the Dean of American composers." He was a leader in the avant-garde modern music movement of the twentieth century. He and a few others of us lived for a while in a crowded apartment on the Upper West Side. Wallingford was a great punster, quite witty. He had a wonderful sense of humor and made us laugh a lot.

114. This was Leonard Lamb, born in Cleveland, Ohio, in 1910.

115. Most likely Geiser is referring to a field hospital in Sabinosa on the coast near Tarragona (see letter dated December 10, 1937.)

116. During the war, the coastal resort town of Benicasim became the site of one of the largest hospitals and a rehabilitation center run by the International Brigades. Medical facilities occupied over fifty buildings in the town. Until it was evacuated in April 1938, the hospital treated over 7,000 patients, including Spaniards and foreign volunteers.

117. Joseph Dallet (1907–37), born to a wealthy family was a graduate of Dartmouth College. After joining the Communist Party, he worked as an organizer in the steel mills of Pennsylvania and Ohio. In 1935, he ran for mayor of Youngstown, Ohio, on the Communist ticket. He was the first commissar of the Mac-Paps and was killed in action at Fuentes de Ebro; Milton Herndon was the brother of Angelo Herndon, a Communist organizer who came to national notice after he was charged with "incitement to insurrection" and sentenced to death in Georgia in 1932. Born in 1910 in Wyoming, Ohio, Milton Herndon was a steel worker. In the mid-1930s he joined the Communist Party and was an organizer in Chicago. In May 1937, he left for Spain and became section leader in the Mackenzie-Papineau Battalion. He was killed in action at Fuentes de Ebro on October 13, 1937.

118. On October 5, 1937, speaking in Chicago, President Roosevelt, proposed that the United States abandon its policy of neutrality in favor of "common action" with other "peace-loving" countries to stop fascist aggression. This was to take the form of a "quarantine" against aggressor nations. Reactions to this so-called "Quarantine Speech" were mixed. While internationalists strongly endorsed Roosevelt's stand, the CPUSA among them, pacifists and isolationists lashed out against the president.

119. Philip Detro was a native of Texas (not Virginia), college educated, a non-Communist, and died from an infected leg wound in 1938; Milton Wolff (1915–2008) rose through the ranks to become the last commander of the Lincoln Battalion. A fictional version of his experiences in Spain was published as *Another Hill* (University of Illinois, 1994).

120. [CG:] I spelled Benicasim variously in my letters, e.g., Bena Casin. I corrected all for the sake of clarity.

121. John Tsanakas was listed as missing in action, presumably killed, during the retreats in 1938.

122. This claim was part of the smear campaign conducted by Communists against the POUM.

123. The CNT, *Confederación Nacional del Trabajo* (National Confederation of Labor), was a confederation of anarcho-syndicalist labor unions. With the onset of the war, the CNT was part of broad anti-fascist coalition; it eventually moved away from its opposition to participation in the electoral and political process as several members of the CNT held various ministries and other high positions in the Republican government; *Solidaridad Obrera* (Workers' Solidarity) was a newspaper published in Catalonia by the CNT.

124. DeWitt Clinton High School in the Bronx; American People's School in New York City.

125. [CG:] American Labor Party, more of a New York State political organization. [The American Labor Party was founded in July 1936 by Sidney Hillman head of the Amalgamated Clothing Workers and David Dubinsky president of the International Ladies Garment Workers Union to channel left-wing and labor support to Franklin D. Roosevelt in New York State. Communists actively supported the ALP.]

126. [CG:] CNT: Anarcho-syndicalist labor organization.

127. In early November 1936, as Franco's troops appeared to be poised to take Madrid, the Republican government moved to Valencia beyond the immediate combat zone. A year later, with the Nationalists closing in on Valencia, the government moved to Barcelona.

128. The SRI, *Socorro Rojo Internacional* (International Red Aid) was the Spanish branch of an international organization established by the Communist International to function as an alternative to the Red Cross. During the Spanish Civil War it provided aid for orphaned and displaced children and reading materials, other supplies, and funds for medical facilities for the troops.

129. [CG:] Tima and Ryah were fellow New York City public school teachers.

130. General José Miaja (1878–1958) was one of the few high-ranking officers to remain loyal to the Republican government. At the onset of war he led the troops that halted the Nationalist advance on Madrid. Later he commanded Loyalist troops in the battles of Jarama, Guadalajara, and Brunete; Diego Martínez y Barrio (1883–1962) was a prominent political figure in the Spanish Republic. During the war, as the founder and leader of the Republican Union Party—one of the components of the Popular Front coalition—he served the Republican government in many capacities, including briefly as prime minister and interim president.

131. In 1937, pro-Roosevelt Republican Fiorello LaGuardia was reelected for a second term as mayor of New York. Crucial to his victory were the endorsement of the American Labor Party and the support of the city's powerful needle trades.

132. November 7 is the anniversary of the Bolshevik Revolution; this is a reference to the anarchist-led insurrection against Bolshevik rule by sailors, soldiers, and civilians on the island of Kronstadt, the naval base of the Soviet fleet, in 1921.

133. Earl Browder (1891–1973) was the head of the CPUSA from the early 1930s to the end of World War II, the period of greatest Communist influence and prestige in U.S. society. In 1937, within the context of the growing global Fascist threat and union support for Roosevelt's domestic policies, the CPUSA openly supported the President along with what Browder termed "the party of the New Deal" composed of the left-wings of the Democratic and Republican parties, the union movement and progressive political parties; [CG:] Earl Browder was the leader of the Communist Party in the United States through this period to the end of the Second World War, and is associated with the Popular Front strategy.

134. The Unified Socialist Youth (*Juventudes Socialistas Unificadas*) was founded by the merger of the youth organizations of the Spanish Socialist and Communist parties in March 1936.

135. The UGT, *Unión General de Trabajadores* (General Union of Workers), is a major Spanish union affiliated with the Spanish Socialist Party.

136. The CGTU was the labor union of the Spanish Communist Party before it joined the UGT in early 1936; [CG:] UGT: Union General de Trabajadores (General Trade Unions) initially influenced most by the Socialist Party. CNT: Confederación Nacional del Trabaj[o], Anarchist-controlled. CGT: Confederación General de Trabajadores, Communist. The CGT[U] joined into the UGT.

137. "Bond's" was a bread factory in the Bronx.

138. *Inprecor* was a multi-lingual magazine published by the Communist International; the *Communist* was the monthly theoretical magazine of the CPUSA.

139. The Sunday edition of the *Daily Worker*.

140. Fred Keller, a working-class Catholic from New York City, became one of the few non-Communists to serve as a commissar, rising to leadership of the Lincoln Battalion in 1938.

141. [CG:] Milton Wolf [*sic*] was the last commander the Lincoln Battalion. Fred Keller took my place when I was wounded.

142. "Arnold" probably refers to Arnold Reid (aka Reisky), a young Communist Party leader in the U.S. who was assigned as liaison officer in Paris for volunteers going into Spain. During the military crisis in 1938, he volunteered to fight and was killed during the Ebro offensive at Gandesa in 1938.

143. [CG:] José Ramos Díaz, Secretary General of the Communist Party of Spain, Partido Comunista Español (PCE).

144. Proportional Representation voting system; Peter V. "Pete" Cacchione (1897–1947) was a local Communist leader. In 1937 he ran unsuccessfully for the New York City Council; Mike Quill (1905–66) was the leader of the New York City subway workers' union and a close ally of the Communist Party. In 1937, he was elected to the New York City Council on the American Labor Party.

145. [CG:] The [American] League Against War and Fascism.

146. [CG:] Not the best writer, but a lot better than most.

147. [CG:] Bernard Walsh survived Spain. [Eds.: Bernard Walsh (1912–2004), a sculptor, was in the first group of Lincoln volunteers.]

148. [CG:] Nathan Hale Branch member.

149. The Battle of Teruel (December 1937–February 1938) was one of the decisive battles of the war. Republican troops occupied the city after bloody fighting. Eventually, however, superiorly equipped Nationalist troops were able to retake the city.

150. Vachel Lindsay Blair, a native of Cleveland, Ohio, deserted from the Lincoln Battalion and returned to the United States.

151. [CG:] These two of my four sisters made their lives' careers as nurses.

152. The "Quarantine" speech of October 5, 1937.

153. [CG:] Milton Rappaport was Sylvia's family relative. [Eds.: Milton Rappaport was killed in the Lincoln Battalion's first action at Jarama in February 1937.]

154. [CG:] David McKelvey White had been an English instructor at Brooklyn College. His father was the governor of Ohio. Dave went on to become the secretary of the Friends of the Abraham Lincoln Battalion, and kept count of who was going in and who was coming out of Spain, who was killed, wounded, etc. Soon after I returned from Spain he took me down to Washington, D.C., to tell of my experiences, and to warn of what I was told by the Italians who captured me (see my autobiography, and/or *Prisoners of the Good Fight*, p. 69 ff.). [Eds.: David McKelvey White fought with the machine gun company at Brunete and was then sent home to work for the Friends of the Abraham Lincoln Brigade and later VALB.]

155. Elizabeth Gurley Flynn (1890–1964) was a labor leader and feminist activist. She joined the CPUSA in 1936.

156. [CG:] Tima, Ryah and Sylvia had moved in to a two-story apartment in the famous Chelsea Hotel—famous not for its prices but for the number of notable artists, musicians, poets and intellectuals who lived there over the years.

157. The BMT (Brooklyn–Manhattan Transit Corporation) was one of the New York City's subway companies.

158. [CG:] That is Ruth Watt, George's wife; Sue Young is unidentified.

159. Everett Hobbs was killed on the Jarama front in February 1937.

160. [CG:] Sam and Ernie worked in the Bronx. Uncle Sam and Adele had an apartment I could sleep over in the Bronx. This Grace was Impy's sister who lived in the Chelsea with Tima, Ryah and Impy.

161. See the letter to Impy dated February 12, 1938, and the letter to Mrs. Lubell dated February 13, 1938.

162. *Art Front* was the monthly journal of the left-wing Artists' Union, published in New York from 1934 to 1937. Several future Lincoln Brigade volunteers contributed articles and artwork.

163. In the 1920s and 1930s, "darb" was slang for something that was "excellent" or "remarkable."

164. This letter is in ALBA #4, box I, folder 13, "Geiser Sylvia: Incoming correspondence from Ben Findley, Paul Wendorf, Unidentified, 1937–1938."

165. Harold L. Ickes was secretary of the interior. At the end of December 1937, taking his cue from the French Socialist leader Léon Blum's campaign against the *deux cents familles* that controlled France's economy, Ickes attacked "America's sixty families."

166. Published in 1937, *From Bryan to Stalin* is the autobiography of Communist leader William Z. Foster.

167. [CG:] This letter is only two pages that are clearly just a portion of a full letter. There was no date other than "Wednesday Eve.," but the subject matter indicates the most appropriate place for insertion into the chronological continuum of the letters.

168. [CG:] My friend Gil Green was a leader in the New York YCL.

169. Sydney Cohen was an English-born Canadian volunteer, killed in Spain in March 1938.

170. Maury Maverick (1895–1954) was a Democratic congressman from Texas; Tom Mooney Garden refers to Madison Square Garden.

171. [CG:] A popular Marxist literary periodical.

172. The ASU held its third conversion at Vassar College in December 1937.

173. Dr. Henry Noble MacCracken was the president of Vassar College; the World Youth Congress (WYC) was founded to promote peace and international cooperation among the youth of the world. The first meeting, sponsored by the League of Nations Association, had been held in Geneva in 1936. The second took place in New York City and Vassar College, with over 700 representatives from 54 countries attending in August 1938. Several student and youth organizations, including the ASU, argued for the organization to endorse "collective security" against fascism.

174. Juan Negrín (1892–1956) was named prime minister of the Spanish Republican government in May 1937; Cortes is the Spanish parliament.

175. [CG:] Former Finance Minister Dr. Juan Negrín took over as Prime Minister from Largo Caballero in May 1937. They were both members of the Socialist Party of Spain, but Negrín's dynamism was more inspirational to the people and forces of the Republic, and much more acceptable by the Communist Party.

176. Hans Amlie, whose brother Thomas was a U.S. congressional representative from Wisconsin, went to Spain as part of a small contingent organized by the Socialist Party that was named in honor of the party's leader, the "Eugene Debs Column." When the group reached Paris, however, they could not arrange to cross the border into Spain without assistance from the Communist Party. Eventually the men were integrated into the Fifteenth Brigade. Amlie, who had served seven years in the U.S. Army, was promoted to commander of the Lincoln-Washington Battalion at Brunete. He was wounded at Belchite and returned to home to speak publicly on behalf of Republican Spain; [CG:] Hans Amlie was commander of the Lincolns, and a decent man.

177. Sam Baron, editor of the newspaper *Socialist Call*, visited Republican Spain to investigate political disputes between Communists, Socialists, and other left-wing groups. His criticism of the government's Communist leadership led to his brief arrest by Spanish authorities.

178. Juan Modesto (1906–69) was a Communist and prominent officer in the Republican army; Edward Cecil-Smith, a former Canadian army officer, commanded the Mac-Pap Battalion at Teruel and the Ebro offensive of 1938.

179. Joseph Lash was executive secretary of the ASU.

180. Possibly this is a reference to Celeste Strack, former member of the NSL. At the time she was secretary of the high school section of the ASU.

181. William Lawrence (aka Lazar) helped to organize the first volunteers of the Lincoln Battalion in New York City in 1936. He later served as commissar of the American base at Albacete, dealing mostly with matters of personnel.

182. [CG:] That was Herman Engert.

183. This was a collection of writings, photographs, and woodcuts published on the 150th anniversary of the U.S. Constitution and the eighteenth anniversary of the founding of the Communist Party by the Ohio Historical Commission of the Communist Party of the USA, Cleveland 1937. The publication included brief biographies of "One Hundred and Fifty Ohio Boys" fighting in Spain.

184. Marion Merriman, wife of the Lincoln Battalion's commander Robert Merriman, went to Spain when her husband was wounded and stayed to become the battalion secretary, one of two U.S. women formally part of the International Brigades. (The other was Evelyn Hutchins, a truck driver.) She kept a diary in Spain that became the basis of a memoir, *American Commander in Spain* (University of Nevada Press,1986), coauthored with Warren Lerude.

185. Possibly Benjamin Stolberg, a journalist for Scripts-Howard and member of the American Committee for the Defense of Leon Trotsky.

186. [CG:] David McKelvey White was working for the Friends back in the States; this letter is in David McKelvey White Papers, ALBA #70, box 1, folder 4.

187. Herbert Matthews (1900–77) was the *New York Times* correspondent in Republican Spain. The *Times* also sent William Carney to cover the Franco side. The two often filed contradictory stories. Matthews's memoir of the Spanish Civil War was published as *Two Wars and More to Come* (Carrick & Evans, 1938).

188. Toivo Suoniemi (aka Suni) was a Finnish-born Canadian volunteer in both the Washington and Mac-Pap Battalions. He died in Florida in 1993; Henry Bushka was a Finnish American, killed during the retreats in 1938; Connors is probably Herbert Connor from Maryland, killed during the retreats in 1938.

189. Max Schwartzberg was a Polish-American volunteer wounded at Belchite; Frank Buturla was a seaman from New York. He returned from Spain in 1939.

190. The name Joe Sameres does not appear on any official list of U.S. volunteers; [CG:] Samores are traditional camping treats.

191. This was a much publicized exchange between a member of the Soviet Young Communist League and Joseph Stalin. In his reply the Soviet dictator described his views on "building Socialism in one country." In 1938 the exchange was translated into English as a pamphlet, titled *Joseph Stalin: A Letter to Ivanov* by the CPUSA's International Publishers.

192. [CG:] Thomas was the leader of the Socialist Party in the United States.

193. On March 12, in what became know as the *Anschluss,* Hitler sent his army across the border into Austria and annexed it into Nazi Germany.

194. Major Allan Johnson (aka McNeil), born in Scotland in 1899 and a former U.S. Army officer, commanded the Fifteenth Brigade training base at Tarazona.

195. [CG:] I was captured on April Fools' Day and spent the next year as a Prisoner Of War as documented in my book: *Prisoners of the Good Fight: The Spanish Civil War 1936–1939 Americans Against Franco Fascism,* (Westport, Conn.: Lawrence Hill, 1989).

196. This letter is in ALBA #4, box I, folder 13, "Geiser Sylvia: Incoming correspondence from Ben Findley, Paul Wendorf, Unidentified, 1937–1938."

197. Carl Geiser recounted the details of how he fell into Fascist hands in his book *Prisoners of the Good Fight* published in 1986. What follows is an excerpt from the chapter titled "How I was Captured."

SUGGESTED READINGS

Baxell, Richard, *Unlikely Warriors: The British in the Spanish Civil War and the Struggle Against Fascism*. London: Aurum, 2013.

Bessie, Dan, ed., *Alvah Bessie's Spanish Civil War Notebooks*. Lexington: University Press of Kentucky, 2002.

Carroll, Peter N., *The Odyssey of the Abraham Lincoln Brigade: Americans in the Spanish Civil War*. Stanford: Stanford University Press, 1994.

Carroll, Peter N. and James D. Fernández, eds., *Facing Fascism: New York and the Spanish Civil War*. New York: New York University Press, 2007.

Cohen, Robert, *When the Old Left Was Young: Student Radicals and America's First Mass Student Movement, 1929–1941*. New York: Oxford University Press, 1993.

Geiser, Carl, *Prisoners of the Good Fight: Americans Against Franco's Fascism*. Westport, Conn.: Lawrence Hill & Company, 1986.

Graham, Helen, *The Spanish Civil War: A Very Short Introduction*. New York: Oxford University Press, 2005.

Nelson, Cary and Jefferson Hendricks, *Madrid 1937: Letters of the Abraham Lincoln Brigade from the Spanish Civil War*. New York: Routledge, 1996.

Neugass, James, *War is Beautiful: An American Ambulance Driver in the Spanish Civil War*. Edited by Peter N. Carroll and Peter Glazer, New York: The New Press, 2008.

Ottanelli, Fraser M., *The Communist Party of the United States: From the Depression to World War II*. New Brunswick, N.J.: Rutgers University Press, 1991.

Petrou, Michael, *Renegades: Canadians in the Spanish Civil War*. Vancouver, B.C.: University of British Columbia Press, 2008.

Preston, Paul, *The Spanish Civil War: Reaction, Revolution, and Revenge*. New York: W.W. Norton, 2007.

Preston, Paul, *The Spanish Holocaust: Inquisition and Extermination in Twentieth-Century Spain*, New York: W.W. Norton, 2012.

INDEX

Abraham Lincoln Battalion. *See* Abraham Lincoln Brigade
Abraham Lincoln Brigade, 37, 39, 44–45; composition of, 10–11, 30, 149–50; first volunteers arrive in Spain, 9; merged with Washington battalion, 43; Ohio volunteers, 200n183; "Song of the Lincoln Battalion," 80, 195n105; recruitment, 9–10. *See also* George Washington Battalion
Ades, Bernard, 51, 192n65
Adirondacks, 5, 29, 33, 45, 148, 159, 184
African Americans, 5, 30, 70, 190n33, 194n90
Almeria (Spain), 26, 189n20
Álvarez del Vayo, Julio, 47, 192n58
American Labor Party (ALP), 91, 106, 197n125
American League against War and Fascism, 4–5, 113
American League for Peace and Democracy, 5
American Student Union, 4, 107, 143, 147, 153, 194n99, 200n172
American Youth Congress, 143, 193n86, 194n99, 200n173
Amlie, Hans, 144, 173, 200n176
Anarchists, 61–62, 86, 93, 98, 102–3, 198n136. *See also* Confederación Nacional del Trabajo (CNT)
Anschluss, 177, 201n193
Anderson, Paul, 24, 29, 66, 189n15, 190n30
Aragon front, 75, 193n79, 194n94
Asturias, 194n100

Barber, Ben, 80, 195n104
Barcelona, 93, 197n127
Barcelona uprising. *See* "May Days" (1937)
Baron, Sam, 144, 200n177
Basque children (refugees), 32, 190n38
Bates, Ralph, 32, 130, 190n37
Belchite, battle of, 67–69, 70, 71–73, 75, 193n79, 194n94
Benicasim (International Brigades hospital), 85, 87, 88, 89, 90, 91, 92, 96, 196n116, 197n120
Bessie, Alvah, 193n81
Bilbao, 32, 33, 37, 46, 190n38, 190n39, 194n100
Blair, Vachel Lindsay, 123, 199n150
"Bonus marchers," 3
Browder, Earl, 100, 106, 198n133
Brunete, battle of, 11, 39, 66, 75, 191n47
Bushka, Henry, 159, 201n188
Buturla, Frank ("Bat"), 160, 201n189

Caballero, Francisco Largo, 80, 86, 144, 166, 195n102, 200n175
Cacchione, "Pete," 111, 198n144
The Cauldron (newspaper), 3
Censorship, 47, 192n61
Christ Reformed Church, 2, 3
Civilian Conservation Corps, 5
Cleveland State University. *See* YMCA School of Technology
CNT. *See* Confederación Nacional del Trabajo
Cohen, Sidney, 141, 200